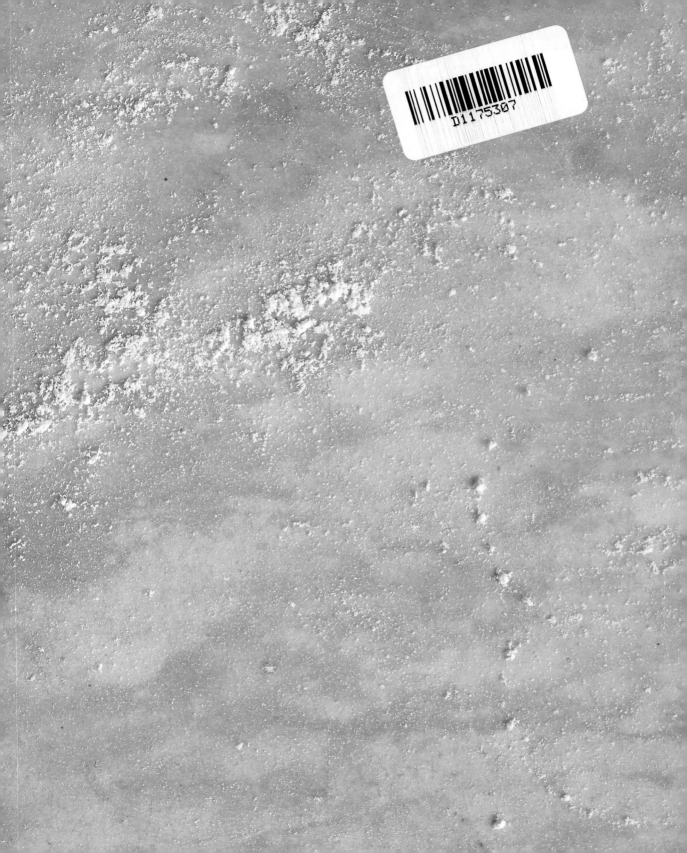

the
baker

the
baker

LEANNE KITCHEN

MURDOCH BOOKS

contents

introduction

The art of the baker is a highly esteemed one. Turning unpromising-looking flour mixtures into delicious treats invariably draws sighs of appreciation and wonderment, especially from those who claim they can't bake. Few aromas are as inviting as those that waft from an oven loaded with baked goodies, and few gestures demonstrate care and nurture like the act of baking.

Of course, it could be asked, with every imaginable baked good so readily available these days (and very affordably so) from supermarkets, grocers and specialist cake and bread shops — not to mention all those packet mixes for cakes and muffins — what is the point of doing your own baking at home, from scratch?

Once upon a time, before widespread industrialisation and the rise of big food businesses, if people wanted to put bread on their table, or enjoy some sweet or savoury baked morsel, they had little choice but to make their own. Today life is remarkably different to what it was even 50 years ago, but there still remain compelling reasons to bake at home.

An obvious one is that it allows you to exercise complete control over what you eat. Aside from the baked goods offered by small, boutique-style producers of cakes, bread and the like (some of whom may also conform to organic practices), there are some fairly questionable ingredients lurking in mass-produced bakery items — extra fats and oils, emulsifiers, colours, preservatives, stabilisers and loads of salt.

Mostly, home-made baked goods contain nothing more than fresh eggs and unsalted butter, flour, sugar, a few raising agents, milk or other liquids, and perhaps a few other ingredients such as nuts, chocolate and dried fruits — and many of these items can even be organic if you wish.

Another reason to bake at home is because it's easy. True, there are some basic techniques to master, but with a little practice these will become second nature. There's little to top the sense of satisfaction and fulfilment that inevitably follows a successful baking session. Baking, with its many fascinating processes — rising, puffing, crisping — is as close to alchemy as cookery gets; there's something magical in the transformation that takes place in the oven (or in the skillet, pudding basin or waffle iron) when doughs, batters and pastries cook to perfection.

Also, as anyone who loves to bake will quickly tell you, it is a soothing past-time and extremely good for the soul. Harking back to a less-hurried age, the art of baking forces us to slow right down and patiently work and wait while those transformative processes (creaming butter and sugar, chilling pastry, the rising of a yeasted dough) take their course.

The following information will help take some of the 'mystery' out of baking and explain the kitchenware you'll need, as well as the basic techniques and ingredients you'll be using, to help give you the very best results from baking at home, every time.

EQUIPMENT

In days gone by, all baking was literally done 'by hand' — that is, without the aid of the labour-saving devices we so rely on nowadays. Butter and sugar mixtures were laboriously worked into a creamy fluff in a bowl using just a wooden spoon, and egg whites and cream were whipped or thickened with the aid of a birch or wire whisk and a very strong arm (the first egg beater wasn't patented until 1870). You couldn't buy pre-ground nuts, self-raising flour or handy little melt-able nibs of chocolate at the supermarket — everything was chopped, ground, candied or mixed entirely from scratch.

Mercifully, baking today involves far less physical exertion and time than it once did. But, perhaps more than any other kitchen-based discipline, having the correct ingredients and equipment is still of the utmost importance when baking. You can bake on an impromptu whim but, unless you have the appropriate hardware at hand (including the right-sized cake or baking tins), success can't be guaranteed. The following are items essential to successful baking — but first, a quick word on the importance of measuring.

Measuring can make or break your baking. While some recipes are a bit 'forgiving', many are not and rely for success on rigid ratios of flour, fat, liquid and sugar. If these ratios are out of alignment, particularly with cakes and pastry, the results can be a little discouraging. The best way to guard against this is to measure your ingredients carefully and accurately.

Measuring by weight (using electronic scales) is far preferable to measuring by volume — when using cups, you can easily compact dry ingredients or heap them in the cup, giving an inaccurately heavy result. Flour, in particular, can be overly aerated, and is best measured by weight rather than volume.

SCALES

Even though most ingredients can be measured by volume using graduated measuring cups, many, for the sake of accuracy, are best measured by weight, using scales. Flour, as explained above, is one such ingredient. Using cups can give inconsistent results as dry ingredients can get compacted, or become aerated and therefore lighter.

Modern digital scales are relatively affordable, durable if looked after, and highly accurate — some to the nearest gram or fraction of an ounce. Many models can switch between metric and imperial readings and can be 'zeroed' so you can weigh several ingredients, one after the other, into the same bowl.

MEASURING CUPS AND MEASURING JUGS

Measuring cups are best for measuring soft ingredients such as yoghurt or jam, while measuring jugs are best for liquids. Measuring cups typically come in sets of 60 ml (2 fl oz/¼ cup), 80 ml (2½ fl oz/⅓ cup), 125 ml (4 fl oz/½ cup) and 250 ml (9 fl oz/1 cup) measures and are usually made of plastic or metal.

Buy the best-quality, most durable set of measuring cups you can afford, and make sure they have perfectly straight sides to make levelling off easier (avoid scoop-shaped ones). Stainless steel is by far the best material as plastic can warp, crack or melt, and ceramic can chip or smash.

If you need to measure thick, viscous or sticky substances such as honey or peanut butter in a cup, a good trick is to grease the inside of the cup first with butter to make it easier to remove.

Hard-wearing glass measuring jugs are a better choice than metal or plastic alternatives as they are much easier to see into. Choose measuring jugs that feature good spouts for pouring, and also have clear markings for easy measuring.

MEASURING SPOONS

These are vital for accurate measuring of dry and liquid ingredients that are used in critically small amounts, such as extracts, yeast, bicarbonate of soda (baking soda) and baking powder. They come in a set of graduated sizes. Some start at 1/8 teaspoon and others from 1/4 teaspoon. Next will be 1/2 teaspoon, 1 teaspoon, then 1 tablespoon. They are usually metal or plastic (metal ones tend to be more durable). Look for a good-quality set with no joins between the spoon heads and handles. Always level off the ingredient being measured for most accurate results.

One teaspoon is 5 ml in volume. This book uses 20 ml (4 teaspoon) tablespoons, so if you happen to be using a 15 ml (3 teaspoon) tablespoon, simply add an extra teaspoon for each tablespoon specified in the recipe. This is particularly important for baking powder, powdered gelatine, bicarbonate of soda (baking soda), flour and cornflour (cornstarch).

MIXING BOWLS

Bowls are so fundamental to baking and it is important to have good ones. Avoid plastic bowls — these can scratch, melt or crack and over time can also become tainted by strong flavours, or can even become greasy. Glass and ceramic are good materials for bowls — their weight makes them stable on the bench for all the mixing, rubbing in and whisking they are likely to see, and they are particularly durable. Stainless steel bowls are good too. Excellent heat conductors, they are useful when you need to melt or heat ingredients over a saucepan of simmering water.

Make sure you have a good variety of sizes; chances are you will need more (and bigger) bowls than you imagine!

ELECTRIC BEATERS AND STAND MIXERS

When making simple cakes, biscuits (cookies) and the like, hand-held electric beaters work well. They will cream butter and sugar, whisk egg whites and beat volumes of air into foam-type cakes with reasonable efficiency. They are relatively inexpensive, portable, and store easily in a utensil draw. They consist of two attachable beaters that fit into a unit holding the motor and have a range of beating speeds.

However, electric beaters cannot be used for heavy-duty mixing (such as kneading bread dough), are likely to have a shorter lifespan than a heavy-duty stand mixer, and will take a little longer to cream or mix than a stand mixer. Also, you need to stand and hold electric beaters while using them.

A heavy-duty stand mixer is the tool of choice for serious bakers and professionals. Highly durable, these mixers come with a range of beating attachments (a whisk, a paddle and a dough hook are the most common) and a large metal bowl. They have a range of adjustable speeds, and motors powerful enough to cope with large cake batters and batches of bread dough.

Choose the best-quality stand mixer you can afford and it will reward you with years of faithful service. It is also a good idea to purchase an extra mixing bowl and a second paddle and whisk so you can perform several tasks, if the recipe demands it, without having to stop and clean equipment halfway through.

Whisks

Even if you use electric beaters for heavy-duty jobs, hand-held wire whisks are endlessly useful. They make short work of lumpy melted mixtures, especially those involving chocolate. They're also useful for quickly combining eggs and liquids when making muffins and certain cakes.

There's a vast array on the market (coil whisks, ball whisks, looped silicone-coated whisks and double rotating turbo whisks, to name a few) but really, it's best to keep your whisk selection simple and to buy good-quality whisks. Several sizes of wire balloon-type whisks, as well as a tiny whisk for smoothing small quantities, are all you need. Go to a chef-supply shop and buy what the professionals use.

Grater

These days, as well as the classic box-style graters, there are some fantastic slim-line microplane graters available. The main applications for these in the baker's kitchen are grating fruits and vegetables, citrus zest, chocolate, hard cheese, nutmeg and ginger. Choose a quality grater made of stainless steel, with a variety of grating planes to cope with a wide range of ingredients.

Food processor

This gadget, now common in many kitchens, takes the elbow grease out of many a tiresome task, such as finely chopping nuts and chocolate and making breadcrumbs. Although some cookbooks recommend using a food processor for making pastry, it is better to make pastry by hand — with a food processor it is easy to overmix the dough, making it tough.

As with all kitchen appliances, choose the best food processor you can afford and it will last you a very long time. It's also handy to have a mini-processor for grinding whole spices or small quantities of an ingredient. Often, hand-held immersion or 'stick' blenders have a small processor attachment; the processing option the more powerful ones provide is more than adequate for most baking purposes.

Spatula

Rubber spatulas come in a variety of forms and shapes — some are thin, plastic and moulded from one piece; others have wooden, metal or plastic handles and a rubber or plastic head. Some are flexible, some not. Rubber spatulas are useful for scraping out bowls, mixing ingredients and folding in ingredients, and it is useful to own a variety of types and sizes.

Another type of spatula, also called a palette knife in some circles, has a blunt, rounded metal blade. These are another baking essential — useful for flipping pancakes and pikelets (griddle cakes), spreading icings (frostings) and fillings, loosening biscuits (cookies) on trays, and loosening cakes in tins. The blades vary in size and can be straight or off-set.

Knives

You'll need a good-quality, long-bladed serrated knife for cutting cakes widthways through the middle when you want to fill them, for slicing biscotti between bakings, and of course for slicing bread and cakes into serving portions. You'll also require an all-purpose chef's knife for chopping items such as nuts, dried fruits and chocolate. It isn't worth buying poor-quality knives — purchase the best ones you can afford and they will last your lifetime and well beyond.

Measuring tape

Having one of these is more useful than you'd think. Imagine you're about to make a cake and you need to check the dimensions of what you hope is the perfectly sized cake tin. Without a tape measure you'll have to guess, and this could lead to choosing the wrong tin — and disaster. Similarly, when a recipe says to roll a piece of pastry out to a specific diameter or thickness, why guess when you can use one of these? Get a ribbon-style one that's laminated with plastic. It will last for ages and won't take up any room in your gadget drawer.

Pastry brushes

You will find that you'll need a few different sizes of these. A thick, good-quality artist's brush is good for painting edges of tarts or small pastry items with egg yolk mixture, while a broader brush is ideal for painting glazes onto pie tops, cakes and loaves of bread. Pastry brushes come in many grades of quality — avoid cheaper ones as they will shed plastic bristles all over your baked goods. Also, choose natural (animal) bristles rather than plastic as they will be much easier to keep clean. Make sure the bristles are securely sealed into the handle.

CUTTERS

From simple circles or squares to elaborate flower, bell or gingerbread-man shapes, biscuit (cookie) cutters come in many very different forms and sizes. A scone, for example, needs only a simple, round cutter, but certain occasions such as Christmas and children's birthday parties cry out for specially shaped, decorative biscuits. Cutters should have a sharp edge so they cut through dough cleanly and easily; you shouldn't need to use much pressure. Metal cutters tend to do a neater job than those made of plastic. Check their construction though — some cutters have seams that are not well aligned and these will affect the neatness of the final shape.

ROLLING PIN

Professionals use straight, solid, wooden rolling pins for most efficient rolling. Choose one that is about 45 cm (18 inches) long and 5 cm (2 inches) in diameter, and also one without handles as this will give you so much more control over your rolling. This type of all-purpose rolling pin will make short work of most dough, including 'laminated' pastry doughs (those made with alternating layers of dough and butter, such as puff pastry).

The rolling pin should be smooth, with no dings or dents in the wood. Don't immerse your wooden rolling pin in water to clean it — a good wipe with a damp cloth should suffice.

BAKING BEADS/PIE WEIGHTS

When baking blind (see pages 18 and 174), you need something to hold down the baking paper lining the pastry case, to stop the pastry puffing up during baking. You can use dried beans (such as chickpeas or red kidney beans) or even dried rice, and reuse these as many times as you like, or you can buy dedicated pie weights. These are small balls about the size of a pea, made of metal or ceramic. If you use these, you don't need to first line the pastry shell with baking paper, although you'll need to wash the weights after use.

You can also buy a long pie 'chain' which you coil over the base of the pastry case, then remove after baking using a pair of tongs. You will need one about 3 metres (10 feet) long for best results.

NON-STICK BAKING MATS/SILICON LINERS

Negating the need to grease and flour baking trays, baking mats are typically made from silicon. They sit on the surface of the baking tray; items such as biscuits (cookies) and the like are baked directly on top of them. Silicon mats can be used again and again — they simply need a wash in soapy water and a good drying off. They are sold in a variety of sizes.

BAKING TRAYS/COOKIE SHEETS

These are essential for baking biscuits (cookies). They come in different sizes and it is best to get the biggest one that will fit in your oven. You'll need several so you can bake two trays at a time (although not all recipes allow you to do this), or at least have a second tray ready to go into the oven the minute the first tray is baked. Baking trays should be heavy enough to not bend or buckle when heated. You can get non-stick trays, but these tend to have very dark surfaces and are not recommended as they cause biscuits to brown too quickly. Choose trays with shiny metal surfaces for best results, and line them with baking paper if you want to keep them clean during baking.

CAKE AND MUFFIN TINS

Cake tins vary in size. Generally their size relates to their width in centimetres or inches across their top, although some manufacturers measure across the base, so check when purchasing. It is vital to have the correct size tin for whatever recipe you are making, otherwise cooking times and the mixture's ability to rise correctly will be affected. Unless you steadfastly bake just one or two types of cakes, for example, you will need a variety of sizes — and for some recipes (such as those with separate layers) you may need two or three of the same size.

Buy good-quality tins with strong construction and tight seams (if there are seams). Many have a non-stick surface — this is handy but not essential.

Spring-form tins, which have a removable base that is released by opening a sprung latch on the tin's side, are necessary for cheesecakes and any delicate cake where removal from a conventional tin is tricky. Make sure the latches are strong — weak ones that spring open while the tin is being filled or during baking spell disaster. There are other types of tins with removable bases that have no latch — you simply push the cake, on the base, up through the hooped side to remove.

Other types of tins include tube (or ring) tins, and bundt (kugelhopf) tins, which are designed around a central tube. Their design facilitates quick, even baking and is particularly useful for rich, yeasted cakes, coffee cakes and pound cakes.

Angel food tins and Swiss-roll (jelly-roll) tins are needed when baking those particular types of cakes.

Muffin tins come in a variety of sizes, colours and finishes, including non-stick and Teflon. You can bake any muffin mixture in any sized tin, but the baking times will be affected. Generally, darker-coloured muffin tins bake faster than light-coloured metal tins. This is also true of loaf (bar) tins, which are useful for quickbreads, cakes and loaves of yeasted bread.

A modern innovation in bakeware is silicon. Goods bake well in silicon and its big advantages are that it doesn't rust, it is very easy to store and it also cools quickly once taken out of the oven. Some brands are rather expensive, but price is no guarantee of quality, so do your homework before making major purchases (there are countless helpful user-review resources posted on the internet).

PIE AND TART TINS

These come in a plethora of sizes, shapes, depths and surface finishes. They can be made of ceramic, glass, aluminium, tinned steel or silicon. Some have straight sides, others sloping; some have smooth sides, while others are fluted.

The most common sizes for large pies are 23 cm (9 inch), 25 cm (10 inch) and 30 cm (12 inch) and they come in a range of depths. The most useful depths are those around 4–5 cm (1 1/2–2 inches); shallower ones won't hold enough filling. Smaller pie dishes are great for individual pies and these generally measure around 13 cm (5 inches).

Avoid dark-coloured metal tins (such as non-stick ones) as they cause pastry to brown too quickly. Non-stick surfaces are not necessary when cooking pastry, as its high fat content makes it unlikely to stick. Clear glass dishes allow you to see when the pastry is cooked, but really the only other advantage of glass and ceramic dishes over metal ones is that they look nicer if you are serving the tart straight from the oven.

Tart tins and quiche tins have straight or fluted sides and usually a removable base. They tend to be quite shallow and can be rectangular, square or round, although there are some with sloping, fluted sides that are quite deep. There are also individual-sized tart tins.

When washing any metal tin that doesn't have a non-stick surface, make sure it is perfectly dry afterwards (let it dry in a cooling oven) as some metal finishes can rust.

CAKE TESTER

This is one of the smallest, least expensive and most useful tools available to the baker. A cake tester will stop you poking a wooden skewer into your cake — these are quite thick and will ruin the appearance of a cake, especially if used several times.

A cake tester is simply a thin, straight length of metal mounted onto a small plastic grip. You just push it into the middle of a cake then withdraw it — the tester should come out clean when the cake is done (although very rich fruitcakes and brownies will still be a little sticky in the middle, even when properly cooked).

WIRE COOLING RACKS

Most recipes for baked goods give specific cooling instructions and tell you when to turn the item 'onto a wire rack' to cool. Wire racks aid quick, even cooling by allowing air to circulate around all sides of baked goods — otherwise, if the baked goods are left in their tins or on trays, they will sweat and turn soggy as they cool.

Racks come in various shapes and sizes. You are better off with a few large rectangular ones that can accommodate a few batches of goods rather than small round ones. It is better to have too much cooling rack than not enough. Very good-quality ones will last a long time. Cheaper ones have wires that tend to come loose at their joins, or can fly off completely, which can be very dangerous. Choose ones with tightly spaced grids so smaller goods can't slip between the wires, and make sure the racks are very strong as some cakes are heavier than you'd think.

A NOTE ON OVENS AND TIMING

Not every oven will bake in exactly the same way. No matter how accurately your oven is calibrated, it is bound to have some quirks. It is so important to know 'how' your oven bakes — is it 'hot' and does it cook too fast? Or does it err on the slightly cool side and bake things more slowly? Does it have 'hot spots' — small zones where heat seems to accumulate and cause uneven baking? Are the seals around the door in good condition? If not, they can cause heat to escape and your oven to run cool. Because these various scenarios are very common, it is advisable to use an oven thermometer (see page 18). These inexpensive devices hook onto an oven rack and measure the true heat inside your oven.

When baking in a conventional oven, most goods should be placed on the centre shelf of the oven for cooking. Avoid baking cakes near the top or the bottom of the oven as they will cook too quickly nearer the heat source. When two cakes are in the oven together, make sure there is plenty of room between the tins so air can circulate. When baking several trays of biscuits (cookies) at a time, place one rack two-thirds up in the oven and the second two-thirds down — then switch the trays halfway through baking to ensure the biscuits cook and brown evenly.

Convection (fan-forced) ovens work by circulating air around the oven, eliminating hot spots. This allows you to bake on any shelf of the oven and to bake multiple goods at a time. They also bake more quickly than conventional ovens. The recipes in this book have been developed for conventional ovens, so if you have a fan-forced oven, reduce the oven temperature given in the recipe by about 20°C (68°F) and decrease the baking time by 10–20%.

Always use a timer (see below) when baking. Set the time recommended in the recipe, then check if the goods are cooked. Similarly, let your nose be your guide — the smell of a fully cooked cake will fill your kitchen, so if you think it is ready before the timer goes off, remove it from the oven. Times are a guide only, and they may be out by 5–10 minutes on either side of the suggested cooking time, depending on how your oven bakes.

OVEN THERMOMETER

Unless you regularly have your oven calibrated, chances are it will be out in its accuracy by at least a few degrees — perhaps more. Ovens are also prone to 'hot spots' where they run at a higher temperature, and it is very useful to know where these are. For these reasons an oven thermometer — an inexpensive little thermometer that clips onto an oven rack — is indispensable. It can also stay in the oven permanently — there's no need to remove it when you're not baking.

TIMER

Setting a timer when you pop something into the oven will help ensure perfectly baked goods every time. Battery-powered digital timers tend to be more accurate than mechanical versions. Some are also portable — you can hang them around your neck so that if you venture out of the kitchen while something is in the oven there is little chance of forgetting it. Choose a timer with a loud, long ring and large, clear numerals. Some timers measure in increments of minutes, others go down to seconds. Most ovens also have an in-built oven timer.

TERMS AND TECHNIQUES

The following are basic terms and techniques common to baking. The techniques are not difficult to perfect, but a basic understanding of them will bring better results to your baked goods.

BAKING BLIND

Pastry shells and pie cases are often 'baked blind' before a filling is added, to stop the pastry becoming wet and soggy. Before being placed in the preheated oven, the pastry base is first pricked all over with a fork to stop it rising during baking, and the pastry case is then lined with baking paper and half-filled with baking beads, dried beans or dried rice. (This stops the pastry rising and puffing during blind-baking, so the base stays flat and even for the filling.) The pastry is then baked for a short time and allowed to cool, before being filled and baked for a second time. For more on baking blind, see page 174.

BEATING

Beating involves repetitive, vigorous mixing to lighten a mixture, change its consistency or make it smooth. Batters and creamed butter and sugar mixtures are those most commonly beaten. Before electric beaters were invented, beating was done with a wooden spoon.

BLENDING

Blending is where ingredients (one is usually a liquid or a fat) are combined until smooth — this can be done using an electric beater, food processor, whisk or wooden spoon, depending upon the ingredients being blended (most recipes will suggest an appropriate method).

CURDLING

A mixture is curdled when it separates into solids and liquids. In baking, a common scenario for curdling is when eggs are added to creamed butter and sugar. When making cakes, always have your eggs at room temperature, and add them slowly to the creamed butter mixture, beating well before adding more egg. This will help prevent the mixture curdling.

Acidic substances, such as lemon juice, can also cause curdling, especially when added to dairy products such as milk and cream.

If your mixture does curdle, it won't ruin your cake. To bring it back together again, stir a little of the dry ingredient mixture into it.

DUSTING

Dusting is when a light, even scattering of plain (all-purpose) flour is scattered over a work surface, rolling pin or the inside of a baking tin, to stop the dough or pastry sticking.

Baked goods are also often dusted with icing (confectioners') sugar once they have cooled — the best way to do this is by putting the icing sugar in a fine, small sieve and shaking it over the top.

Sometimes finely chopped nuts, poppy seeds, sesame seeds or even cocoa powder can be used for dusting.

FOLDING

Folding involves the careful incorporation of one mixture into another. Usually it is a lighter, aerated mixture that is being mixed into a heavier mixture — for example, whisked egg whites into a cake batter. Care needs to be taken in this process that no air is lost, or the resulting mixture won't be as light and fluffy. The best tool for folding is a large, fairly flat metal spoon.

GREASING

Most tins, trays and dishes need to be greased before baking so that cake batters and the like don't stick to the tin during baking. Butter is the best fat for this — oils tend to be too heavy. Often a light dusting of flour is also required after greasing (your recipe will tell you when to do this).

MIXING

To mix is to stir, or use some other method, to combine several ingredients together until they are completely amalgamated. It could be all dry ingredients you are mixing, or a mixture of wet and dry — the principle is still the same.

PINCH

A pinch (usually of salt or some ground spice) is the amount you can hold between the tips of your forefinger and thumb. This is not an exact measurement — but for the record, a pinch is about 1/16 teaspoon.

SIFTING

A sifter is an apparatus with a fine wire mesh, through which dry ingredients — typically fine powders such as flour, icing (confectioners') sugar, cocoa powder and cornflour (cornstarch) — are passed. This is done to lighten the ingredient or the mixture and to remove any small lumps.

STIRRING

Stirring is when ingredients are mixed together to combine them. Depending on the recipe, either a large metal spoon, a rubber spatula, a whisk or a wooden spoon are used for this. Use a definite circular motion to amalgamate ingredients thoroughly, but never overmix — especially where flour is involved — or you can cause the mixture to toughen.

WHIPPING OR WHISKING

Whipping/whisking is a form of beating. A wire whisk, or wire whisk attachments for an electric beater, are used instead of a wooden spoon or beater attachments. The purpose of whisking is to aerate a mixture significantly, giving great volume to the mixture and also a dramatic change in its consistency. The most likely ingredients to be whipped are eggs (either whole or separated, and usually in tandem with sugar) and cream, but sometimes other mixtures are whipped to lighten them.

INGREDIENTS

As with all forms of cookery, for the best possible results, always bake using the best ingredients available.

BAKING POWDER

Baking powder is a relatively modern invention and is composed of bicarbonate of soda (baking soda), acidic salts (usually monocalcium phosphate and sodium aluminium sulphate), tartaric acid and cornflour (cornstarch), which absorbs moisture while the powder is in storage. One of the acidic salts reacts with liquid and another reacts with heat, both actions causing the powder to give off carbon dioxide and cause the mixture to rise.

Slightly more flexible than bicarbonate of soda, baking powder allows for some delay between mixing and baking, which is especially useful for mixtures that require refrigerating or resting before baking. Because the acids perfectly balance the alkaline soda, baking powder does not leave a 'soapy' taste, which can sometimes occur when using bicarbonate of soda alone (see below).

Some bakers and consumers prefer the aluminium-free baking powder sold in health-food stores, both because they believe it gives a more tender result in baked goods and because of concerns about ingesting aluminium.

It is very easy to mix up your own. To replace 1 teaspoon of commercial baking powder, mix together 1/4 teaspoon bicarbonate of soda, 1/2 teaspoon cream of tartar and 1/2 teaspoon cornflour. Make it as you need it, as it does not store well.

BICARBONATE OF SODA

The leavening properties of bicarbonate of soda have been known since ancient times. Also known as baking soda or sodium bicarbonate, bicarbonate of soda is derived from a naturally occuring mineral called trona. A very alkaline substance, it works by reacting with moisture and with acidic ingredients such as vinegar, citrus juice, sour cream, fruits, buttermilk or yoghurt, releasing carbon dioxide. Heat also activates it a little — so as soon as a batter containing bicarbonate of soda is mixed, it should be immediately placed in a preheated oven. If it sits around for a while, the released gas will disperse and the cake (or muffins) will not rise as well during baking.

Goods leavened with bicarbonate of soda need to contain sufficient acid ingredients to neutralise the soda, so be careful if substituting acidic ingredients in a recipe (note that molasses, honey, cocoa powder, maple syrup and brown sugar are, to varying degrees, acidic). Bicarbonate of soda that is not properly neutralised makes baked goods taste 'soapy'; using too much also gives a soapy taste.

As a raising agent, bicarbonate of soda is about four times stronger than baking powder, so if you wish to use baking powder instead, use 4 teaspoons for every 1 teaspoon of bicarbonate of soda. Baking powder, however, will not subdue acidic flavours as soda does and the final taste will be changed.

Stored in an airtight container in a cool, dark place, bicarbonate of soda will keep for up to 1 year. Unless specific instructions say otherwise, always sift it with dry ingredients first to ensure even distribution through a mixture.

BUTTER

It is best to use unsalted butter in baking as its flavour is sweeter and more neutral than salted butter. Bear in mind that salt is a preservative, so unsalted butter is more perishable. Unsalted butter will keep, tightly wrapped in plastic and refrigerated, for up to 2 weeks; you can also freeze it for up to 4 months. Butter is around 80% fat — the rest is liquid and milk solids.

Before baking a cake or biscuits (cookies), always ensure your butter is a little soft (leave it at room temperature for a while), particularly when making creamed goods, as hard butter will not mix with sugar and eggs. Also, when you cream butter you are aerating it, an important step in many baked goods, and chilled butter will not aerate.

For pastry, have butter chilled and chopped, but not rock-hard or it will be impossible to rub in.

CHOCOLATE

Chocolate is a complex ingredient. There are three basic types: dark, milk and white. There are many available brands, with quality varying widely. Chocolate, like cocoa, is derived from cacao beans. There are three main varieties of cacao bean — Criollo, Forastero and Trinitario. Criollo is considered the finest and is the rarest. Most chocolate is blended from two or even all three varieties.

Making chocolate is a time-consuming process. The harvested cacao beans are sun-dried, fermented and roasted, then cracked to extract the internal 'nib', which chocolate is made from. These are ground under heated rollers and a thick liquid collected; from this liquid is separated out cocoa butter, the foundation of all good chocolate.

To make chocolate, the cocoa butter and liquor are mixed with sugar; more sugar for milk chocolate than dark (milk chocolate also has milk solids or powder additives). Some dark chocolates have more sugar added than others: hence you can buy unsweetened or bitter chocolate (no sugar added at all; it tastes as bitter as cocoa), bittersweet (a little sugar and some vanilla too), semi-sweet (more sugar than bittersweet) and sweet (rather sugary). White chocolate is made by mixing cocoa butter with sugar, lecithin and vanilla — it has no cocoa liquor in it. Because cocoa butter is expensive, many chocolate producers substitute other cheaper fats for it.

Couverture chocolate has a high cocoa-butter content and is used in professional kitchens for its fine taste and good melting properties.

You will notice on better brands of chocolate a percentage number, which refers to the percentage of cocoa liquor (also called cocoa solids) it contains. A good bittersweet chocolate for baking contains 65–70% cocoa solids; a good semi-sweet around 50%. Unsweetened chocolate has a very high percentage of cocoa butter and liquor. Sweetened dark chocolate is not recommended for baking, and milk chocolate is rarely specified in baking recipes.

Chocolate should be stored in an airtight container in a cool, dry and dark place. Do not store it in the refrigerator as the shift in temperature and humidity can adversely affect its flavour and appearance.

COCOA POWDER

Cocoa — a dark, somewhat bitter chocolatey powder — is made from cacao beans when chocolate is made. The cocoa butter is extracted from the beans and is used to make chocolate, leaving behind a cakey, dry mass, which is processed into cocoa powder.

Cocoa powder used for baking contains up to 25% fat. There are two types of cocoa: regular (or natural) and 'dutched' cocoa. The latter has been treated during processing with an alkali, which softens the bitter, acid flavours natural to cocoa and darkens its colour; it was a Dutch chemist, Coenraad van Houten, who discovered the effects of alkali on cocoa, hence the name. Dutched cocoa will be clearly labelled as such. Some recipes call for dutched or natural cocoa powder — do not substitute one for the other as the flavour may be affected. Natural cocoa works best when bicarbonate of soda (baking soda) is used as a leavener (on account of its acidity); dutched cocoa, as an alkaline, needs baking powder as a leavener.

Cocoa powder should be fine textured and of an even colour. Depending on the brand, it can vary in colour from tan to a deep, chocolatey red.

CREAM OF TARTAR

Cream of tartar is made from tartaric acid. This is a by-product of the wine industry; it is the sediment left in wine bottles after the wine has fermented. The acid firms the protein in egg whites, so cream of tartar is useful in giving stability and volume when whisking egg whites. It is a main ingredient in baking powder, and is sometimes used in recipes in tandem with bicarbonate of soda as it helps the soda release carbon dioxide and thereby leaven baked goods. Cream of tartar is available from supermarkets and keeps for a long time in an airtight container.

EGGS

Eggs are essential to baking. They colour, bind, lighten and help tenderise cakes, muffins and quickbreads, and give structure in recipes where 'soft' or 'cake' flour (see opposite) is used and gluten is not built up. Egg whites, when beaten, hold air particularly well, providing volume and lift in cakes. In pastries they lend colour, flavour and tenderness to crusts. On its own the white, because it contains no fat, would make baked goods a little tough to eat — the yolk, with its high fat content, is what gives baked goods a rich softness or tenderness.

For baking, use eggs at room temperature, not straight from the refrigerator, or they won't beat or amalgamate properly with other ingredients. Bring them out of the refrigerator several hours (or even the night before) you wish to bake and they will slowly warm up. If you have forgotten to remove them from the fridge, you can gently warm them by placing them in a bowl of warm water for 10 minutes.

Sometimes the yolk and white are used separately and need to be separated. The easiest way to do this is using your hands. Break an egg into your hand over a bowl, then allow the white to drip from the yolk between your fingers into the bowl, carefully moving the yolk from hand to hand to detach all the white as necessary. It is vital not to get any yolk into the whites, or traces of any other fat either, as this will stop the whites gaining volume when whipped. If you end up with left-over whites, you can freeze them in airtight containers for up to 2 months. Just be sure to write on the container how many whites there are and the date you froze them. To use frozen whites, simply defrost them in their container overnight, at room temperature. Egg yolks can't be frozen, but will keep in the refrigerator, with plastic wrap pressed gently on them, for 2–3 days.

The recipes in this book are made using 60 g (2¼ oz) eggs.

FLOUR

The flour most commonly used in baking is milled from wheat flour. Flour provides the structure that supports all the other ingredients in a baked item, although some of this structure can also come from eggs. It's the gluten (protein) in flour that gives flour its strength. Gluten is developed in flour when liquid is added to it and also when it is vigorously kneaded (as with bread). The gluten forms a strand-like network in the flour, between which air is trapped, assisting with rising. The starch in flour also contributes to texture as it thickens when wet and holds ingredients together. The natural sugars in flour caramelise during baking, giving colour and deep flavour to baked goods.

Certain flours contain more (or less) protein than others, making some flours more suitable for some types of baked goods than others. For example, high-protein or 'strong' flour is better for making bread, which requires strong gluten networks to support the structure. Strong flour has a protein content of around 16%. Because a more tender result is required in cakes, pastries, most quickbreads and biscuits (cookies), these benefit from the use of a **soft or lower-protein flour** (around 8% protein). If you cannot find a lower-protein flour, plain ('all-purpose') unbleached flour is perfectly fine. If you wish to lighten it slightly, substitute 1 tablespoon cornflour (cornstarch) for 1 tablespoon flour per cup of flour.

Some recipes call for wholemeal (whole-wheat) flour, which still has the bran and germ of the grain left on. It is nuttier-tasting than white flour and gives a heavier result. Because the bran and germ of the wheat contain oil, which quickly turns rancid, wholemeal flour is best stored in the refrigerator.

Self-raising flour is flour that has already had baking powder added to it (at a ratio of 2 teaspoons baking powder per 1 cup of flour). It is convenient to use in certain recipes. However, the baking powder starts to lose its leavening ability after about 6 months, so don't plan on keeping self-raising flour for any length of time.

Oil

Some recipes call for oil instead of butter, and these recipes work because they do not rely on the fat being creamed with sugar for lightness (oil won't cream with sugar). Oil is derived from plant sources, and those chosen for baking tend to have a mild flavour (such as canola or safflower).

Oil tends to produce very tender baked goods as it instantly coats the flour proteins and stops them forming toughening gluten. Baked goods made with oil also stay moist for a good length of time.

Not all recipes will work using oil — unlike butter, it doesn't contribute to the structure of baked goods.

Sugar

Sugar does much more than sweeten baked goods. It caramelises when heated and aids in browning and forming appealing crusts. It inhibits gluten development in flour, encouraging a tender cake. Sugar also attracts and holds moisture, so it helps baked goods remain moist during storage. The best sugars in this regard are liquid ones such as golden syrup, honey or molasses. Granular sugars help stop other dry ingredients sticking together, assisting their even distribution during mixing.

Granulated white sugar is the most common sugar, but the best sugar for most baking is **caster (superfine) sugar**, as its finer grains dissolve more easily, especially during the creaming process. Caster sugar is the same as granulated sugar except the grains are much smaller.

Some recipes call for **soft brown sugar** — fine, granulated sugar with molasses added to it for flavour. Brown sugar also dissolves readily. It is far better to weigh brown sugar than measure it using a cup because cup measures can vary drastically, depending upon how loosely or tightly packed the sugar is. You can use brown sugar instead of white sugar, but remember to weigh it to get the correct amount, not measure it by volume.

Turbinado sugar is similar to brown sugar but is less refined. It is more expensive than brown sugar and can be used in its place.

Icing (confectioners') sugar is a powdered granulated sugar with a little cornflour (cornstarch) added to stop it forming hard lumps. Only use this sugar in baking if a recipe specifically calls for it — you cannot substitute it for caster or granulated sugar. Icing sugar is most often used in icings (frostings), fillings and glazes, and for dusting over baked goods.

Vanilla

The unmistakable perfume of true vanilla adds something magical to many baked goods. Vanilla is derived from the tiny seeds in the long pods of an orchid species native to Mexico. Picked while unripe, the pods undergo a curing process and are sold individually. Vanilla pods are very expensive — and so are any of the products that contain real vanilla. Vanilla extract is made from the seed pods.

Beware of buying artificial vanilla extract or 'essence', which goes by various names and has either 'artificial' or 'imitation' on its label. This is no more than a chemical vanilla flavouring mixed with alcohol. When compared to real vanilla, its flavour is thin, chemical and wholly unconvincing.

It is also possible to buy a thick paste made from vanilla seeds, which is a more convenient way to add vanilla to a cake batter than using the seeds from the pod, as these need to be scraped out using a small sharp knife.

Empty vanilla pods can be used for flavouring custards, fillings and desserts — or added to a well-sealed container of caster (superfine) sugar to create vanilla sugar, which is delightful for baking.

FREEZING AND THAWING

Many, although not all, baked goods can be successfully frozen. Freezing is a convenient storage option as it means you can bake extra batches and stash them away for later use — it's so handy to have a cake to pull out of the freezer when guests are coming over for afternoon tea, or to have containers of biscuits (cookies) or muffins on hand for school lunchboxes or a snack.

Generally, baked items that are unfilled or un-iced (un-frosted) freeze best (although most fillings and icings made with butter or chocolate can also be frozen). As a basic guide, plain cakes, biscuits, muffins, buns and loaves of bread freeze well, while cheesecakes, meringues and fillings or toppings based on cream, fruit or egg whites do not freeze well at all.

All the recipes in this book will indicate if the item is suitable for freezing. Here are some important notes on freezing baked items.

- Anything destined for freezing must be completely cooled down first or condensation will form inside wrappings, ruining the food's texture.
- Overloaded freezers can lead to the formation of large ice crystals which can ruin the texture of frozen baked goods. Always make sure there is plenty of room in your freezer so air can circulate.
- To prevent 'freezer burn', thoroughly wrap items to be frozen. Wrap cakes and loaves of bread in several layers of plastic wrap, then in foil or in a thick, zip-lock bag. Place muffins, biscuits or buns in strong, zip-lock bags or airtight plastic containers. Make sure you eliminate all air from plastic bags, as air can cause your frozen goods to deteriorate.
- Not all plastic is impermeable, so use heavy plastic bags that are specially made for freezing, or your frozen baked goods may pick up odours from other frozen foods in your freezer.
- Freeze large items carefully, making sure nothing heavy is placed on them.
- Never thaw baked goods in the microwave (this causes 'hot spots' to form in the food, which can toughen baked goods considerably). Thaw them slowly at cool room temperature or in the refrigerator overnight, and bring them to room temperature before serving, to help restore flavour.
- Unbaked pastry and many biscuit doughs can be frozen for up to 3 months. Pastry and dough that is intended to be rolled can be frozen either rolled or unrolled — but for convenience it is best to freeze them already rolled. Pastry that you've already rolled to shape can be frozen in baking tins — you can then bake it straight from the freezer without needing to thaw it. As with other baked goods, wrap pastry and biscuit dough well and store it in airtight bags or containers. If you need to roll it, thaw it slowly in the refrigerator so it remains chilled — it will be easier to roll and you'll minimise toughening if you keep it chilled.

quickbreads

These baked goods have something special in common: they are quick and dead-easy to make. Even confirmed non-bakers can effortlessly whip up a shortcake, teacake or the quaintly named parkin. The ingredients are simply amalgamated in a large bowl using a few quick stirs, speedily rolled out and cut into shapes or turned into a tin or onto a baking tray… then into the oven!

In this chapter you'll find no challenging techniques or special equipment. Quickbreads (of which muffins and scones are two of the most popular) are always dough or batter-based and leavened with the help of chemical raising agents — bicarbonate of soda (baking soda) or baking powder — rather than yeast or air, and often use the most basic ingredients.

Quickbreads are reminiscent of that most English of food rituals, afternoon tea, whose origins are believed to rest with a certain Anna, Duchess of Bedford, sometime in the 1840s. Supposedly, the many hungry hours between midday lunch and dinner (not served in those days until 8.30 pm or even later) proved too much for the Duchess, who requested that a pot of tea accompanied by bread and butter and a few small cakes be brought to her rooms in the late afternoon. Soon she was inviting friends to join her for this small meal; and so, legend has it, a new trend was born. Initially fashionable among the upper crust, the afternoon tea habit spread throughout Britain and beyond. While less popular today, the legacy of this snacking meal still persists. In the United States, after-school 'cookies and milk' is pre-dinner fortification in the spirit of afternoon tea. Around the world, many glamorous hotels to this day serve elaborate afternoon teas, and among the older generations of Britons (and those in Britain's former colonies), households still routinely come to a halt for afternoon tea.

SCONES

Scottish in origin, these simple little quickbreads are the heart and soul of Devonshire tea (scones served with jam and whipped or clotted cream for afternoon tea). The first written mention of them was in 1513. Food historians say scones took their name from the Stone of Destiny (or Scone), where Scottish kings were once crowned. The original scones were made from mixtures of flour, soured milk and a raising agent, were cooked as a large, flat round 'cake' on a griddle plate over coals, then cut into triangles. Small round scones became popular in the nineteenth century, as did many other quickbreads and teacakes, thanks to the advent of chemical leaveners.

Scones are quintessentially British — the closest American equivalent is the biscuit, which was developed in the country's Southern states. The main differences between American biscuits and British scones is that biscuits never contain sugar (whereas scones sometimes do) and are designed to be served hot with butter as an accompaniment to a meal. Scones often have dates, raisins or other dried fruits in them — sometimes even spices — and are served with tea or coffee and usually not a meal. Scones can be served hot, warm or at room temperature. Some cooks make savoury scones, adding a sharp-flavoured grated cheese, chopped herbs, cayenne pepper or even chopped, cooked bacon to the basic dough.

Scones are one of the very first items that many young, aspiring home cooks learn to bake. This is no doubt because they are very easy to make and, if a first batch is less than successful, the low cost of the ingredients means this is hardly a disaster. The secret to perfect scones lies in their lightness and to achieve this, a few simple rules need to be observed.

Always have your oven preheated, so the scones don't need to sit around on trays before baking (have your trays greased and dusted with flour before baking too). Always sift the dry ingredients (flour and raising agent), and have all your other ingredients weighed and measured first so the mixing is as speedy as possible. Have your butter chilled but not rock-hard, so that it takes minimal time to rub in. Add the liquid all at once and quickly mix it in to form a dough — using a fork works quite well for this — but be prepared to quickly add a little more if the dough is not soft enough. Use your hands to gently press and pat the dough into a round or square for rolling on a lightly floured surface — do not knead the dough unless you absolutely need to, as this will make for very tough scones (scone dough does not need to be smooth and will always be a little shaggy).

When rolling out the dough, use a rolling pin, and avoid pushing on or stretching the dough too much, as this will also make scones tough. Stamp out rounds using a biscuit (cookie) cutter, without dragging the cutter through the dough, or use a large, lightly floured knife to cut the scones into rounds, squares or rectangles. Place them on a greased and floured baking tray 2–3 cm (3/4–1 1/4 inches) apart to allow for spreading.

After baking, remove the scones from the oven and transfer to a wire rack to cool completely. Some people like to cool their scones wrapped in a tea towel (dish towel), which makes the crust softer. Like many quickbreads, scones don't keep very well — they need to be eaten the day they are made, although they will freeze well in an airtight, zip-lock bag or airtight container for up to 2 months.

Soda bread and damper

Soda bread and damper are made in the same way as scones, except they are baked as a large round 'cake' and sliced when cooled. Damper is a traditional Australian bread, devised by colonists living in the bush. To provide basic sustenance, flour, baking powder and water would be mixed as needed, then cooked into a bread over a low fire (or 'dampened' fire, which some believe is the origin of the bread's name).

Soda bread, made from flour, bicarbonate of soda (baking soda), salt and soured milk, is Irish in origin and another bread devised from simple necessity. Traditionally it had a cross slashed through its surface before baking, supposedly to ward off the devil. Soda bread did not come into being until the early to mid nineteenth century, when bicarbonate of soda became commercially available. The Irish used this widely to replace yeast in home-made breads. Soda bread has a tangy flavour, chewy crust and dense texture and only stays fresh for 2 days. It can be toasted, and part or all of the flour can be made up of white, rye, wholemeal (whole-wheat) flour or a mixture. Sometimes chopped fresh herbs, nuts, grated cheese or dried fruits are added to the dough, and beer or buttermilk used as the liquid.

Muffins

There are two distinct types of muffin: English and American. English muffins are flat, holey, yeast-raised breads that are cooked on a griddle and eaten split and toasted for breakfast or afternoon tea. The muffin recipes in this chapter are American-style: cup-shaped, sweet and cake-like. It is thought that the muffins initially made in America were of the English sort.

The word 'muffin' is believed to derive from the French word *moufflet*, which means 'soft' and is applied to bread. Muffins do indeed have a tender crumb, with a texture a little coarser and heavier than that of cake. It's most likely these little quickbreads were developed in the nineteenth century thanks to chemical leavenings and, at some stage, the invention of small tins to bake them in. Throughout most of the twentieth century, there were just a select few muffin recipes in existence — corn, apple, date, bran, blueberry, oatmeal. During the 1970s and 1980s, muffin recipes seemed to proliferate as cooks tinkered with grated vegetable muffins, cheese and bacon muffins, chocolate muffins, fresh fruit and various grain muffins.

Like scones, muffins will not keep long. They are best eaten the day they are made or frozen for future use (stored in airtight, zip-lock bags, they'll keep for up to 1 month in the freezer). They can be enjoyed warm or at room temperature, buttered or plain. As with scones (and most other baked items), before starting to bake them you should have your oven preheated, your tins prepared and all your ingredients weighed and measured. Muffin tins can either be lightly greased and floured for baking, or lined with decorative paper cases.

Generally, muffins are made by incorporating a liquid mixture into a dry mixture — a process that needs to be done as swiftly as possible. Muffins are particularly susceptible to toughness, and overmixing results in chewy, dry muffins with a holey texture. Use a large metal spoon and stir with swift, certain strokes until the two mixtures are just combined — it doesn't matter if there are a few streaks of flour left; it is better to slightly undermix than overmix. A light dusting of flour over ingredients such as dried fruits will stop them sinking to the bottom of the muffins as they bake.

Fill muffin tins only two-thirds full as the batter will rise significantly during baking. Waste no time getting your muffins into the oven (usually bicarbonate of soda is used as a leavening agent, and this is activated by liquid and heat). When muffins are cooked, a cake tester will withdraw clean, with a few sticky crumbs attached. Remove from the oven and allow to briefly cool in their tins before turning out. Cover them with a tea towel (dish towel) if you like yours with soft tops.

TEACAKES, FRUIT LOAVES AND OTHER QUICKBREADS
Compared to cakes made using the creamed or foamed methods, and breads made with yeast, quickbreads are easy and very forgiving to make. Most contain less sugar and fat than cakes (although most yeasted breads are also quite low in these). For this reason they do not keep as well as baked goods with a higher fat and sugar content. There are some exceptions though, such

as the fruit and tea loaf on page 40, which keeps well and even improves after a day or two. Teacakes, loaves and the like tend to have a texture that is not nearly as refined as a yeast-raised bread or a cake made by creaming or whisking to create air and lift. In many cases, they benefit from being wrapped well and left for 12 hours before cutting; some are too crumbly when sliced immediately after baking. Each recipe will advise you on this count.

Mostly, these quickbreads are meant to be served sliced and slathered with butter. They are perfect for popping in a lunchbox, or enjoying with a relaxed cup of tea or coffee. Many teacakes and fruit loaves are great for toasting too, which is an ideal solution when they begin to go a little stale.

Most often, loaf-shaped tins are the best for baking these in, although bundt tins and other tube-shaped tins are sometimes called for too. When mixing teacakes and fruit loaves, the same rules for making muffins apply — and those for scones too, if the recipe uses the rubbing-in method: measure every ingredient before starting, have your tin prepared and your oven preheated. Use the correct-capacity tin or the cooking time will be affected, and make sure you don't overmix the batter or dough when you're making them as this will make the cake or loaf tough.

Storage times will vary according to each recipe (always use an airtight container). Unless they contain soft, fresh fruit (apple or pear, for example) they can be frozen for up to 2 months, wrapped well in several layers of plastic wrap or sealed in an airtight, zip-lock bag.

TROUBLESHOOTING QUICKBREADS

If your scones are heavy and dense, chances are they were either overmixed, the oven was not hot enough or the dough was too dry. If your oven temperature is too low or if the scones have not had long enough in the oven, they will be sticky in the middle and also a little dense in texture. If your oven temperature is too hot or if the scones have spent too long in the oven, they will be crusty and hard on the outside and dry inside.

With muffins and other quickbreads, make sure you use the stipulated tin size (fill muffin tins no more than two-thirds full) or the mixtures could spill over the sides during baking, or the cooking time may be affected. These goods can rise by as much as half their volume again during baking. If muffins or loaf-type quickbreads are too peaked in the centre and the crust is overly dark, this is most likely because the mixture has been overmixed or the oven is too hot. The texture will be affected too (tough and rubbery), especially if overmixing is the culprit. Make sure your dry ingredients (including the raising agent) are sifted and well combined before adding the wet ingredients, and mix only until just combined.

PARKIN
MAKES 25 PIECES

150 g (5½ oz) unsalted butter, chopped
140 g (5 oz/¾ cup) dark brown sugar
175 g (6 oz/½ cup) treacle or dark
    corn syrup
200 g (7 oz/2 cups) rolled (porridge) oats
125 g (4½ oz/1 cup) plain (all-purpose)
    flour
1 teaspoon bicarbonate of soda
    (baking soda)
1 tablespoon ground ginger
2 teaspoons mixed (pumpkin pie) spice
125 ml (4 fl oz/½ cup) milk

TOPPING
2 tablespoons rolled (porridge) oats
2 tablespoons raw (demerara) sugar

Preheat the oven to 180°C (350°F/Gas 4). Lightly grease a shallow 23 cm (9 inch) square baking tin and line with baking paper, leaving the paper hanging over two opposite sides.

Put the butter, sugar and treacle in a saucepan and stir over low heat until the butter has melted and the sugar has dissolved. Remove from the heat.

Using a food processor, roughly chop the oats, then tip them into a large bowl. Sift in the flour, bicarbonate of soda, ginger and mixed spice. Stir in the treacle mixture and milk, then pour into the prepared tin. Mix together the topping ingredients and sprinkle over the top.

Bake for 40 minutes, or until a cake tester inserted into the centre comes out clean. Remove from the oven and leave in the tin for 5 minutes, before lifting out onto a wire rack to cool completely. Cut into pieces for serving.

Parkin will keep for up to 1 week, stored in a cool place in an airtight container, or can be frozen in an airtight container for up to 8 weeks.

ORANGE TEACAKE
SERVES 10–12

185 g (6½ oz/1½ cups) plain
  (all-purpose) flour
185 g (6½ oz/1¼ cups) wholemeal
  (whole-wheat) flour
3 teaspoons baking powder
¼ teaspoon salt
330 g (11½ oz/1½ cups) sugar
1½ tablespoons grated orange zest
185 g (6½ oz) cold unsalted butter,
  chopped
4 large eggs
250 ml (9 fl oz/1 cup) milk
sifted icing (confectioners') sugar,
  for dusting

Preheat the oven to 180°C (350°F/Gas 4). Grease a 25 cm (10 inch) tube tin and line with lightly greased baking paper.

Sift the flours, baking powder and salt into a large bowl, then tip the husks from the sifter into the bowl. Stir in the sugar and orange zest. Using your fingertips, lightly rub in the butter until the mixture resembles fine breadcrumbs.

In a bowl, whisk together the eggs and milk. Add to the flour mixture and stir together well using a wooden spoon.

Spoon the batter into the prepared tin, smoothing over the surface. Bake for 35–40 minutes, or until a cake tester inserted into the centre of the cake comes out clean. Remove from the oven and leave to cool in the tin for 10 minutes, before turning out onto a wire rack to cool completely.

Just before serving, dust the cake with icing sugar.

Orange teacake will keep for 2–3 days, stored in a cool place in an airtight container, or can be frozen in an airtight container for up to 8 weeks.

BLUEBERRY AND HAZELNUT SHORTCAKE
SERVES 8

100 g (3½ oz/¾ cup) whole hazelnuts
280 g (10 oz/2¼ cups) self-raising flour
1½ teaspoons ground cinnamon
165 g (5¾ oz/¾ cup) raw (demerara) sugar, plus extra, for sprinkling
150 g (5½ oz) unsalted butter, chopped
2 eggs
160 g (5¾ oz/½ cup) blueberry jam
fresh blueberries, to serve
whipped or thick (double/heavy) cream, to serve

Preheat the oven to 180°C (350°F/Gas 4). Lightly grease a 20 cm (8 inch) round, deep cake tin and line the base with baking paper.

Spread the hazelnuts on a baking tray and bake for 5–10 minutes, or until lightly golden. Place in a clean tea towel (dish towel) and rub together to remove the skins, then roughly chop.

Put the flour, cinnamon, sugar, butter and half the hazelnuts in a food processor and blend until the nuts are finely chopped. Add the eggs and blend until just combined. Press half the mixture onto the base of the prepared tin, then spread the jam evenly over the top.

Lightly knead the remaining hazelnuts into the remaining cake dough, then press evenly over the jam layer. Sprinkle with a little extra sugar and bake for 50 minutes, or until a cake tester inserted into the centre of the cake comes out clean. Remove from the oven and leave to cool in the tin for 15 minutes, before turning out onto a wire rack to cool completely.

Cut into wedges and serve with fresh blueberries and cream.

Blueberry and hazelnut shortcake will keep for 2–3 days, stored in a cool place in an airtight container, or can be frozen in an airtight container for up to 6 weeks.

CHEESE SCONES
MAKES 10

250 g (9 oz/2 cups) plain (all-purpose)
   flour, approximately
1 tablespoon baking powder
a pinch of cayenne pepper
30 g (1 oz) cold unsalted butter, chopped
185 ml (6 fl oz/¾ cup) milk

FILLING
40 g (1½ oz/⅓ cup) crumbled goat's cheese
40 g (1½ oz/⅓ cup) grated parmesan cheese
40 g (1½ oz/⅓ cup) grated mature
   cheddar cheese
2 tablespoons chopped flat-leaf (Italian)
   parsley

Preheat the oven to 220°C (425°F/Gas 7). Grease or line a baking tray with baking paper.

Sift the flour, baking powder, cayenne pepper and a pinch of salt into a large bowl. Using your fingertips, lightly rub in the butter until the mixture resembles breadcrumbs. Add the milk and mix to a soft dough using a flat-bladed knife, adding a little extra flour if the dough is too sticky.

Turn the dough out onto a floured work surface and roll out to form a 20 x 25 cm (8 x 10 inch) rectangle. Mix together the filling ingredients and sprinkle over the dough. Starting from the long side, roll the dough up into a cylinder about 20 cm (8 inches) long, then cut into 10 even slices. Transfer to a baking tray, placing the scones cut side down and spacing them 2 cm (¾ inch) apart.

Bake for 10–12 minutes, or until golden, then transfer to a wire rack to cool slightly. Serve warm.

Cheese scones are best eaten the day they are made, but can be frozen in an airtight container for 4–5 weeks.

BANANA MUFFINS
MAKES 12

300 g (10½ oz/2⅓ cups) self-raising flour
75 g (2½ oz/¾ cup) oat bran
170 g (6 oz/¾ cup) caster (superfine)
  sugar
60 g (2¼ oz) unsalted butter, melted
185 ml (6 fl oz/¾ cup) milk
2 eggs
2 ripe bananas, mashed
dried banana slices, to decorate

CREAMY LEMON ICING
100 g (3½ oz/⅓ cup) cream cheese
2 tablespoons icing (confectioners') sugar
2 teaspoons lemon juice

Preheat the oven to 210°C (415°F/Gas 6–7). Lightly grease a 12-hole standard muffin tin.

Sift the flour into a large bowl, stir in the oat bran and sugar and make a well in the centre.

In a bowl, mix together the butter, milk, eggs and mashed banana, then add to the well in the flour mixture. Using a wooden spoon, stir until just combined. Do not overmix — the batter should look quite lumpy.

Spoon the batter into the muffin holes and bake for 15 minutes, or until risen and golden. Remove from the oven, leave to cool in the tin for 2–3 minutes, then turn out onto a wire rack to cool completely.

To make the creamy lemon icing (frosting), beat the cream cheese, icing sugar and lemon juice using electric beaters until light and creamy. Spread over the cooled muffins and top with dried banana slices.

Banana muffins are best eaten the day they are made. Without the icing they can be frozen in an airtight container for up to 8 weeks.

Fruit and tea loaf
SERVES 10–12

500 g (1 lb 2 oz/2¾ cups) mixed dried fruit
185 ml (6 fl oz/¾ cup) strong, hot black tea
flour, for dusting
125 g (4½ oz/⅔ cup) soft brown sugar
1 egg, lightly beaten
125 g (4½ oz/1 cup) plain (all-purpose)
   flour
¾ teaspoon baking powder
1 teaspoon ground cinnamon
¼ teaspoon ground nutmeg
a large pinch of ground cloves
butter, to serve (optional)

Put the dried fruit in a large bowl, pour the hot tea over, then cover with plastic wrap and leave for 3 hours, or overnight.

Preheat the oven to 160°C (315°F/Gas 2–3). Grease a 25 x 11 cm (10 x 4¼ inch) loaf (bar) tin and line the base with baking paper. Dust the sides of the tin with a little flour, shaking off any excess.

Stir the sugar and egg into the fruit mixture, mixing well. Sift the flour, baking powder and ground spices into a bowl, then add the fruit mixture. Using a large slotted spoon, stir together until just combined.

Spoon the mixture into the prepared tin and bake for 1 hour 35 minutes, or until a cake tester inserted into the centre of the loaf comes out clean, covering the top with foil if it browns too quickly. Remove from the oven and allow to cool in the tin before turning out.

Cut into slices and serve with butter, if desired.

Fruit and tea loaf will keep for up to 1 week, stored in a cool place in an airtight container, or can be frozen in an airtight container for up to 8 weeks.

APRICOT AND RAISIN BRAN LOAF

SERVES 6–8

150 g (5^1/$_2$ oz/^{3}/$_4$ cup) dried apricots,
  chopped
160 g (5^1/$_2$ oz/1^1/$_4$ cups) raisins
70 g (2^1/$_2$ oz/1 cup) processed bran cereal
95 g (3^1/$_4$ oz/^{1}/$_2$ cup) soft brown sugar
375 ml (13 fl oz/1^1/$_2$ cups) warm milk
125 g (4^1/$_2$ oz/1 cup) self-raising flour
75 g (2^1/$_2$ oz/^{1}/$_2$ cup) wholemeal
  (whole-wheat) self-raising flour
1 teaspoon mixed (pumpkin pie) spice
sifted icing (confectioners') sugar
  (optional)
butter, to serve

Preheat the oven to 180°C (350°F/Gas 4). Grease an 18.5 x 11 cm (7^1/$_4$ x 4^1/$_4$ inch) loaf (bar) tin and line the base and sides with baking paper.

In a large bowl, mix together the apricots, raisins, bran, sugar and milk. Set aside to stand for 30 minutes, or until the milk has almost been absorbed.

Sift the flours and mixed spice into a bowl, then stir into the fruit mixture to form a thick batter.

Spoon the batter into the prepared tin, smoothing over the surface. Bake for 50 minutes, or until a cake tester inserted into the centre of the loaf comes out clean, covering the top with foil if it browns too quickly. Remove from the oven and allow to cool in the tin for 10 minutes, before turning out onto a wire rack to cool.

Dust with icing sugar if desired. Cut into thick slices and serve with butter.

Apricot and raisin bran loaf will keep for 3–4 days, stored in a cool place in an airtight container, or can be frozen in an airtight container for up to 8 weeks.

DATE AND WALNUT ROLLS

MAKES 2 ROLLS; EACH YIELDS ABOUT 8 SLICES

90 g (3¼ oz/¾ cup) self-raising flour
90 g (3¼ oz/¾ cup) plain (all-purpose)
  flour
½ teaspoon bicarbonate of soda
  (baking soda)
1 teaspoon mixed (pumpkin pie) spice
125 g (4½ oz/1 cup) chopped walnuts
100 g (3½ oz) unsalted butter, chopped
140 g (5 oz/¾ cup) soft brown sugar
250 g (9 oz/1½ cups) chopped pitted
  dates
1 egg, lightly beaten
butter, to serve (optional)

Preheat the oven to 180°C (350°F/Gas 4). Lightly grease two 17 x 8 cm (6½ x 3¼ inch) nut loaf tins and their lids.

Sift the flours, bicarbonate of soda and mixed spice into a large bowl, then stir in the walnuts. Make a well in the centre.

Put the butter, sugar, dates and 125 ml (4 fl oz/½ cup) water in a small saucepan. Stir constantly over low heat until the butter has melted and the sugar has dissolved. Remove from the heat, allow to cool slightly, then add to the well in the flour mixture, along with the egg. Mix well using a wooden spoon.

Spoon the mixture evenly into the prepared tins and set them upright on a baking tray. Bake for 1 hour, or until a cake tester inserted into the centre of the rolls comes out clean. Leave the rolls in the tins with the lids on for 10 minutes, before turning out onto a wire rack to cool.

Cut into slices and serve with butter, if desired.

Date and walnut rolls will keep for up to 5 days, stored in a cool place in an airtight container, or can be frozen in an airtight container for up to 6 weeks.

CRANBERRY CREAM SCONES

MAKES 12

375 g (13 oz/3 cups) plain (all-purpose)
 flour, approximately
1 1/2 teaspoons bicarbonate of soda
 (baking soda)
3 teaspoons cream of tartar
2 teaspoons caster (superfine) sugar,
 plus extra for sprinkling
50 g (1 3/4 oz) cold unsalted butter,
 chopped
150 ml (5 fl oz) pouring (whipping) cream
150 ml (5 fl oz) milk, plus extra, for
 glazing
125 g (4 1/2 oz/3/4 cup) dried cranberries
jam, to serve
thick (double/heavy) cream, to serve

Preheat the oven to 220°C (425°F/Gas 7). Grease or line a baking tray with baking paper.

Sift the flour, bicarbonate of soda, cream of tartar and sugar into a large bowl. Using your fingertips, lightly rub in the butter until the mixture resembles breadcrumbs. Add the cream, milk and cranberries and mix to a soft dough using a flat-bladed knife, adding a little extra flour if the dough is too sticky.

Using lightly floured hands, gently gather the dough together and transfer to a lightly floured work surface. Pat into a smooth ball, then gently press out to a 2 cm (3/4 inch) thickness. Cut the dough into rounds using a 6 cm (2 1/2 inch) cutter, or use a knife dipped in flour to cut the dough into 4 cm (1 1/2 inch) squares.

Place the scones on the baking tray, brush the tops lightly with a little extra milk and sprinkle with a little extra sugar. Bake for 10–12 minutes, or until golden, then transfer to a wire rack to cool slightly.

Serve warm with jam and cream.

Cranberry scones are best eaten the day they are made, but can be frozen in an airtight container for up to 8 weeks.

CLASSIC MUFFINS
MAKES 12

310 g (11 oz/2½ cups) self-raising flour
55 g (2 oz/¼ cup) caster (superfine) sugar
2 teaspoons baking powder
2 eggs
375 ml (13 fl oz/1½ cups) milk
160 g (5¾ oz) unsalted butter, melted

TOPPING
80 ml (2½ fl oz/⅓ cup) pouring
   (whipping) cream
1 tablespoon icing (confectioners') sugar
2 tablespoons strawberry jam,
   approximately

Preheat the oven to 210°C (415°F/ Gas 6–7). Lightly grease a 12-hole standard muffin tin.

Sift the flour, sugar and baking powder into a bowl, then make a well in the centre.

In another bowl, mix together the eggs, milk and melted butter, then add to the well in the flour mixture. Stir gently with a fork or rubber spatula until just combined. Do not overmix — the batter should look quite lumpy.

Spoon the mixture into the muffin holes, smoothing the tops even. Bake for 20–25 minutes, or until golden brown. Remove from the oven, leave to cool in the tin for 2–3 minutes, then turn out onto a wire rack to cool completely.

To make the topping, beat the cream and icing sugar together using electric beaters until soft peaks form. Cut a circle from the top of each muffin, about 2 cm (¾ inch) deep, and cut these circles in half to make 'wings'. Spoon about ½ teaspoon strawberry jam into each muffin, top with the cream mixture and arrange the 'wings' in the cream.

These muffins are best eaten the day they are made. Without the topping they can be frozen in an airtight container for up to 8 weeks.

DOUBLE-CHOCOLATE MUFFINS

MAKES 6 LARGE MUFFINS

250 g (9 oz/2 cups) plain (all-purpose) flour
2¹/2 teaspoons baking powder
30 g (1 oz/¹/4 cup) unsweetened cocoa
 powder
2 tablespoons caster (superfine) sugar
175 g (6 oz/1¹/4 cups) chopped
 good-quality dark chocolate
1 egg
125 g (4 oz/¹/2 cup) sour cream
185 ml (6 fl oz/³/4 cup) milk
90 g (3¹/4 oz) unsalted butter, melted

CHOCOLATE ICING
100 g (3¹/2 oz/²/3 cup) chopped
 good-quality dark chocolate
2 tablespoons pouring (whipping) cream
20 g (³/4 oz) unsalted butter

Preheat the oven to 180°C (350°F/Gas 4). Grease a 6-hole giant muffin tin.

Sift the flour, baking powder and cocoa powder into a large bowl, then stir in the sugar and 125 g (4 oz/³/4 cup) of the chocolate. Make a well in the centre.

In another bowl, mix together the egg, sour cream, milk and melted butter. Pour into the well in the flour mixture and stir with a fork until just combined. Do not overmix — the batter should look quite lumpy.

Spoon the batter into the muffin holes and scatter with the remaining chocolate. Bake for 12–15 minutes, or until the muffins are firm in the centre. Remove from the oven, leave to cool in the tin for 2–3 minutes, then turn out onto a wire rack to cool completely.

Meanwhile, make the chocolate icing (frosting). Put the chocolate, cream and butter in a small saucepan and stir over low heat until the chocolate has melted and the mixture is smooth. Refrigerate until firm, then spread the icing over the cooled muffins.

Double-chocolate muffins will keep for 2 days, refrigerated in an airtight container. Without the icing they can be frozen in an airtight container for up to 6 weeks.

VANILLA CURRANT LOAF
SERVES 8

250 g (9 oz/2 cups) plain (all-purpose) flour
1 tablespoon baking powder
1/4 teaspoon salt
60 g (2 1/4 oz) cold unsalted butter, chopped
115 g (4 oz/1/2 cup) caster (superfine) sugar
75 g (2 1/2 oz/1/2 cup) currants
1 large egg
170 ml (5 1/2 fl oz/2/3 cup) milk
2 teaspoons natural vanilla extract
sifted icing (confectioners') sugar, for dusting, optional
butter or cream cheese, to serve

Preheat the oven to 180°C (350°F/Gas 4). Grease a 21 x 7 x 8 cm (8 1/4 x 2 3/4 x 3 1/4 inch) loaf (bar) tin and line the base and sides with baking paper.

Sift the flour, baking powder and salt into a large bowl. Using your fingertips, lightly rub in the butter until the mixture resembles coarse breadcrumbs. Stir in the sugar and currants, then make a well in the centre.

In another bowl, mix together the egg, milk and vanilla, then pour into the well in the flour mixture. Using a wooden spoon, stir until just combined.

Spoon into the prepared tin, smoothing the top. Bake for 45 minutes, or until a cake tester inserted into the centre of the loaf comes out clean. Remove from the oven and leave to cool in the tin for 10 minutes, before turning out onto a wire rack to cool.

Just before serving, dust with icing sugar if desired. Slice and serve with butter or cream cheese.

Vanilla currant loaf is best eaten the day it is made, but can be frozen in an airtight container for up to 8 weeks.

DAMPER
SERVES 8

375 g (13 oz/3 cups) self-raising flour,
    plus extra, for dusting
1–2 teaspoons sea salt
90 g (3¼ oz) unsalted butter, melted
125 ml (4 fl oz/½ cup) milk, plus extra,
    for glazing
butter, to serve

Preheat the oven to 210°C (415°F/Gas 6–7). Grease a baking tray.

Sift the flour and salt into a bowl and make a well in the centre. Combine the butter, milk and 125 ml (4 fl oz/½ cup) water and pour into the well in the flour mixture. Using a flat-bladed knife, stir until just combined.

Turn the dough out onto a lightly floured surface and knead for 20 seconds, or until smooth. Place the dough on the baking tray and press out to a 20 cm (8 inch) round.

Using a sharp-pointed knife, score the dough into eight sections, about 1 cm (½ inch) deep. Brush with a little extra milk, dust with flour and bake for 10 minutes.

Reduce the oven temperature to 180°C (350°F/Gas 4) and bake for a further 15 minutes, or until the damper is golden and sounds hollow when tapped on the base. Turn out onto a wire rack to cool briefly.

Serve warm or at room temperature, with butter.

Damper is best eaten the day it is made, but can be frozen in an airtight container for up to 8 weeks.

NOTE: If you prefer, you can make four small rounds instead of one large damper and slightly reduce the cooking time. Cut two slashes in the form of a cross on the top of each round.

JAM PINWHEELS
MAKES 12

300 g (10½ oz/2⅓ cups) self-raising flour
30 g (1 oz) cold unsalted butter, chopped
80 g (2¾ oz/⅓ cup) caster (superfine)
  sugar
1 egg
150 ml (5 fl oz) milk
160 g (5½ oz/½ cup) strawberry jam,
  warmed
butter, to serve

Preheat the oven to 200°C (400°F/Gas 6). Grease a 20 cm (8 inch) cake tin.

Sift the flour into a large bowl. Using your fingertips, lightly rub in the butter until the mixture resembles breadcrumbs. Stir in the sugar, then make a well in the centre.

In a small bowl, mix together the egg and milk, then pour into the well in the flour mixture. Using a fork, mix quickly until a soft dough forms, then turn out onto a lightly floured surface and knead lightly. Roll out to form a rectangle about 1.5 cm (⅝ inch) thick.

Spread the jam over the dough, then roll up into a log about 24 cm (9½ inches) long. Cut the roll into 12 even portions, then place them in the prepared tin.

Bake for 15–20 minutes, or until golden and cooked through. Remove from the oven and allow to cool briefly in the tin, before carefully turning out onto a wire rack.

Serve warm, with butter.

Jam pinwheels are best eaten the day they are made, but can be frozen in an airtight container for up to 6 weeks.

yeasted

Yeasted goods boil down to a few simple basics: yeast, salt, a bit of sugar, flour, water. Throw in a little warmth, time and a bit of kneading… and you have bread, adored the world over in its myriad forms, from the flatbreads of the Middle East, the egg-enriched breads of Scandinavia, the dense rye loaves of Eastern Europe to crusty French baguettes, Italian ciabatta and San Francisco sourdough.

Many cooks — even some highly experienced ones — imagine yeast is a difficult, temperamental substance to work with and that using it to make breads, pizza bases and fancy buns is a highly tricky, time-consuming exercise that's best left to the professionals. After all, our cities, suburbs and towns are full of bakeries, bagel shops, pizzerias and the like, and it is so much easier, we tend to think, to buy such basic commodities already bagged up in plastic than sit around and wait for dough to rise at home.

Actually, yeast-based baked goods are really quite simple to make and, with a little forethought, need not be time consuming.

While there are excellent bakers around of high integrity who make hand-made loaves using the best ingredients and processes, the benefits of making your own bread at home are enormous. Just read the ingredient list on any mass-produced loaf and you will see it is loaded with salt, as well as additives such as enzymes and bread improvers that lengthen shelf-life or 'enhance' flavour, colour and texture. For centuries, bread contained nothing more than flour, water, salt and yeast — and there is no reason why it still should not. Mass-produced bread is also bland and predictable, lacking the character and interest of home-made yeasted goods, while those from 'artisan' bakeries can be expensive and not something that everyone can regularly afford. Making your own loaves is highly economical and enables you to use ingredients of your choice, including organic and less refined ones if you prefer (today's ultra-refined milling processes used in modern commercial flours strip out much of the goodness inherent in wheat and other grains).

And there is little else you can create in your own kitchen that will give as much pleasure and sense of achievement as pulling your own crusty, golden, aromatic loaf of hot bread straight out of the oven.

WHAT IS YEAST?

Yeast is a single-celled organism from the fungus family. There are some 600 species that occur in nature in a variety of environments — in our air, soil, vegetation and foods. The yeast used in baking is *Saccharomyces cerevisiae; sacchus* means sugar in Latin and *myces* means fungus. It takes about 25 billion yeast cells to make just 1 gram (a fraction of an ounce) of dried yeast. The yeast used in baking needs sugar for growth, and this sugar is provided in the carbohydrates found in flour. The sugars that the yeast cells feed on ferment and are converted into carbon dioxide, which is essentially a by-product of fermentation. Kneading the dough results in the formation of an elastic structure called gluten, which has an ability to trap carbon dioxide, thus expanding the dough. When the dough is baked, the yeasts are killed off, but by this stage they have already done their work — the expanded structure they have created in the dough remains, and the fermentation process has given the bread its characteristic 'yeasty' smell and flavour.

Yeast cells expand by 'budding' — that is, a 'daughter' cell grows off the side of a mother cell, eventually growing so large it detaches, forming a new cell. Under ideal conditions, this happens quite quickly, and one yeast cell can spawn many daughters before it expires.

Several types of commercial yeasts are available. Firstly, there is **compressed fresh yeast**, which is favoured by professional bakers and chefs. Sold as a moist, beige 'cake' of yeast, it is said to give the most consistent and reliable results. It has a relatively short life span — it will stay fresh in a sealed container in the refrigerator for just 2 weeks, but can be frozen for up to 2 months. As it ages, it gets darker in colour and dries out. Older fresh yeast is not very reliable and will give your bread slightly 'off' yeasty aromas. When it is frozen and thawed, it turns liquid and must be used straight away.

Active dried yeast is a granular form of dehydrated yeast and is sold in sachets or canisters in supermarkets. It is popular with most home bakers because it is a stable yeast with a relatively long shelf life (but always check the expiry date on the packaging before buying). Dried yeast sold in foil sachets has been treated with nitrogen gas and doesn't require refrigeration until the packet is opened. Active dried yeast is usually first activated in a little warm liquid, generally with a pinch of sugar, until it foams (this takes about 10 minutes), before being added to the other bread ingredients. Most of the recipes in this chapter use active dried yeast.

Instant active yeast, also called **fast-acting yeast**, is a relatively recent innovation. It is even more dehydrated than active dried yeast and does not need rehydrating before use. However, because it works so rapidly, the finished goods are overly 'yeasty' with none of the complex flavours that can only result when a dough is allowed to rise and ripen at a slower pace. Essentially, the faster the dough rises, the less developed the flavours will be.

Which brings us to the original yeast, **wild yeast**. As previously noted, yeasts occur naturally in the air. The original breads, first made millennia ago, harnessed these yeasts. No doubt this first happened by accident — perhaps some baker noticed that his dough mysteriously rose when exposed to the air, and developed delicious fermented flavours and aromas as a result. Early yeasts were incorporated into recipes by letting doughs sit out for a period of time to 'sour'. These wild yeast cultures, once established in a dough mixture, were carefully maintained — some dough from each batch was saved to 'start' the next batch of dough. Before the development of commercial yeast, all leavened bread was made from sourdoughs. Sourdough breads are still made using wild yeast cultures — some of which are decades, if not centuries, old. As long as a little of the starter mixture from each batch is reserved and fed on fresh flour and water, a wild yeast culture will keep indefinitely. Wild yeasts give a wonderfully deep, tangy flavour to breads but are tricky to deal with. When you harvest yeasts from the air, 'bad' yeasts can also be attracted to the dough, and these will give strong, 'off' flavours to the bread.

Yeast conversions

10 g (¹/₄ oz) fresh yeast = 5 g (2 teaspoons) active dried yeast, or 3.5 g (1¹/₂ teaspoons) instant active yeast.

SALT

Salt has many functions in a bread dough. It retards yeast, allowing for its slow growth in the dough, and therefore development of flavour. Salt contributes to the strengthening of the gluten strands, which makes for a better-textured, well-risen bread. It also kills bacteria, helps the baked bread retain moisture and also helps preserve it. The correct ratio of salt to flour also improves the taste and appearance of the crust and helps to preserve the colour and flavour of the flour. For best results use a good, fine sea salt in your bread rather than commercial iodised salt, which can impart a nasty flavour.

FLOUR

Wheat is the primary flour used in bread-making, although a proportion of any number of other flours (such as corn, buckwheat, rye, barley, millet, oat and potato) are also used in bread doughs. Wheat flour is mainly used as it is unique in its composition — it contains proteins called glutenin and gliadin which, in combination with water, form gluten, that stretchy, elastic network that gives bread its necessary structure.

A grain of wheat contains bran (the fibrous coating), a starchy inner part, and the germ, which is high in oil and is found at the base of the grain. White flour has had the bran and germ removed. One advantage of this is that white flour lasts longer than wholemeal (whole-wheat) flour (which is milled from the entire grain) as the oils in wheatgerm go stale quickly. Wholemeal flour should be stored in the refrigerator, inside a sealed zip-lock bag, and used within 6 weeks of milling.

Essentially, there are two types of wheat: 'hard' and 'soft'. Of the two, 'hard' wheat has a harder structure and contains more gluten-forming proteins — a great advantage for bread bakers. This type of flour is sold as **strong flour**, and is sometimes also labelled bread flour.

Durum wheat is a high-proten, hard wheat flour; its inner layer (or endosperm) is known as semolina. Durum wheat produces flour with an exceptionally fine flavour and the highest protein content of all, but the gluten it forms is not as elastic as other wheat flours, so it is usually used in tandem with plain bread flour to avoid unpleasantly chewy results.

LIQUID

Water is the most commonly used liquid in bread, although sweet loaves, buns and yeast-raised cakes use milk. Liquid is used to bind the ingredients together. The liquid should be just warm — too hot and it will kill the yeast; too cold and the yeast will be sluggish to activate. Test the temperature by putting a little on the underside of your wrist — it should feel barely warm (about body temperature).

Tap water can be used for bread-making, but if it is very 'hard' (acidic and full of minerals) or 'soft' (alkaline and mineral-poor) it can affect the final result. Very hard water can produce tough bread that takes a very long time to ferment, while very soft water will produce a soft, sticky dough. Sometimes bakers add a small amount of ascorbic acid (vitamin C) to their baking water if it is overly soft, or more yeast to counteract very hard water. If you have very hard or soft tap water, you can use bottled mineral water (but not distilled water) instead. Chlorine in tap water will disperse if it is left to stand, uncovered, for several hours.

Milk in yeast doughs helps brown the crust as it contains a milk sugar, lactose, that yeast does not consume. Milk also contains protease, a substance which can break down the proteins in flour, weakening the dough. Heat renders protease harmless, so it is advisable to heat milk to simmering point, then cool it, before adding it to yeasted doughs.

Other liquids — buttermilk, yoghurt, sour cream and even beer — are often used in bread, and each imparts its own flavour and texture. Potato water (the cooled, unsalted water saved after potatoes have been boiled) is often used in breads because it adds a mellow flavour and helps bread stay moist.

FATS AND OILS

Butter and oil are the two fats you are most likely to add to bread doughs. Unsalted butter is usually called for so that the salt balance in the dough is not upset. Fat can have one of two very different effects, depending on the quantity added: a very little (about 1% of the dough's weight) lubricates the gluten and promotes gluten expansion, while a large amount retards expansion as it makes the dough heavy and slows yeast activity, leading to very long fermenting times. For this reason, loaves containing a lot of fat are generally raised first; the fat is then added for an additional rising. Fat gives a more tender crumb and helps the loaf (or buns or cake) last longer.

A STEP-BY-STEP GUIDE TO LOVELY LOAVES

The following method assumes the use of active dried yeast, the best of the most readily available commercial yeasts. Use the conversion guide on page 57 to substitute instant active yeast or fresh yeast instead. Instant yeast can just be added directly to the flour mixture — it does not require an initial 'start' (foaming) in warm water. The following method also assumes hand mixing and kneading, but these can be done in a heavy-duty stand mixer, with the dough hook attached.

- Sprinkle the yeast and a pinch of sugar over the warmed liquid. Leave to stand in a draught-free place for about 10 minutes — the yeast should have dissolved and formed a bubbling, foamy surface on the liquid. If it hasn't, the yeast is dead, so try again using a new batch of yeast.

- Combine the yeast liquid with the remaining liquid in the recipe and stir into the dry ingredients. Mix well to form a dough. Even though most bread recipes give exact quantities for liquid and flour, natural variations (in the humidity of the flour or of the atmosphere, for example) mean that sometimes you may have a dough that is too wet, so you need to add a little extra flour, or one that is too dry and that requires a little extra liquid. With experience you will know when a dough is the correct consistency. Resist the temptation to add too much flour too early — dough will firm up and become smooth during kneading, and too much flour results in a tough bread. If in doubt, err on the side of a slightly wet dough — it is easier to add a little extra flour than it is to incorporate extra liquid.

- Turn the dough out onto a floured surface and knead until smooth and elastic — the surface of the dough should be 'baby's-bottom smooth', and an indentation made by your finger should slowly spring back. This process, depending on the type of dough, can take up to 10 minutes by hand. Kneading, when done well, is a rhythmic action which involves sinking the heel of your hand into the middle of the dough and pushing it firmly away from you, giving the dough a half-turn, folding it over onto itself, then pushing it down from the middle again. To do this smoothly requires practice, but is a skill worth acquiring. Fortunately, however, even the most inexpert kneading will lead to acceptable results! Dough is tough and resilient and does not reward tentative kneading — you can be quite forceful with it. Insufficient kneading will result in a bread with a less than optimal structure; it will not rise properly or have the best texture.

- Shape the dough into a ball, place in a large, lightly oiled bowl, turning to coat the dough in the oil, then cover tightly with plastic wrap and leave to rise until doubled in bulk. Most recipes will say to leave dough in a warm place, but this is not necessary. As long as there are no cold draughts, which could kill the dough if strong enough, the dough will rise at room temperature or even in a cool place — it will just take longer. There are distinct advantages to a longer rising. Firstly, the slower the rising, the better developed the flavours of the finished bread will be. Secondly, a slower rising could well be more convenient for the cook — you can let the dough rise in the refrigerator overnight, then give it a second rising the next day. While yeast won't tolerate sudden shifts in temperature (as with a strong draught), constant cold temperature will not kill the yeast; it merely retards its growth. In fact, unbaked yeast doughs can even be frozen for several weeks without much harm. If you choose to rise dough in the refrigerator overnight, bring it to room temperature before preparing it for its second rise.

- Once the dough has risen to twice its original size, it is then 'knocked' down — many recipes say to 'punch' it down, although such a vigorous action as punching is hardly required. All you need to do is gently deflate the dough — pushing a clenched, lightly floured fist into the middle of the dough is sufficient for this.
- Next, the dough is shaped (your hands are best for this) and placed in a baking tin, although many loaves and buns are free-form and are simply shaped, then placed directly on a greased baking tray for a second rising before baking. Place the shaped dough into the tins or on the tray, seam side down.
- At this point, the top of the shaped dough is often glazed or scored. Usually, this second rising is much shorter than the initial one, although the time varies between recipes: some doughs need just a brief second rising, while some need to double in size again. Cover the rising dough with a damp tea towel (dish towel) and leave to rise at ambient room temperature. Do not 'force' the rise by placing the dough in a warm place or you will sacrifice flavour — but do make sure there are no cold draughts that could harm the yeast.
- The baking temperature will depend on the style of bread you are making. Some (particularly very crusty loaves) require quite high oven temperatures, while others need a slower baking. Breads high in sugar or fat can sometimes brown too quickly — if this happens protect the crust with a sheet of foil.
- The traditional way to test if bread is cooked is to remove it from its tin (turn it out into a folded tea towel to protect your hands from the heat), turn it upside down and tap the base with your knuckles — it should sound hollow.
- Do not leave bread to cool in the tin as condensation will cause the crust to go soggy. For super-crisp crusts, crusty loaves can be cooled out of their tins and in the oven with the door ajar. Other breads should be immediately removed from the tin or baking tray and transferred to a wire rack to cool. Always allow bread to cool before cutting it — bread sliced or broken then eaten hot from the oven risks drying out, as this allows precious moisture to escape.
- Fresh bread should be stored in a paper or cloth bag in a cool place; after about 24 hours it will quickly turn stale. Don't store bread in the refrigerator as this will dry it out. Bread can be successfully frozen for 3–4 weeks, but make sure it is well sealed (zip-lock bags, with all the air removed, are best). Ice that forms on the bread in the freezer will turn it soggy upon thawing.

CHOCOLATE BREAD
SERVES 10

2¹/₂ teaspoons active dried yeast
55 g (2 oz/¹/₄ cup) caster (superfine) sugar
375 g (13 oz/3 cups) strong flour
30 g (1 oz/¹/₄ cup) unsweetened cocoa
  powder
¹/₄ teaspoon sea salt
50 g (1³/₄ oz) unsalted butter
185 g (6¹/₂ oz/1¹/₄ cups) chopped
  good-quality dark chocolate
1 egg, lightly beaten
¹/₂ teaspoon natural vanilla extract
mascarpone or ricotta cheese, sweetened
  to taste with ¹/₂–1 tablespoon icing
  (confectioners') sugar, to serve

Pour 185 ml (6 fl oz/³/₄ cup) warm water into a small bowl. Sprinkle with the yeast and a pinch of the sugar and leave in a draught-free place for 10 minutes, or until foamy.

Combine the remaining sugar in a bowl with the flour, cocoa powder and salt.

Put the butter and half the chocolate in a heatproof bowl and place over a saucepan of simmering water, ensuring the base of the bowl doesn't touch the water. Stir frequently, until the chocolate has melted.

Remove from the heat and stir in the egg and vanilla until well combined, then pour into the flour mixture. Add the yeast mixture and mix together using a wooden spoon, then turn out onto a lightly floured work surface and knead for 10 minutes, or until the dough is smooth and elastic.

Place the dough in a large oiled bowl, turning to coat in the oil. Cover with plastic wrap and leave to rise in a draught-free place for 1¹/₂–2 hours, or until doubled in size.

Knock back the dough by punching it gently, then turn out onto a lightly floured work surface. Using your hands, press out to 1 cm (¹/₂ inch) thick, then scatter with the remaining chocolate. Roll the dough into a log.

Transfer to a greased baking tray, cover with a damp tea towel (dish towel) and leave to rise for 1 hour, or until doubled in size. Meanwhile, preheat the oven to 180°C (350°F/Gas 4).

Bake the bread for 45–50 minutes, or until it is light brown and sounds hollow when tapped on the base. Turn out onto a wire rack to cool.

Serve at room temperature with sweetened mascarpone or ricotta.

Chocolate bread will keep for 5 days, stored in a cool place in an airtight container, or can be frozen in an airtight container for up to 6 weeks. After the first day, fresh chocolate bread is best served lightly toasted.

CHEESE AND HERB PULL-APART
SERVES 10

2 teaspoons active dried yeast
1 teaspoon caster (superfine) sugar
500 g (1 lb 2 oz/4 cups) plain
   (all-purpose) flour
1¹/₂ teaspoons sea salt
2 tablespoons chopped parsley
2 tablespoons chopped chives
1 tablespoon chopped thyme
60 g (2¹/₄ oz/¹/₂ cup) grated cheddar
   cheese
milk, for glazing

Pour 60 ml (2 fl oz/¹/₄ cup) warm water into a small bowl. Sprinkle with the yeast and the sugar and leave in a draught-free place for 10 minutes, or until foamy.

Sift the flour and salt into a large bowl. Make a well in the centre, then pour the yeast mixture and 250 ml (9 fl oz/ 1 cup) warm water into the well. Mix using a wooden spoon until a soft dough forms, then turn out onto a lightly floured work surface and knead for 10 minutes, or until smooth.

Place the dough in a large oiled bowl, turning to coat in the oil, then cover with plastic wrap and leave to rise in a draught-free place for 1 hour, or until doubled in size.

Knock back the dough by punching it gently, then turn out onto a lightly floured work surface and knead for 1 minute. Cut the dough in half, then cut each half into 10 even portions. Form each piece into a disc about 6 cm (2¹/₂ inches) in diameter. Mix together the herbs and cheese and spread the mixture over half the discs, leaving a border around the edge. Top with the remaining discs, pressing around the edges to seal.

Grease a 21 x 10.5 x 6.5 cm (8¹/₄ x 4¹/₄ x 2¹/₂ inch) loaf (bar) tin. Stand the dough pieces upright in the prepared tin, fitting them all in snugly. Cover with plastic wrap and leave in a draught-free place for 30 minutes, or until the dough is well risen. Meanwhile, preheat the oven to 210°C (415°F/Gas 6–7).

Lightly brush the dough with a little milk, then bake for 30 minutes, or until the bread is brown and crusty and sounds hollow when tapped on the base. Turn out onto a wire rack to cool.

Serve warm or at room temperature.

Cheese and herb pull-apart is best eaten the day it is made, but can be frozen in an airtight container for up to 6 weeks.

WHITE DINNER ROLLS
MAKES 12 ROLLS

1 teaspoon active dried yeast
2 1/2 teaspoons caster (superfine) sugar
250 g (9 oz/2 cups) plain (all-purpose)
 flour
1/2 teaspoon sea salt
1 tablespoon dried full-cream (whole)
 milk powder
1 1/2 tablespoons oil
milk, for glazing
poppy seeds, sesame seeds, caraway seeds,
 sea salt flakes or plain flour, to decorate

Pour 60 ml (2 fl oz/1/4 cup) warm water into a small bowl. Sprinkle with the yeast and 1/2 teaspoon of the sugar and leave in a draught-free place for 10 minutes, or until foamy.

Combine the flour, salt, milk powder and remaining sugar in a bowl. Make a well in the centre, then pour the oil, yeast mixture and 125 ml (4 fl oz/1/2 cup) warm water into the well. Mix to form a soft dough, then turn out onto a lightly floured work surface and knead for 10 minutes, or until smooth and elastic, adding a little extra flour if the dough is sticky.

Place the dough in a large oiled bowl, turning to coat in the oil. Cover with plastic wrap and leave to rise in a draught-free place for 1 hour, or until doubled in size.

Knock back the dough by punching it gently, then turn out onto a lightly floured work surface and knead for 1 minute. Divide into 12 even portions and form into rolls. To make spiral rolls, roll each portion into a 30 cm (12 inch) rope, coil tightly and tuck under the ends to seal. Alternatively, tie the ropes to make knot rolls. Or simply shape the dough into ovals and leave plain, or cut a diagonal slash over the top using a sharp, lightly floured knife.

Space the rolls apart on two lightly greased baking trays and cover loosely with a damp tea towel (dish towel). Leave to rise for 20 minutes. Meanwhile, preheat the oven to 180°C (350°F/Gas 4).

Brush the rolls with a little milk, then sprinkle with your choice of seeds, sea salt flakes or flour. Bake for 15–20 minutes, or until lightly browned. Transfer to a wire rack to cool.

White dinner rolls are best eaten the day they are made, but can be frozen in an airtight container for up to 6 weeks.

BEIGLI

MAKES 2 ROLLS; EACH YIELDS 10 SLICES

185 ml (6 fl oz/³/4 cup) milk, warmed
2 teaspoons active dried yeast
115 g (4 oz/¹/2 cup) caster (superfine)
   sugar
500 g (1 lb 2 oz/4 cups) strong flour,
   approximately
220 g (7³/4 oz) unsalted butter, softened
2 eggs, lightly beaten, plus extra,
   for glazing
1 teaspoon grated lemon zest

WALNUT FILLING
400 g (14 oz/4 cups) walnuts
165 g (5³/4 oz/³/4 cup) sugar
75 g (2¹/2 oz/¹/2 cup) currants
1 teaspoon finely grated lemon zest

Pour 80 ml (2¹/2 fl oz/¹/3 cup) of the warm milk into a small bowl. Sprinkle with the yeast and a pinch of the sugar and leave in a draught-free place for 10 minutes, or until foamy.

Sift the flour into a large bowl and lightly rub in the butter with your fingertips until the mixture resembles fine breadcrumbs. Make a well in the centre, then add the yeast mixture, the remaining milk and sugar, the eggs and lemon zest to the well. Mix to a dough using a flat-bladed knife, then turn out onto a lightly floured work surface and knead for 10 minutes, adding a little extra flour if the dough is sticky.

Place the dough in a large oiled bowl, turning to coat in the oil. Cover with plastic wrap and leave to rise in a draught-free place for 2 hours, or until doubled in size.

Meanwhile, make the walnut filling. Roughly chop the walnuts in a food processor, then tip into a large heatproof bowl. Combine the sugar and 250 ml (9 fl oz/1 cup) water in a saucepan and stir over medium heat until the sugar has dissolved. Bring to the boil, then reduce the heat and simmer for 10 minutes, or until the syup has reduced and thickened slightly. Pour the syrup over the chopped walnuts, stir in the currants and lemon zest and mix well. Set aside to cool.

Knock back the dough by punching it gently, then knead on a lightly floured work surface for 2–3 minutes. Cut the dough in half, then roll each portion into a 22 x 36 cm (8¹/2 x 14 inch) rectangle. Spread the filling over each sheet of dough, leaving a 2.5 cm (1 inch) border on all sides. Roll each sheet up from the short end to enclose the filling, then place on a greased baking tray, seam side down.

Cover with a tea towel (dish towel) and leave to rise in a draught-free place for 1¹/2 hours, or until doubled in size. Meanwhile, preheat the oven to 200°C (400°F/Gas 6).

Brush the loaves with extra beaten egg and prick the tops in six places with a fork. Bake for 35–40 minutes, or until golden brown, covering loosely with foil if the loaves brown too quickly. Turn out onto a wire rack to cool.

Beigli is best eaten the day it is made, but can be frozen in an airtight container for up to 6 weeks.

Hot cross buns

MAKES 16

4 teaspoons active dried yeast
80 g (2³/₄ oz/¹/₃ cup) caster (superfine) sugar
625 g (1 lb 6 oz/5 cups) strong flour
1¹/₂ teaspoons mixed (pumpkin pie) spice
1 teaspoon ground cinnamon
1 teaspoon ground nutmeg
¹/₂ teaspoon sea salt
250 ml (9 fl oz/1 cup) milk, warmed
100 g (3¹/₂ oz) unsalted butter, melted
2 eggs
200 g (7 oz/1¹/₃ cups) currants
70 g (2¹/₂ oz/¹/₃ cup) mixed peel (mixed candied citrus peel)

GLAZE
2 tablespoons caster (superfine) sugar

CROSSES
60 g (2¹/₄ oz/¹/₂ cup) plain (all-purpose) flour

Pour 60 ml (2 fl oz/¹/₄ cup) warm water into a small bowl. Sprinkle with the yeast and a pinch of the sugar and leave in a draught-free place for 10 minutes, or until foamy.

In a bowl, mix together the flour, ground spices and salt and set aside.

Put the milk, butter, remaining sugar, eggs and 125 g (4¹/₂ oz/1 cup) of the flour mixture in the bowl of an electric mixer fitted with a dough hook attachment. Mix for 1 minute, or until smooth, then add the yeast mixture, currants and mixed peel and stir to combine. Add the remaining flour mixture, 125 g (4¹/₂ oz/1 cup) at a time, mixing well after each addition. As the dough becomes sticky and more difficult to mix, set the mixer to the lowest speed and knead for 5 minutes. Alternatively, mix the dough by hand using a wooden spoon, then turn out onto a lightly floured work surface and knead for 5 minutes, or until smooth and elastic.

Place the dough in a large oiled bowl, turning to coat in the oil. Cover with plastic wrap and leave to rise in a draught-free place for 1¹/₂–2 hours, or until doubled in size.

Knock back the dough by punching it gently, then turn out onto a lightly floured work surface. Divide the dough into 16 even portions. Roll each portion into a ball, then place on two greased baking trays about 4 cm (1¹/₂ inches) apart.

Cover with a damp tea towel (dish towel) and leave for 30 minutes, or until doubled in size. Meanwhile, preheat the oven to 180°C (350°F/Gas 4).

To make the glaze, combine the sugar and 2 tablespoons water in a small saucepan. Slowly bring to the boil over high heat, then remove from the heat and set aside.

To make the crosses, put the flour in a small bowl and gradually add 60 ml (2 fl oz/¹/₄ cup) water, stirring to form a dough. Roll out the dough on a lightly floured work surface to a 2 mm (¹/₁₆ inch) thickness. Cut into 5 mm (¹/₄ inch) wide strips, about 12 cm (4¹/₂ inches) long. Brush the strips with water and place two strips over each bun to form a cross.

Bake for 15–20 minutes, or until golden brown. Remove from the oven and brush the hot buns with the glaze, then turn out onto a wire rack to cool.

Hot cross buns are best eaten the day they are made, but can be frozen in an airtight container for up to 6 weeks.

RYE BREAD
MAKES 1 LOAF

185 ml (6 fl oz/³/4 cup) milk, warmed
2 teaspoons active dried yeast
1 teaspoon caster (superfine) sugar
200 g (7 oz/2 cups) rye flour, plus extra,
    for dusting
165 g (5³/4 oz/1¹/3 cups) strong flour
1 teaspoon sea salt

Pour the warm milk into a small bowl. Sprinkle with the yeast and sugar and leave in a draught-free place for 10 minutes, or until foamy.

Sift the flours and salt into a large bowl and make a well in the centre. Add the yeast mixture and 185 ml (6 fl oz/³/4 cup) warm water to the well. Using a wooden spoon or your hands, gradually incorporate the flour and mix to form a dough. Turn the dough out onto a lightly floured work surface and knead for 10 minutes, or until smooth and elastic.

Place the dough in a large oiled bowl, turning to coat in the oil. Cover with plastic wrap and leave to rise in a draught-free place for 1–1¹/2 hours, or until doubled in size.

Knock back the dough by punching it gently, then turn out onto a lightly floured work surface. Knead for 1 minute, or until smooth, then shape into an 18 cm (7 inch) circle. Using a sharp, lightly floured knife, score a shallow cross into the top of the loaf, then lightly dust with a little extra rye flour.

Lightly grease a baking tray and dust lightly with flour. Place the dough on the baking tray, cover with plastic wrap or a damp tea towel (dish towel) and leave to rise in a draught-free place for 1 hour, or until doubled in size. Meanwhile, preheat the oven to 180°C (350°F/Gas 4).

Bake the bread for 40–45 minutes, or until it is golden brown and sounds hollow when tapped on the base. Turn out onto a wire rack to cool completely before slicing.

Rye bread is best eaten the day it is made, but can be frozen in an airtight container for up to 6 weeks.

PLUM AND ROSEMARY FLATBREAD
SERVES 6

60 ml (2 fl oz/¼ cup) milk, warmed
2½ teaspoons active dried yeast
115 g (4 oz/½ cup) caster (superfine) sugar
2 eggs, lightly beaten
grated zest of 1 lemon
2 teaspoons finely chopped rosemary
250 g (9 oz/2 cups) strong flour
150 g (5½ oz) unsalted butter, softened
10 plums, halved and stoned, or 800 g
   (1 lb 12 oz) tinned plums, drained
whipped cream or mascarpone cheese,
   to serve

Combine the warm milk and yeast in the bowl of an electric mixer. Stir in 55 g (2 oz/¼ cup) of the sugar, the eggs, lemon zest and half the rosemary, then add the flour. Using the beater attachment, mix for 1 minute, or until a soft dough forms. Add the butter, then mix for 1 minute more, or until the dough is smooth, shiny and thick. Alternatively, mix the dough by hand using a wooden spoon.

Place the dough in a large oiled bowl, turning to coat in the oil. Cover with plastic wrap and leave to rise in a draught-free place for 1–1½ hours, or until doubled in size.

Grease a 25 cm (10 inch) spring-form cake tin or a loose-based flan (tart) tin. Knock back the dough by punching it gently with lightly floured hands (the dough is very soft). Place the dough in the prepared tin. Moisten the palms of your hands with water and press the dough into the edge of the tin. Arrange the plums, cut side up, over the top, pressing them gently into the dough. Cover with plastic wrap and leave to rise for 30 minutes.

Meanwhile, preheat the oven to 200°C (400°F/Gas 6).

Sprinkle the plums with the remaining sugar and scatter with the remaining rosemary. Bake for 10 minutes, then reduce the oven temperature to 180°C (350°F/Gas 4) and bake for a further 20 minutes, or until the flatbread is light golden and slightly 'spongy' when pressed in the centre. Turn out onto a wire rack and leave to cool slightly.

Serve warm, cut into wedges, with whipped cream or mascarpone cheese.

Plum and rosemary flatbread is best eaten the day it is made.

SARDINE AND SILVERBEET WHOLEMEAL PIZZA
MAKES TWO 30 CM (12 INCH) PIZZAS

2 teaspoons active dried yeast
a pinch of caster (superfine) sugar
300 g (10½ oz/2⅓ cups) strong flour
115 g (4 oz/¾ cup) wholemeal
  (whole-wheat) flour
1½ teaspoons sea salt flakes
2½ tablespoons olive oil

TOPPING
2½ tablespoons olive oil
1 large onion, finely chopped
5 garlic cloves, thinly sliced
1 bunch of silverbeet (Swiss chard), stems
  removed and discarded, and the leaves
  washed, dried and chopped
85 g (3 oz/⅔ cup) raisins, roughly
  chopped
150 g (5½ oz/1½ cups) grated parmesan
  cheese
a large pinch of chilli flakes, or to taste
2 x 100 g (3½ oz) tins of sardines in oil,
  drained

Pour 60 ml (2 fl oz/¼ cup) warm water into a small bowl. Sprinkle with the yeast and sugar and leave in a draught-free place for 10 minutes, or until foamy.

Put the flours and sea salt flakes into the bowl of an electric mixer fitted with a dough hook attachment. Make a well in the centre and pour the yeast mixture into the well. With the mixer set to the lowest speed, gradually add 250 ml (9 fl oz/1 cup) warm water and the olive oil. Mix for 3 minutes, or until a soft dough forms. Increase the speed to medium and knead for 7 minutes, or until the dough is smooth and elastic (it will be very soft). Alternatively, mix the dough by hand using a wooden spoon, then turn out onto a lightly floured work surface and knead for 7 minutes, or until smooth and elastic.

Place the dough in a large oiled bowl, turning to coat in the oil. Cover with plastic wrap and leave to rise in a draught-free place for 1½ hours, or until doubled in size.

Meanwhile, make the topping. Heat the olive oil in a large saucepan. Add the onion and garlic and stir over medium–high heat for 3 minutes, or until soft and lightly golden. Add the silverbeet and raisins, then cover and cook for 3 minutes, or until the silverbeet has wilted, stirring often. Remove from the heat and allow to cool slightly, then stir in the parmesan and chilli flakes and season with sea salt and freshly ground black pepper.

Preheat the oven to 220°C (425°F/Gas 7). Lightly grease two 30 cm (12 inch) pizza trays. (Alternatively, the pizzas can be baked directly on a pizza stone.)

Knock back the dough by punching it gently, then turn out onto a lightly floured work surface. Cut the dough in half and roll each out to form a 30 cm (12 inch) circle. Place on the pizza trays, scatter with the silverbeet mixture, then arrange the sardines over the top. Bake for 15–20 minutes, or until the pizza bases are crisp and golden. Serve hot.

Parmesan grissini
Makes 32

1 teaspoon active dried yeast
a pinch of caster (superfine) sugar
1 tablespoon extra virgin olive oil
250 g (9 oz/2 cups) strong flour
60 g (2¼ oz/⅔ cup) grated parmesan
 cheese
1 teaspoon sea salt

Pour 170 ml (5½ fl oz/⅔ cup) warm water into a small bowl. Sprinkle with the yeast and sugar and leave in a draught-free place for 10 minutes, or until foamy. Stir in the olive oil.

Put the flour in a large bowl, add the parmesan and salt and stir well. Pour in the yeast mixture and stir until a dough forms. Turn the dough out onto a lightly floured work surface and knead for 5 minutes, or until smooth and elastic.

Place the dough in a large oiled bowl, turning to coat in the oil. Cover with plastic wrap and leave to rise in a draught-free place for 1 hour, or until doubled in size. Meanwhile, preheat the oven to 200°C (400°F/Gas 6).

Lightly grease two baking trays. Knock back the dough by punching it gently, then turn out onto a lightly floured work surface and cut in half. Roll out one piece of dough to form a 20 x 16 cm (8 x 6¼ inch) rectangle, then cut it into 16 strips about 1 cm (½ inch) wide. Using your hands, gently roll each strip to form a 22–24 cm (8½–9½ inch) long stick, then place on one of the baking trays. Repeat with the second piece of dough and place on the other baking tray.

Bake for 17–20 minutes, or until the grissini are golden and crisp. Turn out onto a wire rack to cool.

Grissini will keep for up to 7 days, stored in an airtight container. If they become soft, heat them in a 180°C (350°F/Gas 4) oven for 5 minutes to crisp up.

SAFFRON CURRANT BREAD
SERVES 12

110 g (3³/4 oz/³/4 cup) currants
2 tablespoons dry sherry or rum
60 ml (2 fl oz/¹/4 cup) milk
¹/4 teaspoon saffron threads
2¹/2 teaspoons active dried yeast
115 g (4 oz/¹/2 cup) caster (superfine)
    sugar
125 g (4¹/2 oz) unsalted butter, softened
3 eggs
¹/2 teaspoon sea salt
25 g (1 oz/¹/4 cup) ground almonds
grated zest of 1 orange
375 g (13 oz/3 cups) plain (all-purpose)
    flour
icing (confectioners') sugar, for dusting

Put the currants in a small bowl, pour the sherry over and set aside to soak for 30 minutes.

Meanwhile, warm the milk in a small saucepan over medium heat until it reaches simmering point, then remove from the heat. Stir in the saffron and set aside for 20 minutes to infuse.

Pour 60 ml (2 fl oz/¹/4 cup) warm water into a small bowl. Sprinkle with the yeast and a pinch of the sugar and leave in a draught-free place for 10 minutes, or until foamy.

Grease a 25 cm (10 inch) ring tin.

Using electric beaters, cream the butter and remaining sugar until light and fluffy. Add the eggs one at a time, beating well after each addition. Add the salt, the milk and yeast mixtures, ground almonds, orange zest and currant mixture and beat gently to combine. Add the flour, 60 g (2¹/4 oz/¹/2 cup) at a time, and mix until incorporated. With the mixer set to the lowest speed, beat the mixture for a further 5 minutes, or until the dough is soft, shiny and elastic.

Spoon the dough into the prepared tin and cover with plastic wrap. Leave to rise in a draught-free place for 1¹/2–2 hours, or until doubled in size. Meanwhile, preheat the oven to 180°C (350°F/Gas 4).

Bake the bread for 35–40 minutes, or until it is golden and a cake tester inserted into the centre comes out clean. Remove from the oven and leave to cool in the tin for 10 minutes, before turning out onto a wire rack to cool.

Just before serving, dust with icing sugar.

Saffron currant bread is best eaten the day it is made, but can be frozen in an airtight container for up to 6 weeks.

ORANGE AND BLUEBERRY ROLLS

MAKES 20

250 ml (9 fl oz/1 cup) milk, warmed
4 teaspoons active dried yeast
80 g (2¾ oz/⅓ cup) caster (superfine)
   sugar
125 g (4½ oz) unsalted butter, softened
1 teaspoon sea salt
80 ml (2½ fl oz/⅓ cup) orange juice
2 eggs, lightly beaten
375 g (13 oz/3 cups) strong flour
icing (confectioners') sugar, for dusting

FILLING
100 g (3½ oz) unsalted butter, softened
115 g (4 oz/½ cup) caster (superfine)
   sugar
grated zest of 2 oranges
270 g (9½ oz/1¾ cups) fresh blueberries

Pour 100 ml (3½ fl oz) of the warm milk into a small bowl. Sprinkle with the yeast and a pinch of the sugar and leave in a draught-free place for 10 minutes, or until foamy.

Put the remaining milk and sugar in the bowl of an electric mixer with the butter and salt. Using the beater attachment, mix until the butter has just melted. Add the orange juice, eggs and yeast mixture and mix to combine. With the mixer set to the lowest speed, gradually add the flour, 60 g (2¼ oz/½ cup) at a time, mixing until a soft, smooth dough forms.

Place the dough in a large oiled bowl, turning to coat in the oil. Cover with plastic wrap and leave to rise in a draught-free place for 1 hour, or until doubled in size.

To make the filling, cream the butter, sugar and orange zest in a small bowl using electric beaters until pale and fluffy.

Turn the dough out onto a lightly floured work surface and divide in half. Roll each piece into a 25 x 15 cm (10 x 6 inch) rectangle. Spread half the filling mixture over one rectangle, then arrange half the blueberries over the top. Repeat with the remaining dough, filling and blueberries. Starting from the long side, roll up each rectangle to form a cylinder. Using a lightly floured, serrated knife, cut each cylinder into 10 even rolls.

Grease two 20 cm (8 inch) round spring-form cake tins. Arrange half the rolls, cut side up, in each tin. Cover with a damp tea towel (dish towel) and leave to rise in a draught-free place for 45 minutes, or until doubled in size. Meanwhile, preheat the oven to 180°C (350°F/Gas 4).

Bake the rolls for 25–30 minutes, or until they are golden and coming away from the side of the tins. Remove from the oven and leave to cool in the tins for 5 minutes, then turn out onto a wire rack to cool. Dust with icing sugar to serve.

Orange and blueberry rolls are best eaten the day they are made.

SIMPLE WHITE BREAD

MAKES 1 LOAF

2 teaspoons active dried yeast
1 teaspoon caster (superfine) sugar
450 g (1 lb/3²/₃ cups) strong flour
2 teaspoons sea salt

Pour 150 ml (5 fl oz) warm water into a small bowl. Sprinkle with the yeast and sugar and leave in a draught-free place for 10 minutes, or until foamy.

Combine the flour and salt in the bowl an electric mixer fitted with a dough hook attachment and make a well in the centre. Add another 150 ml (5 fl oz) warm water to the yeast mixture, then pour the mixture into the well. With the mixer set to the lowest speed, mix for 2 minutes, or until a dough forms. Increase the speed to medium and knead the dough for a further 10 minutes, or until smooth and elastic. Alternatively, mix the dough by hand using a wooden spoon, then turn out onto a lightly floured work surface and knead for 10 minutes, or until smooth and elastic.

Place the dough in a large oiled bowl, turning to coat in the oil. Cover with plastic wrap and leave to rise in a draught-free place for 1–1¹/₂ hours, or until doubled in size.

Knock back the dough by punching it gently, then turn out onto a lightly floured work surface. Shape into a rounded oval and transfer to a greased baking tray.

Cover loosely with a damp tea towel (dish towel) and leave to rise again in a draught-free place for 30 minutes, or until doubled in size. Meanwhile, preheat the oven to 190°C (375°F/Gas 5).

Using a sharp, lightly floured knife, make three diagonal slashes, about 4 cm (1¹/₂ inches) apart, across the top of the loaf. Bake for 40 minutes, or until the bread sounds hollow when tapped on the base. Turn out onto a wire rack to cool completely.

This bread is best eaten the day it is made, but can be frozen in an airtight container for up to 6 weeks.

PUMPERNICKEL ROLLS

MAKES 12 LUNCH ROLLS OR 16 DINNER ROLLS

90 g (3¼ oz/¼ cup) molasses
30 g (1 oz) unsalted butter
3 teaspoons active dried yeast
30 g (1 oz/¼ cup) unsweetened cocoa powder
1 tablespoon soft brown sugar
1½ tablespoons caraway seeds
2 teaspoons fennel seeds
1 teaspoon sea salt
300 g (10½ oz/3 cups) rye flour, plus extra, for dusting
375 g (13 oz/3 cups) strong flour

Put the molasses, butter and 500 ml (17 fl oz/2 cups) water in a small saucepan over low heat. Stir until the butter has melted, then remove from the heat and allow to cool slightly.

Combine the yeast, cocoa powder, sugar, caraway seeds, fennel seeds, salt and 200 g (7 oz/2 cups) of the rye flour in a large bowl. Pour in the butter mixture and, using a wooden spoon, mix until well combined. Mix in the remaining rye and strong flour, then turn out onto a lightly floured work surface and knead for 5 minutes, or until smooth and elastic.

Place the dough in a large oiled bowl, turning to coat in the oil. Cover with plastic wrap and leave to rise in a draught-free place for 45–60 minutes, or until doubled in size.

Knock back the dough by punching it gently, then turn out onto a lightly floured work surface and divide into 12 even portions (or 16 if making dinner rolls). Shape each portion into a round, then roll to form an oval shape.

Transfer the rolls to two greased baking trays and dust the tops with extra rye flour. Using a sharp, lightly floured knife, make three 1 cm (½ inch) deep cuts across the top of each roll. Cover with a damp tea towel (dish towel) and leave to rise in a draught-free place for 45 minutes, or until doubled in size. Meanwhile, preheat the oven to 180°C (350°F/Gas 4).

Bake the dinner rolls for 25–30 minutes, and the lunch rolls for 35 minutes, or until they sound hollow when tapped on the base. Turn out onto a wire rack to cool.

Pumpernickel rolls are best eaten the day they are made, but can be frozen in an airtight container for up to 6 weeks.

NOTE: These rolls are delicious served with cheese, smoked salmon and dill pickles.

FRUIT AND NUT BREAD
MAKES 1 LOAF

280 g (10 oz/2¼ cups) plain (all-purpose)
  flour, approximately
2 teaspoons active dried yeast
1 teaspoon mixed (pumpkin pie) spice
2 tablespoons caster (superfine) sugar
2 teaspoons grated orange zest
40 g (1½ oz/⅓ cup) sultanas
  (golden raisins)
35 g (1¼ oz/¼ cup) currants
1 tablespoon mixed peel (mixed candied
  citrus peel)
30 g (1 oz/¼ cup) chopped pecans
1 egg
80 ml (2½ fl oz/⅓ cup) orange juice
30 g (1 oz) unsalted butter, melted
oil or melted butter, for brushing

GLAZE
1 tablespoon milk
1 tablespoon sugar

Sift the flour into a large bowl. Add the yeast, mixed spice, sugar, orange zest, sultanas, currants, mixed peel and pecans and mix well. Make a well in the centre.

In another bowl, mix together the egg, orange juice, butter and 80 ml (2½ fl oz/⅓ cup) warm water, then pour into the well in the fruit mixture. Mix to a soft dough using a wooden spoon.

Turn the dough out onto a lightly floured work surface and knead for 10 minutes, or until smooth and elastic, adding a little extra flour if the dough is sticky.

Place the dough in a large oiled bowl, turning to coat in the oil. Cover with plastic wrap and leave to rise in a draught-free place for 45 minutes, or until well risen.

Knock back the dough by punching it gently, then turn out onto a lightly floured work surface and knead for 1 minute. Shape into an oblong or round and place in a greased 20 x 10 cm (8 x 4 inch) loaf (bar) tin, or on a greased baking tray, patting out to a 23 cm (9 inch) circle.

Brush the loaf with oil or melted butter. Cover with a tea towel (dish towel) and leave to rise in a draught-free place for 30 minutes. Meanwhile, preheat the oven to 180°C (350°F/Gas 4).

Bake the bread for 20–30 minutes, or until it is light brown and sounds hollow when tapped on the base. Turn out onto a wire rack to cool.

While the bread is still hot, brush with the combined glaze ingredients. Serve warm or cold.

Fruit and nut bread is best eaten the day it is made, but can be frozen in an airtight container for up to 6 weeks.

DRIED TOMATO AND THYME FOUGASSE
MAKES 8

1 ½ teaspoons active dried yeast
a pinch of caster (superfine) sugar
1 ½ teaspoons sea salt flakes, plus extra,
    for sprinkling
2 teaspoons finely chopped thyme
150 g (5 ½ oz/1 cup) sun-dried tomatoes,
    drained well (see Note), patted dry
    and chopped
2 ½ tablespoons extra virgin olive oil,
    plus extra for brushing
450 g (1 lb/3 ⅔ cups) plain (all-purpose)
    flour

Pour 125 ml (4 fl oz/½ cup) warm water into a small bowl. Sprinkle with the yeast and a pinch of the sugar and leave in a draught-free place for 10 minutes, or until foamy.

Transfer the yeast mixture to the bowl of an electric mixer fitted with a dough hook attachment. Add 185 ml (6 fl oz/¾ cup) warm water and the remaining ingredients. With the mixer set to a low speed, mix for 7 minutes, or until the dough is smooth and elastic (it will be quite soft). Alternatively, mix the dough by hand using a wooden spoon, then turn out onto a lightly floured work surface and knead until smooth and elastic.

Place the dough in a large oiled bowl, turning to coat in the oil. Cover with plastic wrap and leave to rise in a draught-free place for 1 ½–2 hours, or until doubled in size.

Knock back the dough by punching it gently, then turn out onto a lightly floured work surface and cut into 8 even portions. Using a floured rolling pin, roll out each piece to form an 18 x 9 cm (7 x 3 ½ inch) oval shape. Place them on a board and, using a sharp, lightly floured knife, cut angled slits into each half of the ovals, cutting through to the board, but not through the edges of the dough. Gently pull the cuts apart to form long gaps.

Transfer to two greased baking trays and brush with olive oil. Cover with a damp tea towel (dish towel) and leave to rise in a draught-free place for 20–25 minutes, or until slightly risen and puffy. Meanwhile, preheat the oven to 200°C (400°F/Gas 6).

Sprinkle the fougasse with a little extra sea salt and bake for 20 minutes, or until golden and crisp. Turn out onto a wire rack to cool.

Fougasse is best eaten the day it is made, but can be frozen in an airtight container for up to 6 weeks.

NOTE: If your sun-dried tomatoes have been preserved in oil, use the oil in the fougasse instead of the extra virgin olive oil.

Finnish cardamom rings

Makes 16

4 teaspoons active dried yeast
115 g (4 oz/^{1}/$_2$ cup) caster (superfine)
  sugar
200 ml (7 fl oz) evaporated milk
2 eggs
75 g (2^1/$_2$ oz/^{1}/$_2$ cup) wholemeal
  (whole-wheat) flour
500 g (1 lb 2 oz/4 cups) strong flour
1^1/$_2$ teaspoons ground cardamom
1^1/$_2$ teaspoons sea salt
50 g (1^3/$_4$ oz) unsalted butter, softened

GLAZE
1 egg
60 ml (2 fl oz/^{1}/$_4$ cup) milk

Pour 125 ml (4 fl oz/^{1}/$_2$ cup) warm water into a small bowl. Sprinkle with the yeast and 1 teaspoon of the sugar and leave in a draught-free place for 10 minutes, or until foamy.

In a small bowl, mix together the evaporated milk and eggs.

Put the wholemeal flour, 250 g (9 oz/2 cups) of the strong flour, the cardamom, salt and remaining sugar in the bowl of an electric mixer fitted with a dough hook attachment. Make a well in the centre, then pour the yeast and evaporated milk mixtures into the well. With the mixer set to the lowest speed, mix for 1 minute, or until a dough forms. Add the butter and mix to combine well. Add the remaining flour, 60 g (2^1/$_4$ oz/^{1}/$_2$ cup) at a time, and knead for 10 minutes, or until the dough is smooth and elastic (it will be very soft). Alternatively, mix the dough by hand using a wooden spoon, using your hands to incorporate the flour when the mixture becomes too difficult to mix with a spoon. Turn out onto a lightly floured work surface and knead for 10 minutes, or until smooth and elastic.

Place the dough in a large oiled bowl, turning to coat in the oil. Cover with plastic wrap and leave to rise in a draught-free place for 1–1^1/$_2$ hours, or until doubled in size.

Knock back the dough by punching it gently, then turn out onto a lightly floured work surface. Divide the dough into 16 even portions. Using your hands, roll each piece out to about 25 cm (10 inches) long, then join the ends to form a ring. Gently press the joins to seal.

Place on two lightly greased baking trays, cover loosely with a damp tea towel (dish towel) and leave to rise in a draught-free place for 45 minutes, or until doubled in size. Meanwhile, preheat the oven to 180°C (350°F/Gas 4).

Whisk together the glaze ingredients and brush over the rings. Bake for 18–20 minutes, or until golden. Remove from the oven and turn out onto a wire rack to cool.

Finnish cardamom rings are best eaten the day they are made, but can be frozen in an airtight container for up to 6 weeks.

SALLY LUNN TEACAKE

SERVES 6–8

2 teaspoons active dried yeast
1 teaspoon caster (superfine) sugar
3 eggs
185 ml (6 fl oz/³/₄ cup) milk, warmed
2 teaspoons natural vanilla extract
115 g (4 oz/¹/₃ cup) honey
125 g (4¹/₂ oz) unsalted butter, melted
500 g (1 lb 2 oz/4 cups) plain
   (all-purpose) flour
¹/₂ teaspoon sea salt

GLAZE
1 tablespoon sugar
1 tablespoon milk

Pour 60 ml (2 fl oz/¹/₄ cup) warm water into a small bowl. Sprinkle with the yeast and sugar and leave in a draught-free place for 10 minutes, or until foamy.

Put the eggs, milk, vanilla, honey, butter, half the flour, the salt and the yeast mixture in a large bowl. Beat well using electric beaters or a wooden spoon. Stir in the remaining flour to make a thick batter. Cover with plastic wrap and leave to rise in a draught-free place for 1–1¹/₂ hours, or until well risen.

Grease a 25 cm (10 inch) round, deep cake tin and line the base with baking paper.

Stir down the batter, spoon into the prepared tin, then smooth the surface even using lightly oiled hands. Cover with plastic wrap and leave to stand in a draught-free place for 1 hour, or until the dough has risen to the top of the tin. Meanwhile, preheat the oven to 180°C (350°F/Gas 4).

Bake the teacake for 35–40 minutes, or until a cake tester inserted into the centre comes out clean. Remove from the oven, mix together the glaze ingredients and brush over the top.

Bake for a further 5 minutes, then turn out onto a wire rack and leave to cool for 20 minutes. Serve warm.

Sally Lunn teacake will keep for up to 5 days, stored in a cool place in an airtight container, or can be frozen in an airtight container for up to 4 weeks.

NOTE: Sally Lunn teacake is traditionally served in the following way, usually for afternoon tea. Allow the cake to cool completely, then cut it horizontally into three layers of even thickness. Using an oven grill (broiler), toast the slices on both sides, then butter each side. Reassemble the layers, slice and serve.

FINGER BUNS
MAKES 12

750 g (1 lb 10 oz/6 cups) plain
  (all-purpose) flour
35 g (1¼ oz/⅓ cup) full-cream (whole)
  milk powder
3 teaspoons instant active yeast
115 g (4 oz/½ cup) caster (superfine)
  sugar
60 g (2¼ oz/½ cup) sultanas
  (golden raisins)
½ teaspoon sea salt
60 g (2¼ oz) unsalted butter, melted
1 egg
butter, to serve

GLAZE
1 egg yolk
1½ teaspoons water

GLACÉ ICING
155 g (5½ oz/1¼ cups) icing
  (confectioners') sugar
20 g (¾ oz) unsalted butter, melted
a few drops of pink food colouring

Put 375 g (13 oz/3 cups) of the flour in a large bowl with
the milk powder, yeast, sugar, sultanas and salt. Mix together
and make a well in the centre.

In another bowl, mix together the butter, egg and
250 ml (9 fl oz/1 cup) warm water. Add to the well in the
flour mixture. Stir for 2 minutes, or until well combined.
Add enough of the remaining flour to make a soft dough.

Turn out onto a lightly floured work surface and knead
for 10 minutes, or until the dough is smooth and elastic,
adding a little extra flour if the dough is sticky.

Place the dough in a large oiled bowl, turning to coat
in the oil. Cover with plastic wrap and leave to rise in a
draught-free place for 1 hour, or until well risen.

Knock back the dough by punching it gently, then
knead for 1 minute. Divide into 12 even portions and shape
each into an oval about 15 cm (6 inches) long. Place on two
large greased baking trays, 5 cm (2 inches) apart. Cover
with plastic wrap and leave to rise in a draught-free place
for 20–25 minutes, or until well risen. Meanwhile, preheat
the oven to 180°C (350°F/Gas 4).

Mix together the glaze ingredients and brush over
the buns. Bake for 12–15 minutes, or until firm and golden.
Remove from the oven and transfer to a wire rack to cool.

To make the glacé icing (frosting), sift the icing sugar
into a bowl, add the butter and 2–3 teaspoons water and stir
until smooth. Mix in the food colouring, then spread the icing
over the buns.

Serve the buns with lashings of butter.

Finger buns are best eaten the day they are made.
Without the icing they can be frozen in an airtight container
for up to 6 weeks.

PRETZELS

MAKES 12

150 ml (5 fl oz) milk, warmed
1 teaspoon active dried yeast
1/4 teaspoon caster (superfine) sugar
185 g (6 1/2 oz/1 1/2 cups) strong flour
1/4 teaspoon sea salt
30 g (1 oz) unsalted butter, melted
1 egg yolk, lightly beaten
coarse sea salt, for sprinkling

Pour the warm milk into a small bowl. Sprinkle with the yeast and sugar and leave in a draught-free place for 10 minutes, or until foamy.

Mix the flour and salt together in a large bowl and make a well in the centre. Add the yeast mixture and butter to the well and stir using a wooden spoon until a dough forms.

Turn out onto a lightly floured work surface and knead for 10 minutes, or until smooth and elastic.

Place the dough in a large oiled bowl, turning to coat in the oil. Cover with plastic wrap and leave to rise in a draught-free place for 1 hour, or until doubled in size.

Knock back the dough by punching it gently, then turn out onto a lightly floured work surface and knead for 2–3 minutes. Divide the dough into 12 even portions. Covering the rest of the dough with a tea towel (dish towel) while working with each piece, roll each portion into a rope about 40 cm (16 inches) long. Circle and knot the rope into a pretzel shape, then place 5 cm (2 inches) apart on a large baking tray lined with baking paper.

Cover with a tea towel and leave to rise in a draught-free place for 20–30 minutes, or until risen slightly. Meanwhile, preheat the oven to 190°C (375°F/Gas 5).

Lightly brush the pretzels with the beaten egg yolk and sprinkle with sea salt. Transfer to the oven, spray twice with water, then bake for 12–15 minutes, or until crisp and golden. Remove from the oven and transfer to a wire rack to cool.

Pretzels are best eaten the day they are made, but can be frozen in an airtight container for up to 6 weeks.

cakes

Cakes come in many guises. There are airy cakes, squidgy cakes, dense cakes and springy cakes. Some ooze creamy fillings, others are drenched with syrup or slathered with a gooey topping. Some cakes are dainty and classic and beg a cup of tea or a snifter of sherry, while others taste best when washed down with a glass of cold milk.

Among the most delicious of cakes are the everyday sorts, which are the focus of this chapter — humble and crumby and comforting. Some are burnished brown, some egg-yolk yellow, while others are speckled with nuts, flecked with chocolate or marbled with colour. Even among the simpler cakes, the possible variations are endless. Amazingly, all cakes boil down to a handful of common ingredients: flour, sugar, eggs, butter, raising agents, maybe a little milk or sour cream and a flavouring of some sort.

Very early cakes amounted to no more than flat rounds of crushed grains, moistened, then baked on a hot stone. Over time these primitive 'cakes' were embellished with nuts, honey, oils and fruits. The ancient Egyptians are thought to be among the earliest cake bakers; their creations were yeast-raised affairs, differentiated from bread by their enrichment with nuts and dried fruits. The Greeks refined early flour-milling practices, enabling them to bake lighter-textured goods, which were sweetened with honey. It is thought the Romans further enhanced their cakes by the addition of butter and eggs; they also made fruitcakes and, so some say, a type of cheesecake.

The word 'cake' comes from the Norse word *kaka* and was adopted into English usage around the thirteenth century. Then, though, 'cake' signified a round, flat loaf of bread — it wasn't until the seventeenth century, with the advent of more reliable ovens, the wider availability of refined sugar and the invention of 'cake hoops' for baking, that anything resembling modern cakes started to appear. Cakes had tended to be sturdy, long-keeping affairs; examples of these are the gingerbreads of medieval Britain, Germany and France, and the dense, heavily spiced 'keeping cakes' like *certosino*, from Italy. Not everyone had access to butter, so cakes were often made using dripping, lard or olive oil.

It wasn't until 1843 that great strides were made in the commercial production of baking powder — a leavening substance containing bicarbonate of soda (baking soda) and an acidic salt. Baking powder provided more predictable, consistent and faster rising than yeast or plain bicarbonate of soda. With this and the technological improvements that were made to ovens, cake-making became even easier and more widespread. In 1896, with the publication of Fannie Farmer's *Boston Cooking-School Cook Book*, standardised measurements, specific baking times and correctly measured temperatures were first extolled.

Interestingly, cake-making as we know it isn't widely found in Asian cultures, except where the influence of colonial Europeans has spawned a few noteworthy examples, such as the Sri Lankan 'love cake' (from the Portuguese) and the Indonesian 'thousand-layer spice cake' (from the Dutch, who called it *spekkoek*).

In the West, domestic cake-baking reached its apogée during the early to mid twentieth century, when it was practically a required part of every housewife's repertoire. This is no longer true of course, and simply buying cakes or making them from cheap, convenient pre-mixes has become accepted practice — but, it has to be said, absolutely nothing comes close to the comforting allure and satisfying flavour of a slice (or two) of home-made cake.

CREAMED CAKES

Also called butter cakes, these are one of the most common types of cake, and are characterised by their tender crumb. Pound cakes, devil's food cake and classic yellow cake are all creamed cakes. The process of creaming suits cakes made with a high proportion of butter, where it equals half the weight of the flour or sometimes even more, as creaming makes it easier to combine the butter with the other ingredients.

These cakes all start with softened butter and sugar that is beaten into a smooth, light and fluffy mass — this creaming process helps the butter hold air, thus lightening the cake and helping it to rise. A solid fat is required; oil can't be substituted. Allow the butter to soften at room temperature — microwaving butter can cause it to melt in places. Melted butter is no good for this type of cake either as its chemical make-up changes during melting.

Use caster (superfine) sugar in these cakes as their fine crystals will dissolve into the butter, whereas the larger crystals of regular granulated white sugar will not. Beat the mixture for at least 5 minutes if using an electric stand mixer or hand-held beaters.

Eggs are added next, one at a time. These need to be at room temperature — cold eggs will make the butter curdle. The butter will also curdle if you add too much egg at once, so make sure you beat well between adding each egg and be sure not to rush this stage. Stop to scrape down the sides of the bowl every now and then to make sure all the mixture is fully incorporated. The entire mixture should be very light and creamy.

If, for some reason, the mixture does curdle, stir in a tablespoon or so of whatever type of flour is being used in the cake.

Next, you need to add your sifted flour and any wet ingredients and flavourings. Often recipes will specify to alternate the dry ingredients with the wet ones. A light hand is vital for mixing in the flour — do not use any type of machine to beat the flour in, as this will work the gluten (proteins) in the flour and toughen the cake. Use a large metal spoon or a spatula to quickly, and lightly, stir in any remaining ingredients, taking care not to overmix.

The mixture should then, without delay, be transferred to a prepared cake tin (already greased and floured or lined with baking paper). Smooth the surface even, making a small dip in the very centre to stop the mixture puffing up, and immediately place in a preheated oven. *Always* preheat your oven, as leavening agents (bicarbonate of soda, baking powder and the like) start to activate upon contact with moisture. Some creamed cakes, such as classic pound cakes, are made without chemical leavening, relying solely on air trapped in the batter for raising, and will lose their volume if left to sit.

To test if your cake is cooked, insert a fine, metal cake tester (see page 15) into the middle of the cake — it should withdraw without any crumbs sticking to it. Do not put a wooden skewer or metal meat skewer into your cake as it will leave a large, ugly hole.

Once the cake is cooked, allow it to cool in the cake tin for the time specified in the recipe, before carefully turning it out onto a wire rack to cool completely. Turning it out too early may cause the cake to collapse, but leaving it to cool completely in the tin will cause the moisture in the cake to condense, making the cake crumb soggy.

TROUBLESHOOTING CREAMED CAKES

Here are some of the most common faults in creamed cakes, and the most likely reasons for them.

- **Dense, heavy texture** — the eggs were not beaten in sufficiently, or the dry ingredients were stirred in too vigorously, making the cake tough.
- **The cake is sunken, with a soggy, dense texture** — the cake wasn't cooked long enough or the oven temperature was too low. There may have been too little flour or too much butter added, or the oven door may have been opened during the early stage of cooking.
- **The top of the cake is dark and the internal texture dry** — the cake has been cooked for too long or at too high a temperature, or the cake was baked in the wrong-sized tin (one that is too large).
- **Peaked or cracked in the middle** — either the cake tin was too small, there was too much raising agent in the batter, or the oven temperature was too high.

FOAM OR WHISKED CAKES

The most common cakes in this category are light sponge cakes, American chiffon and angel food cakes. They all have a very airy texture, achieved by incorporating maximum air into the eggs (or egg whites), which is the principal form of leavening. These light, lower-fat cakes often have some sort of rich filling or topping, on account of their drier texture. Foam-type cakes form the basis of many rich and elaborate European-style cakes and desserts such as trifle, tiramisu and *bouche de noel*.

Some recipes use whole eggs, others yolks or whites, but the basic technique is whisking egg with sugar until billowy and very thick. Hand-held electric beaters or an electric stand mixer with a whisk attachment are best for this job (beating by hand, using a wire whisk, is very laborious). Use a large bowl without any trace of grease when working with egg whites, as grease inhibits the whipping process. A mixture beaten from sugar and whole eggs or egg yolks is thick enough when it will fall back on itself and form wide ribbons; it will be lemon-coloured and its volume will have greatly increased. Egg white and sugar mixtures will be very stiff, thick and glossy.

At this point, flavourings and flour are gently folded in, about one-third at a time. If added all at once, the flour would sink through the mixture and need vigorous, destructive stirring to disperse. Make sure the flour is well sifted; some cooks sift it three times to ensure lightness. Be careful to fold right down to the base of the bowl to stop any lumps of flour accumulating, as these will form hard pockets in the finished cake. To fold the flour in, 'cut' a large metal spoon through the centre of the mixture, then turn the spoon and draw it up along the side of the bowl. Give the bowl a 90-degree turn, and then repeat folding. Don't stir or you'll deflate the mixture.

Once combined, quickly pour the cake batter into a prepared tin and bake in a preheated oven without delay — any sitting around will cause the mixture to lose air and start deflating. These cakes rise dramatically in the oven, although some will fall back a little on cooling.

TROUBLESHOOTING FOAM CAKES

These are the most common faults in foam cakes, and why they occur.

- **Bubbles on the surface of the cake** — the oven temperature was too cool (your oven may need recalibrating).
- **The cake rises unevenly or insufficiently** — either the eggs were not whisked enough, or they were whisked too much and collapsed when the flour was added. Another reason for this is overmixing of the dry ingredients, which deflates the mixture.
- **Pockets of flour in the cake** — the flour wasn't folded in thoroughly.

MELTED CAKES

Cakes made with a high proportion of honey, treacle or other heavy liquid sweetener are generally made by first melting butter with sugar and other sweeteners. Traditional 'boiled' fruitcakes are also made using this method.

Cakes made this way tend to be very moist and sweet — classic examples are gingerbread and honey cake. They also have a more dense texture than creamed or foam cakes and rely completely on chemical leaveners to rise as they contain no (or very few) eggs. Because of their high sugar content, these cakes can burn easily, so keep a special eye on them as many of them tend to be dark anyway (thanks to treacle, molasses or spices in the batter).

These are very easy cakes to make. No special equipment is needed — just a saucepan, a bowl and a spoon to mix. After the combined sweetener/butter mixture has melted and cooled a little, the sifted dry ingredients, liquid (usually milk) and any eggs are stirred in, then the batter is transferred to a tin and baked. Often these cakes need to 'age' for a day or two before serving to develop flavour and improve their texture. On account of their high sugar content, these cakes will stay moist longer than other cakes.

These cakes are ideal for beginners as very little can go wrong with them. The only caution — and this applies to all cakes — is not to overmix when adding the flour, as excessive 'working' of the flour will form gluten, which will cause the cake to be very tough.

TROUBLESHOOTING MELTED CAKES
If things do go wrong, here are the reasons why.

- **The cake sinks in the middle** — the cake was not baked long enough.
- **The surface is dry and crusty** — the cake has been baked for too long and/or the oven temperature was set too high.
- **The top is peaked and cracked** — too much raising agent was used, the cake tin was too small, or the oven temperature was too high.
- **The cake tastes slightly soapy** — there was too much bicarbonate of soda (baking soda) in the mixture.

FRUITCAKES
So often the centrepiece of a special celebration (a wedding, birthday or christening), a traditional cake dense with dried fruits, nuts and spices is not at all difficult to make: the best fruitcakes are no more than alcohol-soaked fruits, held together by a minimum of intensely spiced batter.

Fruitcakes can be costly to make, and their longer preparation and cooking times can seem off-putting. However, these wonderful cakes keep for a very long time, can be made well in advance, and a decent-sized one will feed many. And when you make your own, you can completely control the quality of your ingredients and avoid altogether the garish, sugary, fake-flavoured glacé fruits found in cheap, store-bought examples. If you respect the basic ratios of the recipe, you can substitute some or all of the weight in fruit with whatever you desire: dried peaches, apricots, mangoes, pawpaw, cranberries, figs, prunes, dates or quality Italian glacé cherries and oranges.

Most fruitcakes are made using the creaming method, although some 'boiled' fruitcakes use the melted butter method outlined previously. Before starting, have everything ready — the fruit soaked, the nuts toasted and chopped, citrus zest grated, spices measured, the flour weighed and sifted. (If you're using dried-fruit mixtures that seem a little dried out or 'tired', you can pep them up by rinsing them in boiling water, then soaking them for a few days in brandy, whisky or rum — just remember to drain the fruit very well before using.) Line the side and the base of the cake tin with several layers of baking paper. This insulates the cake from the heat and stops it burning during the long cooking time. Make sure the baking paper fits snugly into the joins of the tin so the baked cake has neat, defined edges.

Metal-surfaced, shiny tins are better for baking fruitcakes than black or non-stick ones as these darker surfaces will make the cake brown too quickly.

Always use a very slow oven. If your oven runs a little hot (as some do), set it 25°C (75°F) lower than the recipe suggests — it won't hurt the cake and you can simply bake it for a little longer. If your cake browns too quickly, cover the top with foil or several layers of baking paper.

When the cake is cooked, a cake tester won't come out entirely clean — it will withdraw moist, but with no sign of raw mixture. The cake will also be slightly risen and will have pulled away a bit from the side of the tin.

Just-baked fruitcakes are surprisingly fragile and it is best to let them cool in their tin. While they are cooling you can prick them deeply all over with a skewer and brush liberally with rum, brandy, whisky or whatever alcohol complements the fruit you have used in the batter. Alcohol not only flavours the cake but helps preserve it.

A cooked fruitcake, wrapped well and stored in a cool, dark place, will keep for several months and even up to a year. (You can also freeze fruitcakes — if wrapped *very* well in foil, then sealed in a zip-lock bag or airtight container, they will keep for 8–12 months.)

Once the fruitcake has cooled, remove it from the tin, wrap several times in plastic wrap, then store in an airtight cake tin or plastic container to protect it from insects. Before doing so you can brush or drizzle it fairly liberally with some more alcohol. It is not necessary to remove the paper lining before wrapping it.

Troubleshooting fruitcakes
Fruitcakes are generally trouble-free, but simple faults can sometimes occur.

- **A darkened top with burnt-looking fruit** — the cake is overcooked, or there was too much sugar in the mixture.
- **A cracked top** — there is too much leavening. Fruitcakes contain very little baking powder or bicarbonate of soda (baking soda). Those small quantites (½ teaspoon or so) in the recipes are not a misprint.
- **The surface is sunken** — the cake has not been baked for long enough, or there may be insufficient raising agent. A sunken surface can also happen when the cake is positioned too low in the oven; it needs to be placed in the middle.
- **The fruit sinks to the bottom** — there is too little raising agent or the batter was insufficiently mixed.

COFFEE CUPCAKES
MAKES 18

185 g (6½ oz) unsalted butter, softened
125 g (4½ oz/⅔ cup) soft brown sugar
2 eggs
3 teaspoons instant coffee granules,
    dissolved in 1 tablespoon warm water
150 g (5½ oz/1¼ cups) self-raising flour
100 ml (3½ fl oz) buttermilk
18 chocolate-coated coffee beans,
    to decorate

COFFEE ICING
250 g (9 oz/2 cups) icing (confectioners')
    sugar
30 g (1 oz) unsalted butter, softened
1½–2 teaspoons instant coffee granules,
    dissolved in 2–3 teaspoons warm water

Preheat the oven to 150°C (300°F/Gas 2) and line one 12-hole standard muffin tin and one 6-hole muffin tin with paper cases.

Using electric beaters, cream the butter and sugar until light and fluffy. Add the eggs one at a time, beating well after each addition, then stir in the coffee.

Sift the flour into a bowl. Using a large metal spoon, gently fold the flour into the butter mixture, alternating with the buttermilk, until just combined and almost smooth.

Spoon the batter into the paper cases and bake for 25–30 minutes, or until the cupcakes are lightly golden and slightly springy to the touch. Remove from the oven and leave to cool in the tins.

To make the coffee icing (frosting), sift the icing sugar into a small bowl, add the butter, coffee granules and 1½ tablespoons boiling water and stir until smooth. Thickly spread the icing over the cooled cupcakes and decorate each with a chocolate-covered coffee bean.

Coffee cupcakes will keep for up to 3 days, stored in a cool place in an airtight container. Without the icing they can be frozen in an airtight container for up to 8 weeks.

ORANGE POPPY SEED CAKE
SERVES 8–10

185 g (6½ oz) unsalted butter, softened
170 g (6 oz/¾ cup) caster (superfine)
  sugar
3 eggs
1 teaspoon natural vanilla extract
2½ tablespoons poppy seeds
1 teaspoon grated orange zest
185 g (6½ oz/1½ cups) self-raising flour
60 g (2¼ oz/½ cup) plain (all-purpose)
  flour
60 ml (2 fl oz/¼ cup) milk

CANDIED CITRUS
2 oranges
2 lemons
520 g (1 lb 2½ oz/2¼ cups) caster
  (superfine) sugar

Preheat the oven to 180°C (350°F/Gas 4). Grease a 22 cm (8½ inch) round cake tin or kugelhopf tin and lightly dust with flour, shaking out any excess.

Using electric beaters, cream the butter and sugar until light and fluffy. Add the eggs one at a time, beating well after each addition. Add the vanilla, poppy seeds and orange zest and stir until well combined.

Sift the flours into a bowl. Using a large metal spoon, gently fold the flour into the butter mixture, alternating with the milk, until just combined and almost smooth.

Spoon the batter into the prepared tin and smooth over the surface. Bake for 45 minutes, or until a cake tester inserted into the centre of the cake comes out clean. Remove from the oven, leave in the tin for 10 minutes, then turn out onto a wire cake rack to cool slightly.

While the cake is baking, prepare the candied citrus. Cut the oranges and lemons into slices about 4 mm (⅛ inch) thick. Place 250 g (9 oz) of the sugar in a heavy-based frying pan with 80 ml (2½ fl oz/⅓ cup) water. Stir over low heat until the sugar has completely dissolved. Bring to the boil, then reduce the heat and simmer. Add a quarter of the fruit slices to the syrup and simmer for 5–10 minutes, or until the fruit is transparent and the syrup is reduced and toffee-like. Lift out the fruit with tongs and cool on a wire rack.

Add an extra 90 g (3¼ oz/heaped ⅓ cup) sugar to the syrup and stir to dissolve. Simmer a second batch of fruit slices in the syrup as before, then remove. Add another 90 g (3¼ oz) sugar to the syrup and stir to dissolve, then simmer a third batch of fruit slices in the syrup, then remove. Repeat with the remaining sugar and fruit slices. Reserve the syrup and allow the candied citrus slices to firm.

Place the warm cake, still on the wire rack, over a tray. Pierce all over with a cake skewer, then pour the hot syrup over, allowing it to soak in — if the syrup is too thick, thin it with a little orange juice. Set the cake on a serving plate and arrange some of the firm candied citrus slices over the top.

Orange poppy seed cake is best served within a few hours of decorating.

Any left-over candied fruit can be kept between layers of baking paper in an airtight container for up to 2 days.

CHOCOLATE MUDCAKE
SERVES 8

185 g (6½ oz/1½ cups) self-raising flour
60 g (2¼ oz/½ cup) plain (all-purpose)
   flour
40 g (1½ oz/⅓ cup) unsweetened
   cocoa powder
250 g (9 oz) unsalted butter, chopped
1 tablespoon oil
200 g (7 oz/1⅓ cups) chopped dark
   chocolate
375 g (13 oz/1⅔ cups) caster (superfine)
   sugar
1 tablespoon instant coffee granules
2 eggs, lightly beaten
ice cream or whipped cream, to serve

CHOCOLATE TOPPING
150 g (5½ oz) unsalted butter, chopped
150 g (5½ oz/1 cup) chopped dark
   chocolate

Preheat the oven to 160°C (315°F/Gas 2–3). Grease a 20 cm (8 inch) round, deep cake tin and line the base and side with baking paper.

Sift the flours and cocoa powder into a large bowl and make a well in the centre.

Put the butter, oil, chocolate, sugar and coffee granules in a saucepan with 250 ml (9 fl oz/1 cup) water. Stir over low heat until the chocolate and butter have melted and the sugar has dissolved. Pour the mixture into the well in the flour, then whisk until just combined. Add the eggs and mix until combined and smooth, taking care not to overbeat.

Pour the batter into the prepared tin and bake for 2 hours, or until a cake tester inserted into the centre of the cake comes out clean. Remove from the oven and allow to cool completely in the tin, then carefully turn the cake out onto a wire rack.

To make the chocolate topping, put the butter and chocolate in a saucepan and stir over low heat until melted and smooth. Remove from the heat and allow to cool slightly.

Trim the top of the cooled cake so it is level, then place the cake, cut side down, on a wire rack over a baking tray. Pour the topping over the cake, letting it run down the side.

Serve with ice cream or whipped cream.

Chocolate mudcake will keep for 2–3 days, stored in a cool place in an airtight container, or can be frozen in an airtight container for up to 4 weeks.

GOLDEN GINGER PEAR CAKE
SERVES 8

85 g (3 oz/^{1}/$_4$ cup) golden syrup or
   light corn syrup
250 g (9 oz/2 cups) self-raising flour
2^1/$_2$ teaspoons ground ginger
140 g (5 oz/^{3}/$_4$ cup) soft brown sugar
125 g (4^1/$_2$ oz) unsalted butter, melted
125 ml (4 fl oz/^{1}/$_2$ cup) buttermilk
3 eggs
2 pears, peeled, cut in half, cores
   removed, then thinly sliced

SYRUP GLAZE
85 g (3 oz/^{1}/$_4$ cup) golden syrup or
   light corn syrup
25 g (1 oz) unsalted butter

Preheat the oven to 180°C (350°F/Gas 4). Grease an 18 cm (7 inch) round, deep cake tin and line the base with baking paper. Pour half the golden syrup over the base of the tin, spreading evenly with a warmed metal spoon.

Sift the flour and ginger into a bowl, then stir in the sugar. In a separate bowl, mix together the melted butter, buttermilk and eggs, then add to the flour mixture and stir until smooth. Stir in the pears.

Spoon the batter into the prepared tin and bake for 1^1/$_2$ hours, or until a cake tester inserted into the centre of the cake comes out clean. Remove from the oven and leave to cool in the tin for 10 minutes, then carefully invert the cake onto a serving plate.

To make the syrup glaze, put the golden syrup and butter in a small saucepan and stir over low heat until the butter has melted and the mixture is smooth. Spoon the glaze over the cake and serve warm.

Golden ginger pear cake is best eaten the day it is made.

Upside-down banana cake
Serves 8

BANANA TOPPING
50 g (1³/4 oz) unsalted butter, melted
60 g (2¹/4 oz/¹/3 cup) soft brown sugar
6 ripe large bananas, halved lengthways

125 g (4¹/2 oz) unsalted butter, softened
230 g (8 oz/1¹/4 cups) soft brown sugar
2 eggs
185 g (6¹/2 oz/1¹/2 cups) self-raising flour
1 teaspoon baking powder
2 large, very ripe bananas, mashed

Preheat the oven to 180°C (350°F/Gas 4). Grease and line the base and sides of a 20 cm (8 inch) round cake tin with baking paper.

To prepare the banana topping, pour the melted butter over the base of the prepared tin and sprinkle with the sugar. Arrange the bananas, cut side down, in a single layer over the base of the tin.

Using electric beaters, cream the butter and sugar until light and fluffy. Add the eggs one at a time, beating well after each addition.

Sift the flour and baking powder into a bowl. Using a large metal spoon, gently fold the flour into the butter mixture with the mashed banana.

Carefully spoon the batter over the banana slices in the cake tin, smoothing over the surface. Bake for 45 minutes, or until a cake tester inserted into the centre of the cake comes out clean. Remove from the oven and leave to cool in the tin for 5 minutes, before turning out onto a wire rack to cool completely.

Upside-down banana cake is best eaten the day it is made.

GLACÉ FRUIT AND NUT CAKE
SERVES 20

50 g (1³/4 oz) unsalted butter, softened
60 g (2¹/4 oz/¹/3 cup) soft brown sugar
2 eggs
125 g (4¹/2 oz/1 cup) plain (all-purpose) flour
1 teaspoon baking powder
1 teaspoon ground nutmeg
2 tablespoons marmalade
200 g (7 oz/1¹/4 cups) chopped pitted dates
185 g (6¹/2 oz/1¹/2 cups) raisins
155 g (5¹/2 oz/1 cup) brazil nuts
140 g (5 oz/²/3 cup) red, yellow and green
    glacé cherries
110 g (3¹/2 oz/¹/2 cup) chopped glacé pear
    or pineapple
120 g (4¹/4 oz/¹/2 cup) chopped glacé
    apricots
120 g (4¹/4 oz/¹/2 cup) chopped glacé
    peaches
120 g (4¹/4 oz/¹/3 cup) chopped glacé figs
100 g (3¹/2 oz/1 cup) walnut halves
100 g (3¹/2 oz/²/3 cup) blanched almonds

TOPPING
2 tablespoons marmalade
2 teaspoons powdered gelatine
150 g (5¹/2 oz/²/3 cup) glacé pear or
    pineapple rings
100 g (3¹/2 oz/¹/2 cup) red, yellow and
    green glacé cherries
40 g (1¹/2 oz/¹/4 cup) blanched almonds

Preheat the oven to 150°C (300°F/Gas 2). Lightly grease and line the base and sides of a 20 x 8 x 7 cm (8 x 3¹/4 x 2³/4 inch) loaf (bar) tin with baking paper.

Using electric beaters, cream the butter and sugar in a bowl until light and fluffy. Add the eggs one at a time, beating well after each addition.

Sift the flour, baking powder and nutmeg into a large bowl. Add the remaining cake ingredients and stir to coat the fruit and nuts in the flour mixture. Add to the butter mixture and stir to combine well.

Spoon the mixture into the prepared tin, pushing it into each corner. Bake for 1¹/2–1³/4 hours, or until a cake tester inserted into the centre of the cake comes out clean, covering the cake with foil if it browns too quickly. Remove from the oven and leave to cool in the tin for 30 minutes, then turn out onto a wire rack to cool completely.

Meanwhile, make the topping. Put the marmalade in a small heatproof bowl, stir in 2 tablespoons water, then sprinkle the gelatine over the top. Set the bowl over a small saucepan of simmering water, ensuring the base of the bowl doesn't touch the water, and stir until the gelatine has dissolved.

Brush the top of the cooled cake with some of the gelatine mixture and arrange the glacé fruit and almonds over the top. Brush or drizzle with the remaining gelatine mixture and allow to set.

Glacé fruit and nut cake will keep for up to 3 months, wrapped in baking paper and stored in a cool place in an airtight container.

NOTE: For a deeper colour, you can toast the blanched almonds for the topping. To do this, spread them in a single layer on a baking tray and bake in a 180°C (350°F/Gas 4) oven for 7 minutes, or until lightly golden.

HONEY ROLL
SERVES 8

90 g (3¼ oz/¾ cup) self-raising flour
2 teaspoons mixed (pumpkin pie) spice
3 eggs
125 g (4½ oz/⅔ cup) soft brown sugar
25 g (1 oz/¼ cup) desiccated coconut

HONEY CREAM
125 g (4½ oz) unsalted butter, softened
80 g (2¾ oz/⅓ cup) caster (superfine)
  sugar
2 tablespoons honey

Preheat the oven to 210°C (415°F/Gas 6–7). Grease a 30 x 25 cm (12 x 10 inch) Swiss roll (jelly roll) tin and line the base with baking paper, leaving the paper hanging over two opposite sides.

Sift the flour and mixed spice onto a large sheet of baking paper three times.

Using electric beaters, whisk the eggs in a large bowl for 5 minutes, or until thick and pale. Add the sugar gradually, beating constantly until the sugar has dissolved and the mixture is pale and glossy. Using a large metal spoon, gently fold in the sifted flour mixture until just combined and almost smooth.

Spoon the batter into the prepared tin, smoothing over the surface. Bake for 12 minutes, or until lightly golden and springy to the touch. Remove from the oven and leave to cool in the tin for 1 minute.

Lay a clean, dry tea towel (dish towel) on a work surface. Cover with a sheet of baking paper, then sprinkle the coconut over the paper.

Turn the cake onto the coconut and leave for 1 minute.

Using the tea towel as a guide, carefully roll the cake, along with the paper, up from the short side. Leave for 5 minutes, or until cool, then unroll the cake and discard the paper.

To make the honey cream, beat the butter, sugar and honey in a small bowl using electric beaters until light and fluffy. Continue beating for 12 minutes, adding a teaspoon of cold water every 2 minutes.

Spread the honey cream over the cake, gently but firmly roll the cake up into a Swiss roll, then trim the ends using a sharp knife. Cut into slices just before serving.

Honey roll will keep for 2 days, wrapped in baking paper and stored in a cool place in an airtight container.

PUMPKIN FRUITCAKE
SERVES 8–10

250 g (9 oz) pumpkin (winter squash),
  peeled and finely chopped
125 g (4½ oz) unsalted butter, softened
140 g (5 oz/¾ cup) soft brown sugar
2 tablespoons golden syrup or
  light corn syrup
2 eggs
250 g (9 oz/2 cups) self-raising flour
185 g (6½ oz/1 cup) mixed dried fruit
2 tablespoons chopped glacé ginger

Preheat the oven to 150°C (300°F/Gas 2). Grease a 20 cm (8 inch) round, deep cake tin and line the base and side with baking paper.

Steam the pumpkin for 10 minutes, or until cooked through. Mash with a potato masher until smooth. Measure out 200 g (7 oz/¾ cup), reserving any remainder for another use, and set aside.

Using electric beaters, cream the butter and sugar until light and fluffy, then add the golden syrup and beat well. Gradually add the eggs, beating well after each addition, then stir in the pumpkin.

Sift the flour into a bowl. Stir in the dried fruit and glacé ginger, then stir the flour mixture into the butter mixture using a large metal spoon until combined.

Spoon the mixture into the prepared tin, smoothing over the surface. Bake for 1 hour 40 minutes, or until a cake tester inserted into the centre of the cake comes out clean. Remove from the oven and leave to cool in the tin for 20 minutes, before turning out onto a wire rack to cool completely.

Pumpkin fruitcake will keep for 4 days, stored in a cool place in an airtight container, or can be frozen in an airtight container for up to 8 weeks.

APPLE AND SPICE TEACAKE
SERVES 8

1 lemon
2 granny smith apples, about 300 g
  (10½ oz) in total
180 g (6 oz) unsalted butter, softened
95 g (3¼ oz/½ cup) soft brown sugar
3 eggs
125 g (4½ oz/1 cup) self-raising flour
75 g (2½ oz/½ cup) wholemeal
  (whole-wheat) flour
½ teaspoon ground cinnamon
125 ml (4 fl oz/½ cup) milk

TOPPING
½ teaspoon mixed (pumpkin pie) spice
1 tablespoon soft brown sugar
25 g (1 oz/¼ cup) flaked almonds

Preheat the oven to 180°C (350°F/Gas 4). Grease a 20 cm (8 inch) spring-form cake tin and line the base with baking paper.

Grate the zest from the lemon, then juice the lemon into a bowl. Cut the apples in half, then cut out the cores and thinly slice the flesh. Toss the apple slices in the lemon juice to stop them browning. Set aside.

Using electric beaters, cream the butter and sugar until light and fluffy. Beat in the lemon zest. Add the eggs one at a time, beating well after each addition.

Sift the flours and cinnamon into a bowl. Using a large metal spoon, gently fold the flour mixture into the butter mixture, alternating with the milk, until just combined and almost smooth.

Spoon half the batter into the prepared tin, then neatly arrange half the apple slices over the top. Spoon the remaining batter over the apples, then press the remaining apple slices around the top. Combine all the topping ingredients and sprinkle over the cake.

Bake for 1 hour, or until a cake tester inserted into the centre of the cake comes out clean. Remove from the oven and leave to cool in the tin for 15 minutes, before turning out onto a wire cake rack to cool completely.

Apple and spice teacake will keep for 2 days, stored in a cool place in an airtight container.

LITTLE JAM-FILLED CAKES
MAKES 12

280 g (10 oz/2¼ cups) self-raising flour
170 g (6 oz/¾ cup) caster (superfine) sugar
2 eggs
250 ml (9 fl oz/1 cup) milk
½ teaspoon natural vanilla extract
75 g (2½ oz) unsalted butter, melted
2 tablespoons strawberry jam, approximately
6 small strawberries, hulled and thinly sliced
icing (confectioners') sugar, for dusting (optional)

Preheat the oven to 200°C (400°F/Gas 6). Grease a 12-hole standard muffin tin.

Sift the flour into a bowl, add the sugar and stir to combine. Make a well in the centre.

In another bowl, whisk together the eggs, milk, vanilla and butter. Pour into the well in the flour mixture and gradually stir until just combined, using a large metal spoon.

Spoon three-quarters of the cake batter into the muffin holes. Top each with about ½ teaspoon of the jam, then cover with the remaining batter. Fan the strawberry slices over each cake, gently pressing them in.

Bake for 20 minutes, or until lightly golden. Remove from the oven and leave to cool in the tin for 5 minutes, before turning out onto a wire rack to cool completely.

Dust with icing sugar if desired.

Little jam-filled cakes are best eaten the day they are made.

JAM AND CREAM SPONGE
SERVES 6–8

60 g (2¼ oz/½ cup) plain (all-purpose) flour
60 g (2¼ oz/½ cup) self-raising flour
4 eggs, separated
140 g (5 oz/⅔ cup) caster (superfine) sugar
icing (confectioners') sugar, for dusting

FILLING
100 g (3½ oz/⅓ cup) jam
125 ml (4 fl oz/½ cup) pouring (whipping) cream, whipped

Preheat the oven to 180°C (350°F/Gas 4). Grease two 20 cm (8 inch) sandwich tins. Sift the flours onto a large sheet of baking paper three times.

In a clean, dry bowl, beat the egg whites using electric beaters until stiff peaks form. Add the caster sugar gradually, whisking constantly until the sugar has dissolved and the mixture is thick and glossy.

Add the egg yolks and whisk for a further 20 seconds, or until combined. Using a large metal spoon, fold in the flour quickly and lightly.

Spread the batter evenly into the prepared tins, then bake for 20 minutes, or until lightly golden and springy to the touch. Remove from the oven and leave to cool in the tins for 5 minutes, before turning out onto wire racks to cool completely.

To make the filling, spread the jam evenly over one cake, then spread the whipped cream over the top. Place the second sponge on top and dust with icing sugar.

Jam and cream sponge is best eaten the day it is made. Without the filling, the sponges can be frozen in an airtight container for up to 1 month.

Carrot and hazelnut cake
Serves 8–10

150 g (5¹/₂ oz/1 cup) finely grated carrot
165 g (5³/₄ oz/1¹/₂ cups) ground hazelnuts
75 g (2¹/₂ oz/³/₄ cup) dry breadcrumbs
a pinch of ground nutmeg
6 eggs, separated
230 g (8 oz/1 cup) caster (superfine) sugar
2 tablespoons sweet sherry

ORANGE GLAZE
150 g (5¹/₂ oz/1¹/₄ cups) icing
   (confectioners') sugar
10 g (¹/₄ oz) unsalted butter, softened
2–3 tablespoons orange juice

Preheat the oven to 180°C (350°F/Gas 4). Lightly grease a 24 cm (9¹/₂ inch) round spring-form cake tin and line the base with baking paper. Dust the side of the tin with a little flour, shaking out any excess.

In a bowl, mix together the carrot and ground hazelnuts. Add the breadcrumbs and nutmeg and mix until combined, then set aside.

In a large bowl, beat the egg yolks and sugar using electric beaters for 5 minutes, or until pale and thick. Stir in the sherry, then gently fold into the carrot mixture using a large metal spoon.

In a clean, dry bowl, beat the egg whites using electric beaters until soft peaks form. Gently fold the egg whites, one-third at a time, into the carrot mixture.

Spoon the batter into the prepared tin and bake for 50 minutes, or until a cake tester inserted into the centre of the cake comes out clean. Remove from the oven and leave to cool in the tin for 10 minutes, before turning out onto a wire rack to cool completely.

To make the orange glaze, sift the icing sugar into a heatproof bowl, then mix in the butter and just enough orange juice to make a soft, slightly runny glaze. Set the bowl over a small saucepan of simmering water, ensuring the base of the bowl doesn't touch the water. Stir for 1–2 minutes, or until the mixture is smooth and glossy.

Pour the glaze over the top of the cake and smooth over with a palette knife. Allow the glaze to set before serving.

Carrot and hazelnut cake is best eaten the day it is made. Unglazed cake will keep for up to 6 weeks, frozen in an airtight container.

MARBLE CAKE
SERVES 10

1 vanilla bean, or 1 teaspoon natural
  vanilla extract
185 g (6½ oz) unsalted butter, softened
230 g (8 oz/1 cup) caster (superfine) sugar
3 eggs
280 g (10 oz/2¼ cups) self-raising flour
185 ml (6 fl oz/¾ cup) milk
2 tablespoons unsweetened cocoa powder
1½ tablespoons warm milk, extra

Preheat the oven to 200°C (400°F/Gas 6). Lightly grease a 25 x 11 x 7.5 cm (10 x 4¼ x 3 inch) loaf (bar) tin and line the base with baking paper.

If using the vanilla bean, split it down the middle and scrape the seeds into a bowl. Alternatively, put the vanilla extract in a bowl.

Add the butter and sugar, then cream using electric beaters until pale and fluffy. Add the eggs one at a time, beating well after each addition.

Sift the flour into a bowl. Using a large metal spoon, gently fold the flour into the butter mixture, alternating with the milk, until just combined and almost smooth. Spoon half the batter into another bowl.

Combine the cocoa powder and extra milk in a small bowl and stir until smooth, then stir into one of the bowls of cake batter, mixing well.

Spoon the two cake batters into the prepared tin in alternating spoonfuls. Using a metal skewer, 'cut' through the mixture four times to create a marbled effect.

Bake for 50–60 minutes, or until a cake tester inserted into the centre of the cake comes out clean. Remove from the oven and leave to cool in the tin for 5 minutes, before turning out onto a wire rack to cool completely.

Marble cake will keep for 3–4 days, stored in a cool place in an airtight container, or can be frozen in an airtight container for up to 6 weeks.

GUINNESS SPICE CAKE
SERVES 10–12

250 ml (9 fl oz/1 cup) Guinness or other
   dark beer
350 g (12 oz/1 cup) molasses
2 teaspoons baking powder
3 eggs
230 g (8 oz/1¼ cups) soft brown sugar
200 ml (7 fl oz) vegetable oil
250 g (9 oz/2 cups) self-raising flour
2½ tablespoons ground ginger
2 teaspoons ground cinnamon
100 g (3½ oz/⅓ cup) marmalade

Preheat the oven to 180°C (350°F/Gas 4). Grease a 2.5 litre (87 fl oz/10 cup) kugelhopf tin and lightly dust with flour, shaking out any excess.

Put the beer and molasses in a large saucepan and bring to the boil. Remove from the heat, add the baking powder and allow the foam to subside.

Using electric beaters, whisk the eggs and sugar together in a large bowl for 1–2 minutes, or until pale and slightly thickened. Add the vegetable oil and whisk to combine, then whisk into the beer mixture.

Sift the flour and ground spices into a large bowl, then gradually whisk in the beer mixture until combined.

Pour into the prepared tin and bake for 1 hour, or until the cake is firm to the touch and a cake tester inserted into the centre comes out clean. Remove from the oven and leave to cool in the tin for 20 minutes, before turning out onto a wire rack to cool completely.

Heat the marmalade in a saucepan over low heat for 3–4 minutes, or until melted. Strain, then brush the marmalade over the cooled cake.

Guinness spice cake will keep for up to 7 days, stored in a cool place in an airtight container, or can be frozen in an airtight container for up to 3 months.

OLIVE OIL AND SWEET WINE CAKE
SERVES 6–8

3 eggs
170 g (6 oz/³/4 cup) caster (superfine) sugar
2 teaspoons finely grated orange zest
2 teaspoons finely grated lemon zest
2 teaspoons finely grated lime zest
125 ml (4 fl oz/¹/2 cup) extra virgin
  olive oil
185 g (6¹/2 oz/1¹/2 cups) self-raising flour
125 ml (4 fl oz/¹/2 cup) dessert wine
icing (confectioners') sugar, for dusting

Preheat the oven to 180°C (350°F/Gas 4). Grease a 20 cm (8 inch) round, deep cake tin and line the base with baking paper. Dust the side of the tin with a little flour, shaking out any excess.

In a large bowl, whisk the eggs and sugar using electric beaters for 3–5 minutes, or until thick and pale. Add the citrus zests and olive oil and beat until combined.

Sift the flour into a bowl. Using a large metal spoon, gently fold the flour into the egg mixture, alternating with the wine, until just combined and almost smooth.

Pour the batter into the prepared tin and bake for 40–45 minutes, or until a cake tester inserted into the centre of the cake comes out clean. Remove from the oven and leave to cool in the tin for 10 minutes, before turning out onto a wire rack to cool completely.

Just before serving, dust with icing sugar.

Olive oil and sweet wine cake will keep for 4 days, stored in a cool place in an airtight container, or can be frozen in an airtight container for up to 3 months.

Mocha lamingtons
Makes 25

125 g (4 1/2 oz) unsalted butter, softened
230 g (8 oz/1 cup) caster (superfine) sugar
1/2 teaspoon natural vanilla extract
2 eggs
250 g (9 oz/2 cups) self-raising flour
250 ml (9 fl oz/1 cup) milk
2 teaspoons instant coffee granules,
    dissolved in 2 teaspoons boiling water

ICING
375 g (13 oz/3 cups) icing (confectioners')
    sugar
60 g (2 1/4 oz/1/2 cup) unsweetened cocoa
    powder
20 g (3/4 oz) unsalted butter
2 teaspoons instant coffee granules
75 g (2 1/2 oz/1 1/4 cups) shredded coconut
90 g (3 1/4 oz/1 cup) desiccated coconut

Preheat the oven to 180°C (350°F/Gas 4). Lightly grease the base of a 23 cm (9 inch) square, shallow cake tin and line the base with baking paper.

Using electric beaters, cream the butter, sugar and vanilla in a bowl until light and fluffy. Add the eggs one at a time, beating well after each addition.

Sift the flour into a bowl. Using a large metal spoon, gently fold the flour into the butter mixture, alternating with the milk, until just combined and almost smooth.

Spoon half the batter into the prepared tin and spread evenly over the base. Stir the dissolved coffee into the remaining cake mixture, then carefully spread over the mixture in the tin.

Bake for 30–35 minutes, or until a cake tester inserted into the centre of the cake comes out clean. Remove from the oven and leave to cool in the tin for 5 minutes, before turning out onto a wire rack to cool completely.

To make the icing (frosting), sift the icing sugar and cocoa powder into a large shallow bowl. Add the butter and coffee granules and gradually whisk in 150 ml (5 fl oz) boiling water until smooth. Put the shredded and desiccated coconut in another large shallow bowl and toss to combine.

Cut the cooled cake into 25 squares.

Using two spoons to hold them, dip the cake squares into the icing to cover, allowing the excess to drip off. (Stir a little boiling water into the icing if it starts to thicken.) Roll the cake squares in the coconut mixture to cover, then place on a wire rack. Repeat with the remaining cake squares.

Mocha lamingtons will keep for up to 3 days, stored in a cool place in an airtight container.

LUMBERJACK CAKE
SERVES 8

200 g (6½ oz) fresh dates, pitted and chopped
1 teaspoon bicarbonate of soda (baking soda)
125 g (4½ oz) unsalted butter, softened
230 g (8 oz/1 cup) caster (superfine) sugar
1 egg
1 teaspoon natural vanilla extract
2 granny smith apples, peeled and grated
125 g (4½ oz/1 cup) plain (all-purpose) flour
60 g (2¼ oz/½ cup) self-raising flour
icing (confectioners') sugar, for dusting

TOPPING
75 g (2½ oz) unsalted butter
95 g (3¼ oz/½ cup) soft brown sugar
80 ml (2½ fl oz/⅓ cup) milk
60 g (2¼ oz/1 cup) shredded coconut

Preheat the oven to 180°C (350°F/Gas 4). Grease a 20 cm (8 inch) spring-form cake tin and line the base with baking paper.

Put the dates in a small saucepan with 250 ml (9 fl oz/1 cup) water and bring to the boil. Stir in the bicarbonate of soda, then remove from the heat. Set aside until just warm.

Using electric beaters, cream the butter and sugar until light and fluffy. Add the egg and vanilla and beat until combined, then stir in the date mixture and grated apple.

Sift the flours into a bowl. Using a large metal spoon, gently fold the flour into the butter mixture until just combined and almost smooth.

Spoon the batter into the prepared tin, smoothing over the surface. Bake for 40 minutes.

Meanwhile, put all the topping ingredients in a small saucepan and stir over low heat until the butter has melted and the ingredients are well combined.

Remove the cake from the oven and carefully spread the topping over the cake. Bake for a further 20–30 minutes, or until the topping is golden and a cake tester inserted into the centre of the cake comes out clean. Remove from the oven and allow the cake to cool completely in the tin.

Place the cooled cake on a serving plate and remove the tin. Just before serving, dust with icing sugar.

Lumberjack cake will keep for 3 days, stored in a cool place in an airtight container.

CHERRY CAKE
SERVES 8–10

210 g (7½ oz/1 cup) red glacé cherries
85 g (3 oz/⅔ cup) plain (all-purpose) flour
90 g (3¼ oz) unsalted butter, softened
145 g (5 oz/⅔ cup) caster (superfine) sugar
2 eggs
1 teaspoon natural vanilla extract
125 g (4½ oz/1 cup) self-raising flour
80 ml (2½ fl oz/⅓ cup) milk

ICING
125 g (4½ oz/1 cup) icing (confectioners') sugar
20 g (¾ oz) unsalted butter

Preheat the oven to 180°C (350°F/Gas 4). Grease a 20 cm (8 inch) kugelhopf tin and lightly dust with flour, shaking out any excess.

Rinse and dry the glacé cherries, then cut each in half. Toss them in a little of the flour and set aside.

Using electric beaters, cream the butter and sugar until light and fluffy. Add the eggs one at a time, beating well after each addition. Beat in the vanilla.

Sift all the flour into a bowl. Using a large metal spoon, gently fold the flour into the butter mixture, alternating with the milk, until just combined and almost smooth. Stir in the cherries.

Spoon the batter into the cake tin, smoothing over the surface. Bake for 35 minutes, or until a cake tester inserted into the centre of the cake comes out clean. Remove from the oven and leave to cool in the tin for 10 minutes, before turning out onto a wire rack to cool completely.

To make the icing (frosting), sift the icing sugar into a small heatproof bowl, then add the butter and 1–2 tablespoons water. Set the bowl over a small saucepan of simmering water, ensuring the base of the bowl doesn't touch the water. Stir until the butter has melted and the icing is glossy and smooth. Drizzle the icing over the cooled cake, allowing it to run down the sides.

Cherry cake will keep for 4 days, stored in a cool place in an airtight container. Without the icing, the cake can be frozen in an airtight container for up to 3 months.

BOILED FRUITCAKE

SERVES 20–24

250 g (9 oz) unsalted butter
185 g (6½ oz/1 cup) soft brown sugar
1 kg (2 lb 4 oz) mixed dried fruit
125 ml (4 fl oz/½ cup) sweet sherry
½ teaspoon bicarbonate of soda
  (baking soda)
185 g (6½ oz/1½ cups) self-raising flour
125 g (4½ oz/1 cup) plain (all-purpose)
  flour
1 teaspoon mixed (pumpkin pie) spice
4 eggs, lightly beaten

Preheat the oven to 180°C (350°F/Gas 4). Lightly grease a 22 cm (8½ inch) round cake tin and line the base and side with a double layer of baking paper.

Put the butter, sugar, dried fruit and sherry in a saucepan with 185 ml (6 fl oz/¾ cup) water, then stir over low heat until the butter has melted and the sugar has dissolved. Bring to the boil, then reduce the heat and simmer for 10 minutes. Remove from the heat, stir in the bicarbonate of soda and set aside to cool.

Sift the flours and mixed spice into a large bowl and make a well in the centre.

Add the beaten eggs to the fruit mixture, mix well, then pour into the well in the flour and mix thoroughly.

Spoon into the prepared tin and smooth over the surface. Bake for 1¼–1½ hours, or until a cake tester inserted into the centre of the cake comes out clean, covering the cake with foil if it browns too quickly. Remove from the oven and leave to cool in the tin for at least 1 hour, before turning out onto a wire rack to cool completely.

Boiled fruitcake will keep for up to 3 months, wrapped well in several layers of plastic wrap and stored in a cool place in an airtight container. It can also be frozen in an airtight container for up to 6 months.

The flavour improves after standing for 3 days.

NOTE: The cake colour will depend on the fruit. For a dark cake, use raisins, currants and sultanas (golden raisins); for a lighter colour, replace one-third to half of the dried fruit with chopped glacé fruit (such as figs, pears, pineapple, cherries and apricots).

POUND CAKE
SERVES 10–12

375 g (13 oz) unsalted butter, softened
375 g (13 oz/1²/₃ cups) caster (superfine)
  sugar
1 teaspoon natural vanilla extract
6 eggs
375 g (13 oz/3 cups) plain (all-purpose)
  flour
1 teaspoon baking powder
60 ml (2 fl oz/¼ cup) milk
icing (confectioners') sugar, for dusting

Preheat the oven to 180°C (350°F/Gas 4). Lightly grease a 22 cm (8½ inch) round cake tin and line the base with baking paper.

Using electric beaters, cream the butter and sugar in a large bowl until light and fluffy. Beat in the vanilla, then add the eggs one at a time, beating well after each addition.

Sift the flour and baking powder into a bowl. Using a large metal spoon, gently fold the flour mixture into the butter mixture, alternating with the milk, until just combined and almost smooth.

Spoon the batter into the prepared tin, smoothing over the surface. Bake for 1 hour, or until a cake tester inserted into the centre of the cake comes out clean. Remove from the oven and leave to cool in the tin for 10 minutes, before turning out onto a wire rack to cool completely.

Just before serving, dust with icing sugar.

Pound cake will keep for up to 1 week, stored in a cool place in an airtight container, or can be frozen in an airtight container for up to 8 weeks.

VARIATIONS
To make **orange pound cake**, add 2 tablespoons finely grated orange zest to the creamed butter mixture and use 60 ml (2 fl oz/¼ cup) orange juice instead of the milk.
To make **hazelnut pound cake**, add 125 g (4½ oz/1 cup) chopped, toasted hazelnuts to the creamed butter mixture before adding the flour.
To make **caraway seed cake**, add 1 tablespoon caraway seeds to the creamed butter mixture before adding the flour.
To make **espresso pound cake**, add 2½ tablespoons very finely ground coffee beans to the creamed butter mixture before adding the flour.
To make **chocolate-chip pound cake**, toss 150 g (5½ oz/1 cup) finely chopped semi-sweet chocolate with 30 g (1 oz/¼ cup) of the flour, then add it to the cake batter after the remaining flour and milk have been added.
To make **vanilla pound cake**, add the scraped seeds from a vanilla bean to the creamed butter mixture.

biscuits

Perhaps it's because they are so easy and so much fun to make that biscuits (cookies) are one of the most commonly made home-baked goods. They come in a multitude of colours and shapes and can be sweet or savoury, hard and crisp, or soft and crumbling. Some are filled, some iced (frosted) — while others have enticing baked-on toppings of sugar, spices, seeds or nuts.

Biscuits can be coarse-textured, based on mixtures of wholesome oats or other grains, seeds and rustic flours. Or they can be refined and pale, and subtly flavoured with lemon, vanilla or just the taste of pure, creamy butter. They can be dense with chocolate or intense with nuts, spices, dried fruits, honey, malt extract or maple syrup.

They can be shaped in endless ways too, depending on the type of dough — some are baked as casual piles of dough or irregular mini-saucers while others are neatly rolled out, then stamped with cutters. Others are shaped by forcing the uncooked dough through decorative piping tubes.

There are thousands of recipes for biscuits worldwide, with each country having its own 'take' on this most versatile — and portable — of foods. In his classic reference book *The Oxford Companion to Food*, Alan Davidson suggests that the Roman cook Apicius gave us the first recipe for a biscuit. This was made when 'a thick paste of fine flour was boiled and spread out on a plate. When it had dried and hardened it was cut up and then fried until crisp then served with honey and pepper.'

It is thought that the ancestors of modern-day biscuits were actually small pieces of cake batter that were cooked first to test the temperature of the oven. Some culinary historians believe that the ancient Persians were the first to bake small cakes as they were among the first to cultivate sugar, a vital ingredient in sweet biscuits. The Muslim conquest of Spain, the Crusades (and the contact with Middle Eastern cultures that resulted), as well as the birth of the spice trade all conspired to move the idea of baking small cakes or biscuits westward throughout Europe.

During the Middle Ages, long-keeping biscuits made with spices, egg whites and honey were popular and many different types were invented. The age of sea exploration led to the development of hard tack, a super-hard type of biscuit that could withstand the rigours of long periods at sea. Stored properly they could last for years, and they sustained those on board when no other food was available.

Scottish, English and Dutch settlers took their own particular styles of biscuit-baking to America where, over time, it evolved into something approaching a national obsession — 'cookies' are an intrinsic part of the Amercian culinary lexicon.

The word 'biscuit' comes from the French words *bis* and *cuit*, which literally mean 'twice cooked' — a reference to early baking techniques that involved two bakings, the second to make biscuits drier and harder and therefore longer lasting. Other countries use an equivalent word for biscuits. In Germany, for example, they are called *zwieback* (literally 'two bake'); in Italy they are called *biscotti* (also meaning twice-baked). In Spanish a word for biscuit is *rosca*, which means 'twisted', as often their doughs were braided before baking. *Rosca* is believed to have given rise to the word 'rusk', a type of very hard, plain biscuit. The American word 'cookie' is thought to derive from the Dutch word *koekje*, a word closely related to the English word 'cake'.

It is probable that biscuits made by creaming butter and sugar weren't developed until the eighteenth century. During the nineteenth century, thanks to the impact of the industrial revolution, flour and sugar became cheap, basic commodities and biscuit-making really took off; the invention of reliable, chemical leaveners also contributed to this trend. It was in the nineteenth century too that industrialised biscuit-making became common (although chocolate-coating was an innovation that did not occur until after the Second World War).

Today, out of sheer convenience, many of us opt to reach for a packet of commercially prepared biscuits, which is a shame. Their texture and flavour have a standardised blandness that is worlds apart from the crusty goodness and quirky irregularity of home-made versions.

MAKING BISCUITS

As with cakes and pastries, the basic ingredients of biscuits are simple: flour, sugar, fat (generally butter) and sometimes eggs. Most biscuits are also made using techniques very similar to those employed in cake-making — namely the creaming method, the melted method and the foamed method. Quite a number are also made by the 'rubbing in' method, where fingers are used to incorporate butter into the dry ingredients; this is essentially the same way most simple pastries are made.

There are many biscuits that fall outside these categories — particularly those from certain European cultures where, for example, olive oil, huge amounts of honey or the twice-cooked method might be used.

There are also many fine, sophisticated biscuits such as those based on meringue or marzipan, or those filled with ganache, glazed with fondant or robed in chocolate, which place greater technical demands on the cook — but for the sake of ease and simplicity, the biscuits in this book reflect a more homey, less complicated style of baking.

Biscuits tend to be categorised by the way they are shaped rather than the way the dough has been mixed — for example, we speak of 'drop' biscuits, 'rolled' biscuits, 'hand-shaped' biscuits and 'piped' biscuits. This is an easier way to think of biscuits than by technique, as some 'drop' biscuits are made by the creamed method and others by the melted method, while some 'rolled' biscuits are made by creaming and others using the rubbing-in method. Baking faults also tend to relate more to a biscuit's shape and general dimensions than to the way the dough was initially put together.

Then there are the various 'bars' or 'slices', which fall somewhere between cakes, biscuits and pastries, but tend to be included in the biscuit family. Some of these resemble quite thin, dense cakes (for example, the ever-popular brownie), while others are more like a pastry (such as linzer slice or bakewell slice) — but in the main, biscuits and slices keep longer than dessert-style pastries.

Bars and slices are a convenient way to bake smallgoods as they don't require shaping before cooking; rather, they are baked as a slab, then allowed to cool before being cut. They are as varied a bunch as individually shaped biscuits, with versions that range from quite delicate to dense and chewy; some comprise several layers, and many have special baked-on toppings or glazes that are spread over later.

Biscuit recipes are a flexible lot. Although they rely on certain ratios of basic ingredients such as fat, sugar, flour and eggs, they will generally tolerate a few substitutions much better than most cake or pastry recipes.

Drop biscuits

These are possibly the easiest of all biscuits to make. You just make your dough, drop it by spoonfuls onto a prepared baking tray, then bake. Doughs for drop biscuits tend to be the softest of all biscuit doughs, with a high moisture content (from butter, eggs or liquid such as milk). For this reason, they need plenty of room to spread on their trays.

If you prefer biscuits that don't spread thinly when baked, you can refrigerate drop-biscuit dough for a few hours or even overnight to firm it up. Bake spoonfuls of the dough straight from the fridge in a preheated oven and it won't spread nearly as much.

A tiny ice-cream scoop is a useful tool for shaping the dough into evenly sized and shaped rounds, giving uniform biscuits.

Rolled biscuits

Rolled biscuits are those where the dough is rolled into a thin, even sheet, then stamped or cut out, using either a sharp knife or special biscuit (cookie) cutters (which come in a variety of shapes and sizes — see page 13).

Usually these doughs, like pastry, are rather fragile — and as in pastry recipes it is often advised to refrigerate the biscuit dough for 20–30 minutes before rolling it. This firms the dough, making it easier to roll, and also lets the gluten in the flour relax, thus avoiding tough biscuits. You don't want the dough too chilled though, or it will be impossible to roll — it should still be pliable. It is also a good idea to chill the dough once it has been rolled, cut out, and is sitting on the baking tray(s), as a chilled mixture will hold its shape better when baking.

Divide the dough in half, or in thirds if the batch is large, and work with one piece at a time — it'll be much easier to roll with a smaller amount. It's best to roll the dough out between two sheets of baking paper, although you can also roll it out on a lightly floured surface. If using a floured surface, try to use as little extra flour as possible on your work surface as the flour will stick to the rolled dough and make the baked biscuits tough — use a pastry brush to brush any excess flour off before baking if necessary. Using baking paper avoids this issue altogether, and also stops the dough sticking to the bench.

Roll from the middle of the dough out towards the edges, and give the dough a 90-degree turn every few rolls so that you are constantly rolling in the same direction and are making an even shape. Don't push too hard on the dough or you will stretch it and the biscuits will be tough. Our recipes will tell you either how thick the dough should be, or how large the piece should be once it has been rolled out.

When using cutters, dip them lightly in flour every so often as you work, to prevent the dough sticking to them. Press them straight down and firmly into the dough without twisting them — twisting the cutters through the dough will ruin a biscuit's shape.

Aim to cut out biscuits as close to each other as possible to avoid having too much left-over dough. You can re-roll the scraps, but only do this once — after that, the dough will become too tough to produce tender biscuits. Use a palette knife or metal spatula to lift the cut shapes onto baking trays so you don't ruin their shape. If time allows, refrigerate until firm before baking.

Refrigerator biscuits

These biscuits are the ultimate in home-baking convenience. Once the dough is made, it is designed to be shaped neatly into logs using baking paper as a guide and either stored in the refrigerator or frozen. When fresh biscuits are wanted, you simply use a sharp knife to cut off rounds of dough, place them on a prepared baking tray and bake.

Mostly, these biscuits are made using the creamed method and are very straightforward to put together. Varying the base recipe is easy too. You can add grated citrus zest, chopped nuts, chopped dried fruits, chopped chocolate, coconut, ground spices or flavoured extracts as the mood strikes you — and you can come up with your own unique flavour combinations (lime and cardamom, orange and coconut, rosewater and pistachio… or try a mocha version made by adding chopped dark chocolate and finely ground coffee beans). Use drops of food colour to tint the dough and play with the possibilities.

You can create spiral effects by placing two different coloured, rolled-out doughs on top of each other, then rolling these tightly into a log. Or you could roll an outside dough around a different-flavoured inner 'sausage' of dough to create a 'dot' effect when the biscuits are cut. The potential for indulging your creative flair is endless.

The trickiest part of making refrigerator biscuits is in forming the dough into a perfectly round roll for refrigerating so that when you slice it for baking, the biscuits will have an even, round shape. Form the dough into a rough log shape and place it down the middle of a large sheet of baking paper on a work surface. Pull one side of the paper over the dough, then use your hands to gently roll it back and forwards until it is the desired length and circumference (use a ruler to measure). A sturdy ruler with a straight edge can be pressed along the dough into the edge of the baking paper, to help form the cylinder. Make sure the paper is very tight and there are no wrinkles in it to mar the surface of the biscuits. (If you like, before rolling, the paper can be sprinkled lightly all over with poppy seeds, sesame seeds, fine desiccated coconut or finely chopped nuts, to form a decorative edge on the biscuits.)

In some recipes the dough is softened slightly at room temperature before slicing; in others it is cut directly from the refrigerator.

To preserve the even roundness, roll the dough gently as you cut it with a sharp knife, using a straight-down slicing action. If the dough softens slightly during cutting, place it back in the refrigerator for 10 minutes or so to firm it up again.

The uncooked dough will keep for 7–10 days in the refrigerator, and up to 3 months in the freezer.

HAND-FORMED BISCUITS

Most likely the biscuits you shape by hand will have been made by the creaming method or the melted method. If the dough is of the rich and soft sort (normally those with a high butter content), chill the mixture for 20 minutes or so to firm it up before shaping.

Lightly flour your hands as you take pieces of the dough to shape, so the dough doesn't stick. Balls are the most common shape for these biscuits. These are placed on prepared baking trays, then flattened slightly (or a lot, depending on the recipe) using your fingers or the tines of a fork.

To make balls, roll pieces the size of a large walnut between your palms, taking care to make the balls a uniform size so they will bake evenly. Don't handle them for any longer than necessary or they will heat in your hands and soften overly.

Other popular shapes are little logs and crescents. For logs, take small amounts of dough and roll into a log shape on a lightly floured board using the palm of your hand, neatening the edges with the sides of your hands as you go. For crescents, do the same, except make the ends a little tapered, then push the ends towards each other on the board to form a crescent.

The ever-popular biscotti are first formed by shaping the dough into several large, long, slightly flattened rolls, which are transferred to a tray and baked. After this they are cooled, sliced on a slight diagonal using a large serrated knife, then baked again in a single layer until hard and dry.

Biscotti dough generally has no (or very little) butter and is quite firm, so it does not need chilling before shaping. Roll the dough into logs on a lightly floured surface using lightly floured hands — the dough is quite robust so it can stand a little more handling than more tender doughs, but even so, don't overwork it. Bake the logs immediately for the required time, cool on wire racks, then cut as described above.

PIPED BISCUITS

Some quite soft mixtures are shaped by being forced through a cloth or plastic piping (icing) bag fitted with a decorative tube, or a special biscuit press, which comes with interchangeable decorative metal plates through which the mixture is extruded. Using either apparatus requires a steady hand and an amount of patience, but they are not hard to use. Smooth mixtures work best here — any lumps of nuts or chocolate, unless they are quite pulverised, will clog the nozzle or disc.

When using a piping bag, just fill it halfway with the mixture, otherwise it will be too difficult to push the mixture out. Twist the top of the bag tightly down to where the dough is so the bag is tight, then pipe shapes directly onto a prepared baking tray. The secret is in the placement of your hands: keep your right hand at the top of the bag, keeping the twist secure and pressing on the contents to squeeze it through the nozzle. Your other hand should be cradling the bag and directing the nozzle to control the shape of each biscuit. You can pipe rings, 'S' shapes, crescents or logs.

A biscuit press has a metal or plastic barrel which you fill with dough, then screw your chosen disc over one end. The other end houses the pressing mechanism. You simply hold the press flat against the baking tray, press to push enough dough through the blade to form a biscuit, then lift the press away and repeat the process until the baking tray is full.

Whichever method you use, be sure to chill the uncooked biscuits thoroughly on their trays before baking to ensure the biscuits retain their decorative shape.

SLICES AND BARS

These are a varied bunch and made by such a mixture of methods. Slices can be as simple as a melted and stirred mixture that is pressed into a tin and baked, then sliced into sturdy pieces — or a crisp, pastry-like mixture with a fruity filling or topping. Soft, cake-like mixtures such as gingerbread are often baked as a slice, and sometimes so too is the simple, biscuity Scottish shortbread. Some slices, influenced by the baking of the Middle East, are even doused in syrup after baking.

What is common to all slices is that they are baked in one piece in a shallow, rectangular or square tin, then cooled and sliced after baking.

Do make sure that the tin is properly prepared (lightly greased and floured or lined with baking paper), or the slice will be impossible to remove. Also make sure you use the tin size stipulated in the recipe. A slice cooked in a tin that is too small will cook more slowly, while a larger tin will create a thinner bar that will cook more quickly.

Some doughs for slices require rolling out — do this between two sheets of baking paper or on a lightly floured work surface. Some mixtures are too soft or crumbly to be rolled out and need to be pressed into the tin — use the back of a spoon to smooth the top as even as possible so the bar bakes through evenly.

When a slice is constructed of several layers, it is important that each layer be allowed to cool before adding the next, unless specified otherwise, especially if that layer is a final one of icing (frosting) or glaze.

For the neatest shape and to minimise crumbling, slices should only be cut when completely cold, unless a recipe says otherwise; some slices, such as brownies, cut better when they have been refrigerated until firm, turned out of the tin and then sliced.

General biscuit baking tips

- Have your eggs at room temperature and, unless using the 'melted' method, the butter softened.
- Weigh and measure ingredients accurately, or the texture and appearance of the baked biscuits could be affected.
- For easy removal of the baked biscuits, use baking trays with no lips or edges. For best results, use heavy, non-shiny metal baking trays instead of dark-surfaced ones, as these can cause the biscuits to brown too quickly. Many good bakers cover the tray with baking paper before placing the biscuits on — this not only avoids the mess of greasing trays, but also helps the biscuits brown evenly.
- Unless a recipe says to cool biscuits on the baking tray, remove them to a wire rack, using a metal spatula, about 2 minutes after they are taken from the oven. If left on the tray, condensation can form on their base and they'll be soggy; others will stick hard to the tray. Allow them to cool completely on the rack before storing.
- Biscuits should be stored in a cool place in an airtight container, with baking paper placed between each layer (exposure to air will make them go soft). Most biscuits can also be frozen for up to 3 months — zip-lock bags are ideal for this, but make sure you remove all the air first or ice will form on the biscuits, making them soggy once thawed.
- The length of time biscuits will keep at room temperature in an airtight container varies from recipe to recipe. Those that have a high fat content (such as shortbread), or a low moisture content (such as biscotti), generally keep the longest.
- Any biscuits that have gone a little soft can be crisped in a preheated 160°C (315°F/Gas 2–3) oven for 4–5 minutes.

TROUBLESHOOTING BISCUITS

Here are some of the most common biscuit faults, and the most likely causes.

The biscuits spread too much during baking

The rate at which a biscuit spreads has much to do with the oven temperature and the melting point of the various ingredients involved. Some ingredients melt at lower temperatures than others — butter, honey, golden syrup, treacle and maple syrup all melt quite quickly, whereas vegetable shortening and sugar have a much higher melting point. Exposure to heat causes the ingredients to start melting, and if this happens before the structure of the biscuits has been set, spreading will result.

Similarly, you will also get excessive spreading if you put biscuits onto a hot baking tray, or into an oven in which the temperature is too low — as you will if there is too much sugar in the mixture (sugar attracts moisture and if there is too much moisture, the flour, which supports the structure of the biscuits, will absorb too much liquid to do its job).

Biscuits made using bicarbonate of soda (baking soda) tend to spread more than those made with baking powder, as acidity levels affect baking and browning times.

The biscuits are tough

Either the dough was handled too much during mixing and/or shaping, there was too much flour in the mixture, or too much extra flour was absorbed during rolling.

The biscuits brown unevenly during baking

This happens when the trays are not rotated during cooking. Most ovens have 'hot spots' — areas where heat accumulates — and biscuits are especially prone to the effects of these. To avoid these, you need to turn trays of biscuits halfway through baking, and if you have two trays in the oven at once, swap their position in the oven.

The biscuits are too thick and not crisp

The mixture being rolled too thickly is an obvious cause of this fault, or there may be too much flour in the mixture or the oven is too hot.

Greasy-textured biscuits

There could be too much butter (or other fat) in the dough, the oven temperature could be too high or, if these are biscuits that benefit from chilling before baking, they may have been insufficiently chilled.

SIMPLE BISCUITS
MAKES ABOUT 50

125 g (4¹/₂ oz) unsalted butter, softened
115 g (4 oz/¹/₂ cup) caster (superfine)
  sugar
1 egg
¹/₄ teaspoon natural vanilla extract
125 g (4¹/₂ oz/1 cup) plain (all-purpose)
  flour
125 g (4¹/₂ oz/1 cup) self-raising flour

Preheat the oven to 160°C (315°F/Gas 2–3). Line two baking trays with baking paper.

Using electric beaters, cream the butter and sugar until light and fluffy. Add the egg and vanilla and beat until combined. Sift the flours into a bowl, then fold into the butter mixture using a large metal spoon to form a soft dough.

Turn the dough out onto a sheet of baking paper and place another sheet of baking paper on top. Roll out the dough until 5 mm (¹/₄ inch) thick. Using cutters, cut out the biscuits and place on the baking trays.

Bake in batches for 10–15 minutes each time, or until lightly golden. Remove from the oven and leave to cool slightly on the baking trays, then transfer to a wire rack to cool completely.

Make up one of the following fillings to sandwich the biscuits together, or simply spread the biscuits with one of the following icings (frostings).

Without an icing or filling, the biscuits will keep for up to 7 days, stored in a cool place in an airtight container, or can be frozen in an airtight container for 10–12 weeks.

VARIATIONS
Caramel filling Melt 30 g (1 oz) butter, 95 g (3¹/₄ oz/¹/₂ cup) soft brown sugar and 160 g (5³/₄ oz/¹/₂ cup) condensed milk in a saucepan. Bring to the boil, then boil for 1 minute, or until the mixture thickens. Allow to cool, then spread between the biscuits. The filled biscuits will keep for 3–4 days.
Vanilla icing Combine 150 g (5¹/₂ oz/1¹/₄ cups) sifted icing (confectioners') sugar, 1 tablespoon softened butter, ¹/₂ teaspoon natural vanilla extract and 2 tablespoons boiling water. Spread over the cooled biscuits. The iced biscuits will keep for 5 days.
Peppermint filling Combine 250 g (9 oz/2 cups) sifted icing (confectioners') sugar, 5–6 teaspoons hot water and a few drops of natural peppermint extract. Spread between the cooled biscuits. The filled biscuits will keep for 5 days.
Lime butter filling Beat 60 g (2¹/₄ oz) softened butter and 125 g (4¹/₂ oz/1 cup) icing (confectioners') sugar until smooth. Beat in the finely shredded zest of 1 lime and 1–2 teaspoons lime juice and spread between the biscuits. The filled biscuits will keep for 5 days.

FIG NEWTONS

MAKES 24

75 g (2½ oz) unsalted butter, softened
2 tablespoons sour cream
140 g (5 oz/¾ cup) soft brown sugar
2 eggs
1 teaspoon natural vanilla extract
375 g (13 oz/3 cups) plain (all-purpose)
   flour
2 teaspoons baking powder
½ teaspoon bicarbonate of soda
   (baking soda)
½ teaspoon ground cinnamon

FILLING
375 g (13 oz) dried figs, stems removed
80 g (2¾ oz/⅓ cup) caster (superfine)
   sugar
1 teaspoon grated lemon zest

Using electric beaters, cream the butter, sour cream and sugar until light and fluffy. Add the eggs one at a time, beating well after each addition — the mixture will appear curdled. Stir in the vanilla.

Sift the flour, baking powder, bicarbonate of soda and cinnamon into a bowl, then stir into the butter mixture until well combined — the mixture will be very soft. Gather the dough into a disc, wrap in a sheet of lightly floured plastic wrap and refrigerate for at least 2 hours.

To make the filling, put the figs in a large saucepan with 250 ml (9 fl oz/1 cup) water. Bring to the boil, then reduce the heat and simmer, covered, for 30 minutes, or until the figs have softened. Add the sugar and lemon zest and simmer for a further 10 minutes. Remove from the heat and allow to cool slightly, then drain off any remaining syrup. Chop the figs in a food processor until smooth, then set aside to cool.

Meanwhile, preheat the oven to 180°C (350°F/Gas 4). Line a baking tray with baking paper.

Divide the dough into three equal portions. Refrigerate two portions, and roll the third out on a lightly floured work surface to a 12 x 28 cm (4½ x 11¼ inch) rectangle. Spread a third of the filling lengthways along one half of the pastry, leaving a 2 cm (¾ inch) border along that side and on the ends. Brush the border with water. Fold the unfilled half over the filling, then press the edges together to seal. Trim 1 cm (½ inch) of pastry from the edges to neaten. Repeat with the remaining dough and filling.

Lift the three rolls onto the baking tray, allowing room for spreading. Refrigerate for 30 minutes.

Bake the rolls for 25 minutes, or until the pastry is cooked through and golden. Remove from the oven and leave to cool for several minutes on the tray, then carefully transfer to a wire rack to cool for 3–4 minutes.

Place the rolls on a cutting board. Using a serrated knife, trim the ends, then cut each roll into slices about 2 cm (¾ inch) thick. Allow to cool completely.

Fig newtons will keep for up to 7 days, stored in a cool place in an airtight container.

RASPBERRY LINZER SLICE

MAKES 24

90 g (3¼ oz) unsalted butter, softened
115 g (4 oz/½ cup) caster (superfine) sugar
1 teaspoon natural vanilla extract
1 egg
85 g (3 oz/⅔ cup) plain (all-purpose) flour
40 g (1½ oz/⅓ cup) self-raising flour
240 g (8½ oz/¾ cup) raspberry jam,
   warmed

HAZELNUT TOPPING
125 g (4½ oz) unsalted butter, softened
80 g (2¾ oz/⅓ cup) caster (superfine)
   sugar
1 egg
60 g (2¼ oz/½ cup) plain (all-purpose)
   flour
1 tablespoon custard powder or instant
   vanilla pudding mix
1 teaspoon baking powder
125 g (4½ oz/1 cup) plain cake crumbs
55 g (2 oz/½ cup) ground hazelnuts
80 ml (2½ fl oz/⅓ cup) milk

Preheat the oven to 180°C (350°F/Gas 4). Lightly grease a 20 x 30 cm (8 x 12 inch) baking tin and line with baking paper, leaving the paper hanging over two opposite sides.

Using electric beaters, beat the butter, sugar and vanilla in a bowl until light and fluffy. Add the egg and beat well.

Sift the flours into a bowl, then fold into the butter mixture using a metal spoon. Spread the mixture evenly over the base of the prepared tin, then spread evenly with the jam.

To make the hazelnut topping, cream the butter and sugar using electric beaters until light and fluffy. Add the egg and beat well. Sift the flour, custard powder and baking powder into a bowl, then fold into the butter mixture with the cake crumbs and ground hazelnuts. Stir in the milk and spread the mixture over the biscuit base.

Bake for 45 minutes, or until firm and golden brown. Remove from the oven and leave to cool completely in the tin, before cutting into squares or fingers.

Raspberry linzer slice will keep for up to 5 days, stored in a cool place in an airtight container, or can be frozen in an airtight container for up to 4 weeks.

PASSIONFRUIT MELTING MOMENTS
MAKES 14

250 g (9 oz) unsalted butter, softened
40 g (1$\frac{1}{2}$ oz/$\frac{1}{3}$ cup) icing (confectioners')
  sugar
1 teaspoon natural vanilla extract
185 g (6$\frac{1}{2}$ oz/1$\frac{1}{2}$ cups) self-raising flour
60 g (2$\frac{1}{4}$ oz/$\frac{1}{2}$ cup) custard powder or
  instant vanilla pudding mix

PASSIONFRUIT FILLING
60 g (2$\frac{1}{4}$ oz) unsalted butter, softened
60 g (2$\frac{1}{4}$ oz/$\frac{1}{2}$ cup) icing (confectioners')
  sugar
1$\frac{1}{2}$ tablespoons strained passionfruit pulp

Preheat the oven to 180°C (350°F/Gas 4). Line two baking trays with baking paper.

Using electric beaters, cream the butter and icing sugar in a large bowl until light and fluffy. Add the vanilla and beat until combined. Sift the flour and custard powder into a bowl, then stir into the butter mixture until a soft dough forms.

Roll level tablespoons of the mixture into 28 balls and place on the baking trays, spacing them well apart to allow for spreading. Flatten the balls slightly with a fork.

Bake for 20 minutes, or until lightly golden, then transfer to a wire rack to cool.

To make the passionfruit filling, cream the butter and icing sugar using electric beaters until light and fluffy, then stir in the passionfruit pulp.

Use the passionfruit filling to sandwich pairs of the cooled biscuits together. Leave to firm before serving.

The biscuits will keep for up to 4 days, stored in a cool place in an airtight container, or can be frozen in an airtight container for up to 6 weeks.

VARIATION
To make a **coffee filling**, dissolve 2 teaspoons instant coffee granules in 2 teaspoons water and beat it into the creamed butter mixture instead of the passionfruit pulp.

Melting moments can also be piped for a decorative finish. Using a large, strong piping (icing) bag fitted with a large star nozzle, pipe the biscuit mixture in heaped rounds, about 3.5 cm (1$\frac{1}{4}$ inches) wide at the base, directly onto two large baking trays lined with baking paper, allowing room for spreading. Refrigerate for 30 minutes, or until firm, then bake as directed above.

Peanut toffee shortbreads

MAKES 18

110 g (3³/₄ oz) unsalted butter, softened
115 g (4 oz/¹/₂ cup) caster (superfine) sugar
1 egg
185 g (6¹/₂ oz/1¹/₂ cups) plain (all-purpose) flour
60 g (2¹/₄ oz/¹/₂ cup) self-raising flour

TOPPING
180 g (6 oz) unsalted butter
185 g (6¹/₂ oz/1 cup) soft brown sugar
2 tablespoons golden syrup or dark corn syrup
¹/₂ teaspoon lemon juice
400 g (14 oz/2¹/₂ cups) roasted unsalted peanuts

Preheat the oven to 180°C (350°F/Gas 4). Lightly grease an 18 x 27 cm (7 x 10³/₄ inch) baking tin and line the base and sides with baking paper, leaving the paper hanging over the two long sides.

Using electric beaters, cream the butter and sugar until light and fluffy. Add the egg and beat well. Sift the flours into a bowl, then fold into the butter mixture using a large metal spoon until just combined. Press the mixture into the prepared tin.

Bake for 15 minutes, or until the shortbread is firm and lightly coloured. Remove from the oven and leave to cool in the tin for 10 minutes.

To make the topping, put the butter, sugar, golden syrup and lemon juice in a saucepan. Stir over low heat until the sugar has dissolved, then simmer, stirring now and then, for 5 minutes. Stir in the peanuts and remove from the heat.

Spread the topping over the shortbread base using two spoons, taking care as the mixture will be very hot.

Bake for a further 5 minutes. Remove from the oven and leave to cool in the tin for 15 minutes, then turn out onto a board and cut into fingers using a large knife.

Peanut toffee shortbreads will keep for up to 1 week, stored in a cool place in an airtight container, or can be frozen in an airtight container for up to 1 month.

BISCOTTI

MAKES ABOUT 40

375 g (13 oz/3 cups) plain (all-purpose)
 flour
170 g (6 oz/³/₄ cup) caster (superfine)
 sugar
3 eggs, lightly beaten
¹/₂ teaspoon baking powder
¹/₂ teaspoon natural vanilla extract
75 g (2¹/₂ oz/¹/₂ cup) blanched almonds
75 g (2¹/₂ oz/¹/₂ cup) pistachio nuts

Preheat the oven to 180ºC (350ºF/Gas 4). Line two baking trays with baking paper.

Sift the flour into a large bowl. Add the sugar, eggs, baking powder, vanilla and a pinch of salt. Using a wooden spoon at first and then your hands, mix until a firm, smooth dough forms. Turn out onto a lightly floured work surface and divide the dough in half. Knead the almonds into one portion, and the pistachios into the other.

Roll each portion into a log about 20 cm (8 inches) long. Place one on each baking tray and press down gently to flatten the logs slightly.

Bake for 25 minutes, or until lightly golden, then remove from the oven and allow to cool slightly. Reduce the oven temperature to 170ºC (325ºF/Gas 3).

Using a large, serrated knife, cut each log on the diagonal into slices 1 cm (¹/₂ inch) thick, then place back on the baking trays.

Bake for a further 15 minutes, or until the biscotti start to brown and are dry to the touch. Remove from the oven and transfer to wire racks to cool.

Biscotti will keep for up to 3 weeks, stored in a cool place in an airtight container, or can be frozen in an airtight container for up to 3 months.

CHOCOLATE FUDGE SANDWICHES

MAKES 20–24

250 g (9 oz/2 cups) plain (all-purpose)
  flour
30 g (1 oz/¼ cup) unsweetened cocoa
  powder
200 g (7 oz) cold unsalted butter,
  chopped
100 g (3½ oz/heaped ¾ cup) icing
  (confectioners') sugar
2 egg yolks, lightly beaten
1 teaspoon natural vanilla extract

FILLING
100 g (3½ oz/⅔ cup) chopped
  good-quality dark chocolate
1 tablespoon golden syrup or dark corn
  syrup
25 g (1 oz) unsalted butter, softened

Sift the flour and cocoa powder into a bowl. Using your fingertips, lightly rub in the butter until the mixture resembles fine breadcrumbs. Sift the icing sugar into the bowl, then stir in using a wooden spoon. Add the egg yolks and vanilla and stir until a soft dough forms.

Turn out onto a lightly floured work surface and shape into a block about 4 cm (1½ inches) deep, 26 cm (2½ inches) long and 6 cm (2½ inches) wide. Wrap in plastic wrap and refrigerate for 30 minutes, or until firm.

Meanwhile, preheat the oven to 200°C (400°F/Gas 6). Lightly grease two baking trays.

Cut the dough into 40–48 slices, about 5 mm (¼ inch) wide, and place on the baking trays, spacing them well apart to allow for spreading.

Bake for 10 minutes, or until firm. Remove from the oven and leave to cool on the trays for 5 minutes, then transfer to a wire rack to cool completely.

Meanwhile, make the filling. Put the chocolate in a small heatproof bowl. Set the bowl over a small saucepan of simmering water, ensuring the base of the bowl doesn't touch the water. Stir until the chocolate has melted, then remove from the heat. Stir in the golden syrup and butter until smooth. Allow to cool a little, then refrigerate for 10 minutes, or until the mixture is thick enough to spread.

Use the chocolate filling to sandwich pairs of the biscuits together.

Chocolate fudge sandwiches are best eaten the day they are made. Unfilled biscuits will keep for up to 3 days, stored in a cool place in an airtight container. The filled biscuits can be frozen in an airtight container for up to 4 weeks.

CASHEW BROWNIES
MAKES 25

175 g (6 oz) unsalted butter, chopped
300 g (10½ oz/2 cups) chopped
  good-quality dark chocolate
2 eggs
230 g (8 oz/1¼ cups) soft brown sugar
40 g (1½ oz/⅓ cup) unsweetened cocoa
  powder
125 g (4½ oz/1 cup) plain (all-purpose)
  flour
80 g (2¾ oz/½ cup) unsalted cashew
  nuts, toasted and chopped

CHOCOLATE ICING
200 g (7 oz/1⅓ cups) chopped
  good-quality dark chocolate
30 g (1 oz/¼ cup) icing (confectioners')
  sugar
125 g (4½ oz/½ cup) sour cream

Preheat the oven to 160°C (315°F/Gas 2–3). Lightly grease a 23 cm (9 inch) square baking tin and line the base with baking paper.

Put the butter and 200 g (7 oz/1⅓ cups) of the chocolate in a heatproof bowl. Set the bowl over a saucepan of simmering water, ensuring the base of the bowl doesn't touch the water. Stir until the chocolate and butter have melted, then remove from the heat and allow to cool.

Using electric beaters, whisk the eggs and sugar in a large bowl for 5 minutes, or until pale and thick. Stir in the cooled chocolate mixture. Sift the cocoa powder and flour into a bowl, then gently fold into the chocolate mixture. Fold in the cashews and remaining chocolate, then pour the mixture into the prepared tin, smoothing over the surface.

Bake for 30–35 minutes, or until just firm to the touch — the brownies may have a slightly soft centre when hot, but will firm upon cooling. Remove from the oven and allow to cool completely in the tin.

Meanwhile, make the chocolate icing (frosting). Put the chocolate in a small heatproof bowl. Set the bowl over a small saucepan of simmering water, ensuring the base of the bowl doesn't touch the water. Stir until the chocolate has melted, then remove from the heat and allow to cool slightly. Sift the icing sugar into the bowl, then stir in the sour cream.

Spread the icing evenly over the cooled brownies. Refrigerate for a few hours or overnight to firm up, then cut into squares.

Cashew brownies will keep for up to 5 days, stored in a cool place in an airtight container, or can be frozen in an airtight container for up to 3 months.

TOLLHOUSE COOKIES
MAKES 40

180 g (6 oz) unsalted butter, softened
140 g (5 oz/3/4 cup) soft brown sugar
115 g (4 oz/1/2 cup) caster (superfine) sugar
2 eggs
1 teaspoon natural vanilla extract
280 g (10 oz/2 1/4 cups) plain (all-purpose)
   flour
1 teaspoon bicarbonate of soda
   (baking soda)
300 g (10 1/2 oz/2 cups) chopped
   good-quality dark chocolate
100 g (3 1/2 oz/1 cup) pecans,
   roughly chopped

Preheat the oven to 190°C (375°F/Gas 5). Line two baking trays with baking paper.

Using electric beaters, cream the butter and all the sugar in a large bowl until light and fluffy. Add the eggs one at a time, beating well after each addition. Stir in the vanilla.

Sift the flour and bicarbonate of soda into a bowl, then fold into the butter mixture using a large metal spoon until just combined. Fold the chocolate and pecans through.

Drop tablespoons of the mixture onto the baking trays, spacing them well apart to allow for spreading.

Bake for 8–10 minutes, or until lightly golden. Remove from the oven and allow to cool slightly on the trays, then transfer to a wire rack to cool completely.

Tollhouse cookies will keep for up to 1 week, stored in a cool place in an airtight container, or can be frozen in an airtight container for up to 10 weeks.

NOTE: Instead of pecans, you can use any nuts such as walnuts, almonds or hazelnuts in these cookies.

REFRIGERATOR BISCUITS
MAKES ABOUT 60

180 g (6 oz) unsalted butter, softened
185 g (6½ oz/1 cup) soft brown sugar
1 teaspoon natural vanilla extract
1 egg
280 g (10 oz/2¼ cups) plain (all-purpose) flour
1 teaspoon baking powder

Using electric beaters, cream the butter and sugar until light and fluffy. Beat in the vanilla and egg. Sift the flour and baking powder into a bowl, then mix the flour into the butter mixture using a flat-bladed knife until a soft dough forms. Gather the dough together, then turn out onto a board and cut in half.

Place one portion on a sheet of baking paper and press lightly until about 30 cm (12 inches) long and 4 cm (1½ inches) thick. Fold the paper around the dough and roll neatly into a log shape. Twist the ends of the paper to seal. Repeat with the remaining dough, then refrigerate for 30 minutes, or until firm.

Meanwhile, preheat the oven to 180°C (350°F/Gas 4). Line two baking trays with baking paper.

Using a large, sharp knife, cut the logs into slices 1 cm (½ inch) thick. Set on the baking trays, leaving 3 cm (1¼ inches) between them. Bake for 10–15 minutes, or until lightly golden.

Remove from the oven and leave to cool on the trays for 3 minutes, then transfer to a wire rack to cool completely.

Refrigerator biscuits will keep for up to 1 week, stored in a cool place in an airtight container, or can be frozen in an airtight container for up to 3 months.

VARIATIONS
Mocha spirals Lightly knead 2 teaspoons cocoa powder into one dough portion and 2 teaspoons coffee powder into the other. Divide both in half again. Roll two different-coloured portions separately to even rectangles 2 mm (⅛ inch) thick, then place one layer on top of the other on a sheet of baking paper. Trim the edges and roll up, Swiss roll (jelly roll) style. Repeat with the remaining dough. Chill, slice and bake as above.
Maple and pecan Add 60 ml (2 fl oz/¼ cup) maple syrup to the creamed butter mixture. Roll the logs in 125 g (4½ oz/ 1 cup) finely chopped pecans before refrigerating. Press a whole pecan into the top of each biscuit before baking as above.
Spicy fruit Add 1 teaspoon mixed (pumpkin pie) spice and ½ teaspoon ground ginger to the flour before sifting. Roll one dough portion on a sheet of baking paper to a rectangle about 2 mm (1/16 inch) thick and trim the edges. Chill until just firm. Spread with 95 g (3¼ oz/½ cup) fruit mince (mincemeat), then roll up, Swiss roll (jelly roll) style. Repeat with the other portion of dough. Chill, slice and bake as above.

JAM DROPS
MAKES 32

80 g (2³/₄ oz) unsalted butter, softened
80 g (2³/₄ oz/¹/₃ cup) caster (superfine) sugar
2 tablespoons milk
¹/₂ teaspoon natural vanilla extract
125 g (4¹/₂ oz/1 cup) self-raising flour
40 g (1¹/₂ oz/¹/₃ cup) custard powder or instant vanilla pudding mix
100 g (3¹/₂ oz/¹/₃ cup) raspberry jam

Preheat the oven to 180°C (350°F/Gas 4). Line two baking trays with baking paper.

Using electric beaters, cream the butter and sugar until light and fluffy. Add the milk and vanilla and beat until combined.

Sift the flour and custard powder into a bowl, then fold the flour mixture into the butter mixture to form a soft dough. Roll heaped teaspoons of the dough into balls and place on the baking trays.

Using the end of a wooden spoon, make an indentation in each ball. Fill each hole with a little jam.

Bake for 15 minutes, or until lightly golden. Remove from the oven and leave to cool slightly on the baking trays, then transfer to a wire rack to cool.

Jam drops will keep for up to 7 days, stored in a cool place in an airtight container, or can be frozen in an airtight container for 10–12 weeks.

TWO-SEED CRACKERS
MAKES ABOUT 30

250 g (9 oz/2 cups) plain (all-purpose)
  flour
1 teaspoon baking powder
½ teaspoon sea salt
2 tablespoons poppy seeds
2 tablespoons sesame seeds
1 teaspoon freshly ground black pepper
60g (2¼ oz) cold unsalted butter,
  chopped
100 ml (3½ fl oz) iced water

Preheat the oven to 180°C (350°F/Gas 4). Line two baking trays with baking paper.

Sift the flour, baking powder and sea salt into a bowl, then stir in the poppy seeds, sesame seeds and pepper. Using your fingertips, lightly rub in the butter until the mixture resembles fine breadcrumbs.

Make a well in the centre, then add the iced water to the well. Using a flat-bladed knife at first and then your hands, mix until a firm dough forms, adding a little more iced water if necessary. Take care not to overmix.

Form the dough into a rough ball, then cut in half. Wrap one portion in plastic wrap and refrigerate.

Roll the other portion out between two sheets of baking paper until 2 mm (¹/₁₆ inch) thick. Using a lightly floured 6 cm (2½ inch) round cutter, cut out rounds from the dough. Place on the baking trays and prick all over with a fork. Repeat with the remaining dough. Re-roll any scraps and cut them into rounds.

Bake for 20–35 minutes, or until lightly golden. Transfer to a wire rack to cool completely.

Two-seed crackers will keep for up to 5 days, stored in a cool place in an airtight container, or can be frozen in an airtight container for up to 8 weeks.

Walnut coffee slice
MAKES 20

125 g (4½ oz/1¼ cups) walnut halves
155 g (5½ oz/1 cup) blanched almonds
2 tablespoons plain (all-purpose) flour
170 g (6 oz/¾ cup) caster (superfine)
  sugar
7 egg whites
chocolate-coated coffee beans, to
  decorate

COFFEE CREAM
200 g (7 oz) unsalted butter, softened
150 g (5½ oz/1 cup) chopped
  good-quality dark chocolate, melted
4 teaspoons instant coffee granules

Preheat the oven to 180°C (350°F/Gas 4). Lightly grease a
23 cm (9 inch) square baking tin and line with baking paper,
leaving the paper hanging over two opposite sides.

Spread the walnuts and almonds on a baking tray and
roast for 7–10 minutes, or until golden. Remove from the oven
and allow to cool slightly, then place in a food processor and
process until finely ground. Tip into a bowl. Sift the flour into
the bowl, add 115 g (4 oz/½ cup) of the sugar and mix well.

In a large, clean, dry bowl, beat the egg whites using
electric beaters until soft peaks form. Whisking constantly,
gradually add the remaining sugar, whisking until the mixture
is thick and glossy and the sugar has dissolved. Using a large
metal spoon, gently fold the nut mixture, one-third at a time,
into the meringue.

Spoon the mixture into the prepared tin, smoothing
over the surface. Bake for 20 minutes, or until springy to the
touch. Remove from the oven and allow to cool in the tin for
5 minutes, then transfer to a wire rack to cool completely.

To make the coffee cream, beat the butter in a small bowl
using electric beaters until light and creamy. Add the cooled
melted chocolate and beat to combine well. Dissolve the
coffee granules in 2 teaspoons water, then add to the chocolate
mixture and beat well. Refrigerate for 5–10 minutes, or until
thickened slightly.

Using a large, serrated knife, cut the cooled slice in half
horizontally to form two layers. Carefully remove the top
layer and spread half the coffee cream over, then replace the
top layer. Spread the remaining coffee cream evenly over
the top, then refrigerate until the cream is firm.

Serve at room temperature, cut into squares and
decorated with coffee beans.

Walnut coffee slice will keep for up to 5 days, refrigerated
in an airtight container, or can be frozen in an airtight container
for up to 8 weeks.

PEAR AND MACADAMIA FINGERS
MAKES 20

90 g (3¼ oz/¾ cup) plain (all-purpose)
   flour
25 g (1 oz) unsalted butter, chopped
1½ tablespoons ground almonds
1½ tablespoons icing (confectioners')
   sugar
1 egg yolk
¼ teaspoon natural vanilla extract

MACADAMIA TOPPING
100 g (3½ oz/¾ cup) roughly chopped
   macadamia nuts
185 g (6½ oz/1 cup) soft brown sugar
150 g (5½ oz) unsalted butter, chopped
1 teaspoon natural vanilla extract
100 g (3½ oz/½ cup) chopped dried
   pears
50 g (1¾ oz/⅓ cup) chopped
   good-quality dark chocolate

Put the flour, butter, ground almonds and icing sugar in a food processor and process until a crumbly mixture forms. Using the pulse button, add the egg yolk, vanilla and just enough iced water to make a firm dough. Turn out onto a lightly floured work surface, gather into a ball, then wrap in plastic wrap and refrigerate for 30 minutes.

Meanwhile, preheat the oven to 180°C (350°F/Gas 4). Lightly grease a 20 cm (8 inch) square cake tin and line the base and sides with baking paper.

Roll out the dough to fit the base of the prepared tin, then ease the dough into the tin. Bake for 15 minutes, or until lightly browned. Remove from the oven and leave to cool completely.

To make the macadamia topping, spread the macadamias on a baking tray and roast for 7 minutes, or until golden.

Put the sugar and butter in a saucepan and stir over low heat until the butter has melted and the sugar has dissolved. Bring to the boil, then reduce the heat and simmer for 1 minute, stirring all the while. Remove from the heat and stir in the vanilla, pears, chocolate and roasted macadamias.

Spread the mixture over the biscuit base and bake for 30 minutes, or until the topping is bubbling. Remove from the oven and allow to cool completely in the tin, before cutting into fingers to serve.

Pear and macadamia fingers will keep for up to 4 days, stored in a cool place in an airtight container, or can be frozen in an airtight container for up to 6 weeks.

CRACKLE COOKIES
MAKES ABOUT 60

125 g (4½ oz) unsalted butter, softened
370 g (13 oz/2 cups) soft brown sugar
2 eggs
1 teaspoon natural vanilla extract
60 g (2¼ oz/⅓ cup) chopped
  good-quality dark chocolate, melted
80 ml (2½ fl oz/⅓ cup) milk
340 g (12 oz/2¾ cups) plain (all-purpose)
  flour
2 tablespoons unsweetened cocoa powder
2 teaspoons baking powder
¼ teaspoon ground allspice
85 g (3 oz/⅔ cup) chopped pecans
icing (confectioners') sugar, for dusting

Using electric beaters, cream the butter and sugar until light and fluffy. Add the eggs, one at a time, beating well after each addition. Stir in the vanilla, chocolate and milk.

Sift the flour, cocoa, baking powder, allspice and a pinch of salt into the butter mixture and mix well. Stir in the pecans, then refrigerate for at least 3 hours, or overnight.

Preheat the oven to 180°C (350°F/Gas 4). Lightly grease two baking trays.

Sift the icing sugar onto a plate. Roll tablespoons of the cookie mixture into balls, then roll each one in the icing sugar to coat. Place on the baking trays, spacing them well apart to allow for spreading.

Bake for 20–25 minutes, or until lightly browned and just firm. Remove from the oven and leave to cool on the trays for 3–4 minutes, then transfer to a wire rack to cool completely.

Crackle cookies will keep for 1 week, stored in a cool place in an airtight container, or can be frozen for up to 3 months.

GREEK SHORTBREAD

MAKES 38

200 g (7 oz) unsalted butter, softened
1 teaspoon finely grated orange zest
250 g (9 oz/2 cups) icing (confectioners')
  sugar
1 egg
1 egg yolk
310 g (11 oz/2½ cups) plain (all-purpose)
  flour
1½ teaspoons baking powder
1 teaspoon ground cinnamon
250 g (9 oz/1⅔ cups) blanched almonds,
  toasted and finely chopped

Preheat the oven to 160°C (315°F/Gas 2–3). Line two baking trays with baking paper.

Put the butter and orange zest in a bowl. Sift half the icing sugar into the bowl, then cream using electric beaters until light and fluffy. Add the egg and egg yolk and beat until well combined.

Sift the flour, baking powder and cinnamon into a bowl. Using a metal spoon, gently fold into the butter mixture along with the almonds until well combined.

Roll level tablespoons of the mixture into logs, then form into crescent shapes and place on the baking trays.

Bake for 15 minutes, or until lightly golden. Remove from the oven and leave to cool on the trays for 5 minutes, then transfer to a wire rack to cool.

While the shortbreads are still warm, dredge with the remaining sifted icing sugar. Just before serving, dust heavily again with icing sugar.

Greek shortbreads will keep for up to 1 week, stored in a cool place in an airtight container, or can be frozen in an airtight container for up to 8 weeks.

FIG AND CINNAMON SLICE
MAKES 15

125 g (4½ oz) unsalted butter, softened
45 g (1½ oz/¼ cup) soft brown sugar
1 teaspoon ground cinnamon
185 g (6½ oz/1½ cups) plain (all-purpose) flour
375 g (13 oz/2 cups) dried figs
1 cinnamon stick
115 g (4 oz/½ cup) caster (superfine) sugar

Preheat the oven to 180°C (350°F/Gas 4). Lightly grease an 18 x 27 cm (7 x 10¾ inch) baking tin and line with baking paper, leaving the paper hanging over the two long sides.

Using electric beaters, cream the butter, brown sugar and cinnamon until light and fluffy, then stir in the flour using a large metal spoon. Press the mixture evenly into the prepared tin.

Bake for 25 minutes, then remove from the oven and leave to cool slightly in the tin.

Meanwhile, put the figs, cinnamon stick and caster sugar in a saucepan with 375 ml (13 fl oz/1½ cups) boiling water. Bring to the boil, then reduce the heat and simmer for 20 minutes, or until the figs have softened and the liquid has reduced by one-third. Remove the cinnamon stick and transfer the mixture to a food processor. Using the pulse button, process until just smooth.

Pour the mixture onto the cooked biscuit base and bake for 10 minutes, or until set. Remove from the oven and leave in the tin to cool completely.

To serve, lift the slice out of the tin using the baking paper and cut into squares.

Fig and cinnamon slice will keep for up to 4 days, stored in a cool place in an airtight container.

BAKEWELL SLICE
MAKES 15

125 g (4$^{1}/_{2}$ oz/1 cup) plain (all-purpose) flour
1 tablespoon icing (confectioners') sugar
50 g (1$^{3}/_{4}$ oz) cold unsalted butter, chopped
1 egg yolk
2 tablespoons iced water

TOPPING
125 g (4$^{1}/_{2}$ oz) unsalted butter, softened
115 g (4 oz/$^{1}/_{2}$ cup) caster (superfine) sugar
4 eggs
125 g (4$^{1}/_{2}$ oz/1$^{1}/_{4}$ cups) ground almonds
2 drops of natural almond extract
160 g (5$^{3}/_{4}$ oz/$^{1}/_{2}$ cup) raspberry jam
25 g (1 oz/$^{1}/_{4}$ cup) flaked almonds
2 tablespoons icing (confectioners') sugar

Sift the flour and icing sugar into a bowl, then add the butter. Using your fingertips, lightly rub in the butter until the mixture resembles breadcrumbs. Add the egg yolk and iced water and mix using a flat-bladed knife until the mixture comes together in beads. Gather into a ball, cover with plastic wrap and refrigerate for 30 minutes.

Meanwhile, preheat the oven to 180°C (350°F/Gas 4). Lightly grease a 20 x 30 cm (8 x 12 inch) baking tin and line with baking paper, leaving the paper hanging over the two long sides.

Roll the dough out between two sheets of baking paper to the size of the baking tin. Remove the top sheet of baking paper and carefully invert the dough into the tin, easing it in and pressing it into the edges.

Bake for 10 minutes, then remove from the oven and leave to cool slightly in the tin.

Meanwhile, make the topping. Using electric beaters, cream the butter and sugar until light and fluffy. Add the eggs one at a time, beating well after each addition, then stir in the ground almonds and almond extract.

Spread the jam over the biscuit base and pour the creamed butter mixture over the top. Sprinkle with the flaked almonds, then bake for 30–35 minutes, or until the topping is firm. Remove from the oven and leave to cool completely.

Sift the icing sugar into a bowl and mix in 2–3 teaspoons warm water to form a free-flowing paste. Drizzle over the slice in a zigzag pattern and leave to set. Trim the edges and cut into squares before lifting out using the baking paper.

Bakewell slice will keep for up to 4 days, stored in a cool place in an airtight container, or can be frozen in an airtight container for up to 8 weeks.

Cinnamon pecan biscuits

Makes 40

100 g (3½ oz/⅔ cup) chopped
  good-quality dark chocolate
125 g (4½ oz) unsalted butter, softened
115 g (4 oz/½ cup) caster (superfine)
  sugar
1 egg
75 g (2½ oz/¾ cup) pecans, finely
  chopped
50 g (1¾ oz/heaped ⅓ cup) self-raising
  flour, sifted
100 g (3½ oz/heaped ¾ cup) plain
  (all-purpose) flour, sifted
2 teaspoons ground cinnamon
40 whole pecans, to decorate
icing (confectioners') sugar, for dusting

Preheat the oven to 180°C (350°F/Gas 4). Line two 32 x 28 cm (12¾ x 11¼ inch) baking trays with baking paper.

Put the chocolate in a small heatproof bowl and set the bowl over a small saucepan of simmering water, ensuring the base of the bowl doesn't touch the water. Stir until the chocolate is melted and smooth. Remove from the heat and allow to cool.

Using electric beaters, cream the butter and sugar in a small bowl until light and fluffy. Add the egg and beat well. Add the cooled melted chocolate and beat until combined.

Transfer the mixture to a large bowl and add the chopped pecans. Sift the flours and cinnamon into the bowl and fold through using a large metal spoon, until the mixture is just combined and a dough forms. Lightly roll 2 teaspoons of the mixture into oval shapes, place on the baking trays and press a whole pecan onto each.

Bake for 10 minutes, or until lightly golden, then transfer to a wire rack to cool completely.

Lightly dust with icing sugar to serve.

Cinnamon pecan biscuits will keep for 2 days, stored in a cool place in an airtight container, or can be frozen in an airtight container for up to 8 weeks.

VARIATION
These biscuits can also be piped for a decorative finish. Using a large, strong piping (icing) bag fitted with a large plain or star nozzle, pipe the biscuit mixture in heaped rounds, about 3.5 cm (1¼ inches) wide at the base, directly onto two large baking trays lined with baking paper, allowing room for spreading. Refrigerate for 30 minutes, or until firm, then bake as directed above.

DIGESTIVE BISCUITS
MAKES 16

125 g (4½ oz) unsalted butter, softened
60 g (2¼ oz/⅓ cup) soft brown sugar
1 tablespoon malt extract
1 egg
125 g (4½ oz/1 cup) plain (all-purpose) flour
150 g (5½ oz/1 cup) wholemeal (whole-wheat) flour
1 teaspoon baking powder
35 g (1¼ oz/½ cup) unprocessed bran
butter or cheese, to serve

Using electric beaters, cream the butter, sugar and malt in a large bowl until light and fluffy. Add the egg and beat well.

Sift the flours and baking powder into a bowl, tipping any husks in the sieve back into the bowl, then stir in the bran. Using a large, metal spoon, fold the flour mixture into the creamed butter mixture until combined. Cover with plastic wrap and refrigerate for 1 hour.

Line two baking trays with baking paper.

Cut the dough in half, then roll out each half between two sheets of baking paper until 5 mm (¼ inch) thick. Cut out rounds of dough using a lightly floured 7 cm (2¾ inch) round cutter, then place on the baking trays. Re-roll any scraps and cut into rounds. Refrigerate on the baking trays for 20 minutes.

Meanwhile, preheat the oven to 180°C (350°F/Gas 4).

Bake the biscuits for 12 minutes, or until firm and golden. Transfer to a wire rack to cool completely.

Serve with butter or cheese.

Digestive biscuits will keep for up to 1 week, stored in a cool place in an airtight container, or can be frozen in an airtight container for up to 8 weeks.

pies and tarts

Any baking aroma is seductive, but among the most divine is the one emanating from a glossy-glazed pie, fresh from the oven and left to cool. A two-crust pie holds the secret of its filling until slices are wedged out — inside might be anything from an oozing, sweet mass of sugar-sweetened berries, apples or lemon or a savoury striation of bacon and hard-cooked egg.

Open-topped pies, such as the various tarts, galettes, quiches and flans, are a similarly varied lot — a baked pastry case can hold anything from a neat overlap of sliced seasonal fruit to a goat's-cheese flavoured custard or a classic filling of sweet, spiced, puréed pumpkin.

With kitchenware stores now stocked with tins of all shapes and sizes, a pie or tart needn't be round either — elegant oblongs, chic squares and cute individual tins of all shapes make for a world of pie possibilities.

Curiously, primitive pie pastries weren't designed to be edible. In medieval Europe for example, when pies were called 'coffyns' (from the Greek word *kophinos*, meaning basket), pastry served as both a cooking container and serving vessel. These were days when cookware and tableware had yet to become widely available or refined. A 'pie' was more akin to a casserole cooked in a rock-hard pastry; this pastry was far too tough to eat, but because it served such a practical purpose, it was an everyday kitchen staple.

It wasn't until the sixteenth century when cookbooks for domestic use began appearing that pie recipes were published — in England and Europe these were always savoury. Food historians believe the Egyptians made the first pies, although these were more like rustic, flat-baked cakes. The Greeks and Romans used thin flour and water-based pastries, which they employed as thin, tight seals around pieces of baked meat — the crust wasn't eaten but was designed to keep all the juices inside. Via the Roman roads into lands of their conquest, many culinary ideas and inventions — including the pie — spread to far-flung nations. It is little wonder that almost every country on earth today has some sort of pie in its traditional culinary repertoire.

During the thirteenth and fourteenth centuries, 'animated pies' became a popular form of entertainment at banquets. Pre-baked pie crusts would be baked with a pastry top, in which were cut several holes. Into these holes would be crammed (after baking) an assortment of live beasts — birds perhaps, or frogs, tortoises or rabbits. The pie would be cut and then, for the entertainment of assembled guests, out would fly, hop or scramble the enclosed beasts. There are even accounts of human dwarves being thus presented in a pie. The nursery rhyme lyric 'four and twenty blackbirds baked in a pie' is a direct reference to this now-curious custom.

The English became very good pie cooks, and their early fillings involved a complexity of flavours. Meat (mutton, game, veal or poultry) would be mixed with a host of spices, dried sweet fruits and suet. It was not unheard of for meat, suet, ginger, cinnamon, cloves, mace, prunes, candied citrus, currants, dates and raisins to all feature together in a pie. The original Christmas fruit mince (mincemeat) pies did indeed contain minced (ground) meat — along with a richness of sweet spices, sugar, dried fruits, alcohol and suet. Dishes such as cottage pie (made from left-over beef roast) and shepherd's pie (using left-over lamb roast) came much later in the piece, well after potatoes were introduced from the New World in the sixteenth century.

The French, not surprisingly, were the ones responsible for refining pastry-making. In 1440 the formation of a trade organisation, the Corporation of Pastry Cooks, effectively took pastry-making away from the Bakers (who also made cakes) and over time, the pastry cooks perfected puff, flaky and fine butter pastries. They expanded their lines of production, making not just the meat and fish pies that were originally their stock-and-trade but sweet pies and flans too. Pie-making also became significant in North America thanks to the early Pilgrim settlers, who experimented with the indigenous fruits and berries when they first arrived and went on to 'invent' a number of now-standard pies — pumpkin and pecan among them.

Today there are literally hundreds of types of pies, ranging from the individual, transportable Spanish empanada, British pasty and Italian calzone to the classic French quiche, tarte tatin or gâteau Basque, and universally popular desserts such as lemon, rhubarb or berry pies, as well as numerous other examples from the Middle East, Asia, Central Europe, Russia and South America. This chapter gathers together a tempting collection of some of the simplest and most loved pies and tarts, and some invaluable tips to guide even the most timid pastry-makers.

TYPES OF PASTRY

At its simplest, pastry consists of no more than a certain ratio of butter to flour. Butter is rubbed into the flour (using fingertips is the classic method), then a little liquid (iced water, milk, beaten egg or a combination of these) is added to bring the dough together and form a firm but pliable mass.

There are many different types of pastry, from the simplest flour-and-butter pie crust to airy flaky or puff pastry; from fine-textured sweet pastry to 'laminated' (or layered) yeast-raised pastry (such as that used in Danish pastry), and unique regional and traditional pastries such as the Greek filo pastry and the English hot-water raised pastry used in pork pies.

Some types of pastry do require patience and advanced cooking skills to perfect, particularly those with a high fat content (these are quite fragile) and the yeasted types, which need some practice to master. This chapter focuses on pastries that use simple techniques and produce alluringly homey results — those you use to make treacle or custard tarts, savoury flans and quiches, fruit pies and sturdy Italian-style crostatas.

An all-purpose pastry, **shortcrust pastry** is good for many sweet and savoury pies and tarts. It is made using butter rubbed into flour, with perhaps a little vegetable fat for added crispness. Generally just iced water is used to moisten the dough. It is possible to vary the flavour of this pastry. For example, you could substitute an amount of wholemeal (whole-wheat), buckwheat or rye flour for some of the plain (all-purpose) flour. You could also substitute some ground almonds or hazelnuts, add a teaspoon of spice such as cinnamon, add some finely grated citrus zest, a little natural vanilla extract, finely chopped herbs or grated cheese.

Rich shortcrust pastry is made using just butter as the fat, with an added egg yolk or two to make it richer. The savoury flavourings suggested for shortcrust pastry above can also be added to it. **Sweet rich shortcrust pastry** is identical to rich shortcrust except it is sweetened with a little sugar. The suggested sweet flavourings above can also be incorporated.

With a high butter content, pâte sucrée is a very rich shortcrust pastry that is sweetened with sugar and enriched with egg yolks. This is used for fruit flans and sweet tarts such as custard tarts. Some recipes cream the butter and sugar first, then stir in the egg yolks and flour, while others use the rubbing-in method. This is a pastry that requires careful attention when making — be sure to weigh and measure all ingredients carefully.

TIPS FOR PERFECT PASTRY

- The golden rule of pastry-making is to keep the ingredients — and the resulting pastry — as cool as possible while you are making it. If it is a particularly hot day, try to find somewhere cool to work, or work in the cool of the early morning or evening and chill the pastry well between mixing and rolling and baking.
- Have your butter cold but not rock-hard. Take it from the refrigerator 15–20 minutes before you wish to make your pastry, and cut it into small pieces to facilitate rubbing in.
- Sift the flour (with a large pinch of fine sea salt if you like) into a large bowl — this will help aerate the flour and produce a lighter dough. If you are using ground nuts, spices or sugar, stir those in now.
- Add the chopped butter all at once then, using the tips of your fingers, 'rub in' the butter until it is evenly distributed through the flour and the mixture looks like coarse breadcrumbs. Keep the palms of your hands out of this process as they are too warm. Add any extra ingredients, such as chopped herbs or grated cheese, at this stage.
- Make a well in the centre of the flour mixture, then add nearly all of the recommended liquid (including any beaten egg yolk). You may need more (or less) liquid, depending on the humidity, temperature and liquid-absorbing qualities of the flour (which can vary from batch to batch). Many recipes recommend using a fork or a flat-bladed knife to mix the dough, but it is also good practice to use your fingers. The techniques of making pastry are best mastered by 'feel' and experience, and only by getting your hands in the dough and 'feeling' when it is ready (enough liquid, for example), can you truly be confident of turning out consistently good results.
- Mix the dough firmly but not too vigorously, until it comes together in small lumps, adding a little extra liquid as necessary. When there is sufficient liquid in the dough, a small piece will hold together when you squeeze it gently between your fingers. If it is too dry, it will be impossible to roll; if it is too wet, it will toughen and shrink when baked.
- *Do not overwork the dough.* The more you handle and 'work' the pastry, the more gluten you will build up and strengthen in the dough, which will make the final result tough to eat. It will probably also shrink when baked.
- Gently push the dough together into a loose ball, place on a lightly floured surface and press it into a smooth, flattened disc, taking care not to knead or handle it too much. Cover it tightly in plastic wrap, then refrigerate for

about 30 minutes to rest. This resting period is vital — it allows any gluten in the dough to relax, and ensures the dough is cold when you roll it. Cold dough is easier to handle than room-temperature dough.

• Some recipes suggest making pastry in a food processor. While this is an option, there are a few cautionary tips to note. If using a machine, have the butter chilled and chopped and process it into the flour using the pulse button, checking the 'rubbing in' process regularly. Leaving the processor running risks heat from the motor warming the mixture and ruining the pastry — and it is easy to overmix this way too. Never mix in the liquid using the food processor — the risk of overmixing is just too great. Only when you mix in the liquid by hand can you 'feel' when enough has been added. It is much better to remove the flour/butter mixture to a large bowl, then mix in the liquid manually.

Rolling out the dough

A really good rolling pin (see page 13) makes the world of difference with pastry-making. Most professionals don't bother with the short rolling pins with handles on each end that are commonly available for domestic use — a long, thinnish pin (sometimes tapered at the ends) is their preference and for good reason. These are lighter than ones with handles, have a wider reach across the dough and are far easier to handle.

As with all steps of pastry-making, the golden rule when rolling is 'don't overwork the dough'. So, don't stretch it while rolling, don't scrape it off the bench and re-roll it unless you really have to (and even then it is a good idea to gently fold it up, wrap it in plastic wrap and rest it in the refrigerator for 20 minutes before attempting to re-roll it), and take care not to stretch it while transferring the rolled dough to a tin.

Always chill your pastry for at least 30 minutes before rolling it out, to allow any gluten that has been worked during mixing to relax. Once removed from its refrigerated rest, stand the dough at room temperature to soften it a little, otherwise it will be too difficult to roll.

The best surfaces for rolling are a large wooden board (make sure it has a smooth, even surface) or a smooth benchtop. Professionals often use a slab of marble for rolling pastry as the natural coolness of the stone prevents dough from becoming too warm. Lightly dust your chosen surface with plain (all-purpose) flour — just use a minimum here as extra flour will coat the pastry and risk making it tough and chewy. Dust both the top of your dough and your rolling pin lightly with flour too.

Always roll pastry away from you, beginning in the centre of the dough and then rolling out towards the edges. Turn your pastry 90 degrees every few rolls so that it doesn't roll too much in one direction — note that you are turning the pastry to roll evenly, never your position at the bench or the direction of the pin. Use even pressure and long roll strokes, but don't push down on the pastry or it will stretch. Evaluate the shape and size of your intended tin so you know what size you are aiming for, being sure to allow plenty for the sides of the tin and for trimming (to give a neat edge).

If any spots of pastry stick to the bench, a palette knife with a broad, flexible blade is the best implement to remove it. Hold the blade as flat as you can against the work surface and gently nudge it under the pastry to loosen. Be sure to lift the pastry and lightly flour that area before proceeding with rolling. Very fragile pastry can be rolled beween two sheets of baking paper to ensure it doesn't stick, break or tear too much.

Once the pastry is rolled to the desired thickness and size, gently roll it around the rolling pin and transfer it to the tin, centering it in the tin as much as you can so you don't need to reposition it. Ease the pastry into the tin, pressing lightly with your fingertips to make sure it goes snugly into all the corners. Rolling the pin over the edges is a good way to trim off the excess dough if the recipe requires you to do so at this stage.

It is always recommended that you rest the rolled pastry in the refrigerator for at least 30 minutes before baking (you can do this while the oven is preheating), to guard against shrinking and toughness during baking.

BAKING BLIND

Baking blind is simply a way to pre-cook pastry so it won't go soggy when the filling is added. It is very easy. You simply take your rolled, chilled, pastry-lined tart tin and prick the pastry base all over with a fork.

Place a piece of baking paper over the pastry, making sure both the base and sides are fully covered, with about 2 cm (3/4 inch) hanging over the upper edge. Crimp the paper around the base and push it into the lower edge of the pastry so it more or less fits inside the pastry case.

The paper is then half-filled with something heavy that will stop the pastry from puffing up in the oven. You can use purpose-made ceramic baking beads (see page 13), or simply dried rice, lentils, split peas or any dried beans you might have on hand (these can be reused many times for blind baking; there is no need to discard them once they've been baked).

Then you simply bake the pastry according to the directions in the recipe — times vary depending upon the size, type of pastry and intended use. Generally, pastry is blind-baked in a fairly hot oven for 10–15 minutes, the baking paper and beads removed, the oven temperature reduced slightly, and the pastry baked again for a short time until it is very lightly golden and feels dry in the centre. Unless the pastry case is being filled with a pre-cooked or gelatine-based mixture (in which case it should be cooked for longer until it is golden and crisp), the object is not to cook the pastry all the way through. Once it is filled, the pastry then goes back in the oven for further cooking, so you don't want to over-do it.

FREEZING DOUGH

Uncooked dough can be frozen quite successfully, either unrolled, or rolled out and placed in a tart or pie tin.

If the dough isn't rolled out, form it into a flattened disc that is close to the shape you want to ultimately roll it into (square, round, rectangular, for example) and wrap it very well in several layers of plastic wrap. Seal it in a zip-lock bag; it will keep in the freezer for up to 8 weeks. Thaw it slowly (in the refrigerator is ideal), then use it as you would freshly made pastry.

Tins lined with uncooked pastry can also be frozen for up to 8 weeks. These should also be very well wrapped and sealed, if possible, inside a zip-lock bag so no ice forms (this will melt and wet the pastry as it thaws).

You can also roll and freeze pastry 'tops', stacking them with a sheet of baking paper in between and freezing them on a large plate, or pre-freezing each piece first on a small baking tray, then stacking them as they freeze.

You can also freeze blind-baked, unfilled pastry-lined tins and cases for up to 10 weeks. Again, wrap these well in plastic wrap and zip-lock bags. Slowly thaw them first, then crisp them up in a 180°C (350°F/Gas 4) oven for 5 minutes before using.

GLAZING AND DECORATING

It takes little effort to decorate even the simplest pie. A glaze of egg yolk mixed with a little water brushed over a pie will bake to a burnished gold, and once you've glazed the unbaked pie you can use a small, sharp knife to score patterns in the glaze, which look striking once baked. Crimping (using your fingers or the tines of a fork) is a simple way to give pie edges a neat finish.

With skill and patience, you can fashion pastry scraps into plaits or twists to place around a pie edge. Scraps are also useful for making into lattices for an open-topped pie, or into patterns such as flowers, leaves or berries to adorn a glazed pie. To give interest to an otherwise plain surface, you can even cut shapes — such as hearts or even just small rounds — out of a rolled pastry top using a shaped cutter before placing it over the filling.

Depending on their filling, glazed pies can even be showered with coarse sugar (raw or even coffee crystals), poppy seeds, a few caraway or cumin seeds, sesame seeds or pumpkin seeds before baking.

BRAMBLE PIE
SERVES 4–6

125 g (4¹/² oz/1 cup) self-raising flour
125 g (4¹/² oz/1 cup) plain (all-purpose) flour
2 tablespoons caster (superfine) sugar
125 g (4¹/² oz) cold unsalted butter, chopped
1 egg, lightly beaten
3–4 tablespoons milk

FILLING
2 tablespoons cornflour (cornstarch)
2–4 tablespoons caster (superfine) sugar, to taste
1 teaspoon grated orange zest
1 tablespoon orange juice
600 g (1 lb 5 oz) brambles (see Note)

GLAZE
1 egg yolk, mixed with 1 teaspoon water

Sift the flours into a large bowl and add the sugar. Using your fingertips, lightly rub in the butter until the mixture resembles fine breadcrumbs. Make a well in the centre, then add the egg and most of the milk to the well. Mix using a flat-bladed knife until a rough dough forms, adding a little more milk if necessary. Turn out onto a lightly floured work surface, then gently press together into a ball. Form into a flat disc, cover with plastic wrap and refrigerate for 30 minutes.

Meanwhile, preheat the oven to 180°C (350°F/Gas 4).

To make the filling, combine the cornflour, sugar, orange zest and orange juice in a saucepan. Add half the berries and stir over low heat for 5 minutes, or until the mixture boils and thickens. Leave to cool, then stir in the remaining berries. Pour into a 750 ml (26 fl oz/3 cup) pie dish.

Cut the chilled dough in half. Roll out one portion on a lightly floured work surface until large enough to cover the top of the dish, trimming away the excess. Roll out the other half and, using heart-shaped pastry cutters of various sizes, cut out some hearts to decorate the pie. Brush the pie with the glaze and bake for 35 minutes, or until golden brown. Serve hot or warm.

Bramble pie is best eaten the day it is made.

NOTE: Brambles include any creeping stem berries, such as boysenberries, blackberries, loganberries and youngberries. You can use just one variety or a combination.

PEACH GALETTES
MAKES 12

400 g (14 oz/3¼ cups) plain
  (all-purpose) flour
165 g (5¾ oz/1⅓ cups) icing
  (confectioners') sugar, plus extra,
  for dusting
200 g (7 oz) cold unsalted butter,
  chopped
2 egg yolks, mixed with 2 tablespoons
  iced water

FILLING
600 g (1 lb 5 oz) firm, ripe peaches,
  stoned and thinly sliced
20 g (¾ oz) unsalted butter, melted
1 tablespoon honey
1 tablespoon caster (superfine) sugar
¼ teaspoon ground nutmeg
25 g (1 oz/¼ cup) flaked almonds, toasted

FOR GLAZING
1 egg yolk
1 tablespoon milk
80 g (2¾ oz/¼ cup) apricot jam

Sift the flour, icing sugar and a pinch of salt into a large bowl. Using your fingertips, lightly rub in the butter until the mixture resembles coarse breadcrumbs. Make a well in the centre, then add the egg yolks to the well. Mix using a flat-bladed knife until a rough dough forms. Turn out onto a lightly floured work surface, then gently press together into a ball. Form into a flat disc, cover with plastic wrap and refrigerate for 30 minutes.

Lightly grease a baking tray or line with baking paper. Roll out the pastry on a lightly floured work surface to 3 mm (⅛ inch) thick. Cut out twelve 12 cm (4½ inch) rounds.

To make the filling, put the peach slices, butter, honey, sugar and nutmeg in a bowl and gently toss together. Divide among the pastry rounds, leaving a 1 cm (½ inch) border around the edge. Fold the pastry over the filling, leaving the centre uncovered, and pleating the pastry edges at 1 cm (½ inch) intervals to fit. Place the galettes on the baking tray and refrigerate for 30 minutes.

Meanwhile, preheat the oven to 200°C (400°F/Gas 6).

To make the glaze, mix together the egg yolk and milk, then brush over the chilled pastry. Bake for 30 minutes, or until golden.

Meanwhile, put the jam and 1 tablespoon water in a small saucepan and stir over low heat until smooth.

Remove the galettes from the oven and brush the jam mixture over the hot galettes. Sprinkle with the almonds, then transfer to a wire rack to cool slightly. Serve warm or at room temperature, dusted with icing sugar.

Peach galettes are best eaten the day they are made.

FREE-FORM APPLE AND CHERRY CROSTADE
SERVES 8

200 g (7 oz/1²/³ cups) plain (all-purpose)
  flour
85 g (3 oz/²/³ cup) icing (confectioners')
  sugar
100 g (3¹/² oz) cold unsalted butter,
  chopped
1 egg yolk, mixed with 1 tablespoon
  iced water

FILLING
20 g (³/⁴ oz) unsalted butter
3 green apples, peeled, cored and cut into
  1 cm (¹/² inch) pieces
60 g (2¹/⁴ oz/¹/³ cup) soft brown sugar
¹/² teaspoon ground cinnamon
¹/² teaspoon ground ginger
¹/² teaspoon lemon juice
2 tablespoons plain (all-purpose) flour
300 g (10¹/² oz/1¹/² cups) pitted fresh,
  frozen or drained tinned cherries

FOR GLAZING
1 egg yolk
1 tablespoon milk
80 g (2³/⁴ oz/¹/⁴ cup) apricot jam

Sift the flour, icing sugar and a pinch of salt into a large bowl. Using your fingertips, lightly rub in the butter until the mixture resembles breadcrumbs. Make a well in the centre, then add the egg yolk to the well. Mix using a flat-bladed knife until a rough dough forms. Turn out onto a lightly floured work surface, then gently press together into a ball. Form into a flat disc, cover with plastic wrap and refrigerate for 30 minutes.

Meanwhile, preheat the oven to 180°C (350°F/Gas 4). Grease and flour a large baking tray.

To make the filling, melt the butter in a saucepan over medium heat, then add the apple, sugar, cinnamon, ginger and lemon juice. Cover and cook for 5 minutes, or until the apple has softened a little. Remove from the heat, allow to cool slightly, then stir in the flour and cherries.

Roll out the chilled pastry on a lightly floured work surface into a round 3 mm (¹/⁸ inch) thick, then ease onto the baking tray. Pile the filling into the centre, leaving a 5 cm (2 inch) border. Fold the pastry edges over the filling, leaving the centre uncovered, and pleating the pastry to fit.

To make the glaze, mix together the egg yolk and milk, then brush over the pastry edges. Bake on the bottom shelf of the oven for 35–40 minutes, or until the pastry is golden. Remove from the oven and leave on the baking tray.

Put the jam and 1¹/² tablespoons water in a small saucepan and stir over low heat until smooth. Brush the jam mixture over the hot crostade and filling. Allow to cool slightly before serving.

Apple and cherry crostade is best eaten the day it is made.

Fresh pear tart
SERVES 6

150 g (5½ oz/1¼ cups) plain
 (all-purpose) flour
55 g (2 oz/¼ cup) caster (superfine) sugar
1 teaspoon grated lemon zest
60 g (2¼ oz) cold unsalted butter,
 chopped
1 egg yolk, mixed with 2 teaspoons
 iced water

MASCARPONE CREAM
125 g (4½ oz) mascarpone cheese
55 g (2 oz/¼ cup) caster (superfine) sugar
1 egg
¼ teaspoon natural vanilla extract
1 tablespoon plain (all-purpose) flour
2–3 tablespoons milk, if needed

FILLING
4 ripe pears
juice of ½ lemon
45 g (1½ oz/⅓ cup) roasted hazelnuts,
 roughly chopped
1½ tablespoons caster (superfine) sugar

GLAZE
1 tablespoon apricot jam
1 teaspoon pear liqueur, or other
 fruit-flavoured liqueur

Sift the flour into a large bowl, then stir in the sugar, lemon zest and a pinch of salt. Using your fingertips, lightly rub in the butter until the mixture resembles breadcrumbs. Make a well in the centre, then add the egg yolk to the well. Mix using a flat-bladed knife until a rough dough forms, adding a little more iced water if necessary. Turn out onto a lightly floured work surface, then gently press together into a ball. Form into a flat disc, cover with plastic wrap and refrigerate for 30 minutes.

Meanwhile, preheat the oven to 190°C (375°F/Gas 5). Grease a 23 cm (9 inch) loose-based tart tin.

On a lightly floured work surface, roll the chilled pastry out until large enough to fit the prepared tin. Roll the pastry around the rolling pin, then lift and ease it into the tin, gently pressing to fit the side. Trim the edges, then prick the base with a fork. Line the pastry case with baking paper and half-fill with baking beads, rice or dried beans. Bake for 15 minutes, then remove from the oven and allow to cool. Meanwhile, reduce the oven temperature to 170°C (325°F/Gas 3).

To make the mascarpone cream, put the mascarpone, sugar, egg, vanilla and flour in a food processor and blend until smooth and well combined — add a little milk if necessary to make it spreadable. Spoon the mascarpone cream into the pastry case, smoothing over the surface.

To make the filling, peel, halve and core the pears, brushing the cut surfaces with lemon juice as you go. Arrange the pear halves like wheel spokes in the tart case, with the wider end of each pear half to the outside — you may need to trim them slightly so they fit snugly. Place a round piece of pear in the centre. Scatter the hazelnuts over, then sprinkle the sugar over the top.

Bake for 45 minutes, or until the pastry is golden, the filling is set and the pears are soft. Remove from the oven and leave to cool slightly in the tin.

To make the glaze, put the jam, liqueur and about 2 tablespoons water in a small saucepan and stir over low heat until smooth. Strain and brush over the pears. Serve warm or at room temperature.

Fresh pear tart is best eaten the day it is made.

RED WINE AND RAISIN TART

SERVES 8

FILLING
200 g (7 oz/1½ cups) raisins
125 ml (4 fl oz/½ cup) red wine
125 ml (4 fl oz/½ cup) blackcurrant juice
½ teaspoon lemon juice
1 cinnamon stick
2 cloves
4 eggs
80 g (2¾ oz/⅓ cup) caster (superfine)
    sugar
15 g (½ oz) unsalted butter, melted

200 g (7 oz/1⅔ cups) plain (all-purpose)
    flour
85 g (3 oz/⅔ cup) icing (confectioners')
    sugar
100 g (3½ oz) cold unsalted butter,
    chopped
1 egg yolk, mixed with 1 tablespoon
    iced water
icing (confectioners') sugar, for dusting
    (optional)

Start by preparing some of the filling. Put the raisins in a heatproof bowl and set aside. Put the wine, blackcurrant juice, lemon juice, cinnamon stick and cloves in a saucepan over medium heat and bring to a simmer. Remove from the heat, then strain the liquid over the raisins and set aside to steep for 2 hours.

Meanwhile, make the pastry. Sift the flour, icing sugar and a pinch of salt into a large bowl. Using your fingertips, lightly rub in the butter until the mixture resembles coarse breadcrumbs. Make a well in the centre, then add the egg yolk to the well. Mix using a flat-bladed knife until a rough dough forms. Turn out onto a lightly floured work surface, then gently press together into a ball. Form into a flat disc, cover with plastic wrap and refrigerate for 30 minutes.

Lightly grease a 34 x 11 cm (13½ x 4¼ inch) rectangular loose-based tart tin. Roll out the pastry on a lightly floured work surface to fit the base and side of the tart tin — it should be about 3 mm (⅛ inch) thick. Roll the pastry around the rolling pin, then lift and ease it into the tin, gently pressing to fit the side. Trim the edges, cover with plastic wrap and refrigerate for 1 hour.

Meanwhile, preheat the oven to 200°C (400°F/Gas 6).

Prick the base of the chilled pastry case with a fork. Line with baking paper and half-fill with baking beads, rice or dried beans. Bake for 10 minutes, then remove the paper and beads and bake for a further 8–10 minutes, or until the pastry is golden. Remove from the oven and allow to cool slightly.

Meanwhile, reduce the oven temperature to 160°C (315°F/Gas 2–3) and finish making the filling. Whisk the eggs, sugar and melted butter in a bowl until well combined. Transfer the raisin mixture to a saucepan and gently heat through — do not allow to boil. Pour the warm raisin mixture over the egg mixture, stirring to combine.

Pour the filling into the tart case and bake for 30–40 minutes, or until the filling has just set. Allow to cool a little, then serve lightly dusted with icing sugar if desired.

Red wine and raisin tart is best eaten the day it is made.

APPLE TARTE TATIN
SERVES 6

100 g (3½ oz) unsalted butter, chopped
185 g (6½ oz/heaped ¾ cup) sugar
6 large pink lady, fuji or golden delicious
    apples, peeled, cored and cut into
    quarters
1 sheet of ready-made butter puff pastry
thick (double/heavy) cream or ice cream,
    to serve

Melt the butter in a frying pan. Add the sugar and stir over medium heat for 4–5 minutes, or until the sugar starts to caramelise. Continue to cook, stirring, until the caramel turns golden brown.

Add the apple quarters to the pan and cook them in two batches over low heat for 20–25 minutes each time, or until they begin to turn golden brown underneath. Carefully turn them over and cook the other side until evenly coloured. Cook off any liquid that comes out of the apples over a higher heat — the caramel should be sticky rather than runny.

Meanwhile, preheat the oven to 220°C (425°F/Gas 7). Lightly grease a 23 cm (9 inch) shallow cake tin (see Note).

Using tongs, arrange the hot apples in the prepared tin, in slightly overlapping circles. Pour the caramel over the top.

Place the pastry sheet over the apples, tucking it down firmly at the edges using the end of a spoon. Bake for 30–35 minutes, or until the pastry is golden and puffed.

Remove from the oven and leave to cool in the tin for 15 minutes, before inverting onto a serving plate.

Remove the baking paper and serve warm or cold with thick cream or ice cream.

Apple tarte tatin is best eaten the day it is made.

NOTE: You could also bake the tarte tatin in a 23 cm (9 inch) ovenproof cast-iron frying pan, as we have done — in which case there is no need to grease a cake tin. After the apples have been cooked, arrange them in the frying pan, place the pastry on top and transfer the pan to the oven to bake the pastry.

COCOA AND DATE CROSTATA

SERVES 12

75 g (2¹/₂ oz/heaped ¹/₂ cup) walnut
  pieces, toasted
215 g (7¹/₂ oz/1³/₄ cups) plain
  (all-purpose) flour
125 g (4¹/₂ oz/1 cup) icing (confectioners')
  sugar
150 g (5¹/₂ oz) cold unsalted butter,
  chopped
2 egg yolks, mixed with 1 tablespoon
  iced water

FILLING

500 g (1 lb 2 oz/2³/₄ cups) pitted dried
  dates
¹/₂ teaspoon natural vanilla extract
2 teaspoons lemon zest
¹/₂ teaspoon ground cinnamon
¹/₂ teaspoon ground ginger
30 g (1 oz/¹/₄ cup) unsweetened cocoa
  powder
1 tablespoon soft brown sugar
¹/₄ teaspoon bicarbonate of soda
  (baking soda)

FOR GLAZING

1 egg yolk
1 teaspoon caster (superfine) sugar
¹/₄ teaspoon ground cinnamon

Put the walnuts in a food processor and blend until finely ground. Tip into a large bowl. Sift the flour and icing sugar into the bowl and stir together well. Using your fingertips, lightly rub in the butter until the mixture resembles breadcrumbs. Make a well in the centre, then add the egg yolks to the well. Mix using a flat-bladed knife until a rough dough forms, adding a little more iced water if necessary. Turn out onto a lightly floured work surface, then gently press together into a ball. Form into a flat disc, cover with plastic wrap and refrigerate for 30 minutes.

Meanwhile, preheat the oven to 180°C (350°F/Gas 4). Grease a deep, 25 cm (10 inch) loose-based tart tin.

To make the filling, put the dates, vanilla, lemon zest, cinnamon, ginger, cocoa powder, sugar and 250 ml (9 fl oz/ 1 cup) water in a heavy-based saucepan over medium heat. Bring to a simmer, then add the bicarbonate of soda, stir to combine and set aside to cool. Transfer to a food processor and, using the pulse button, blend until a coarse paste forms. Set aside.

Roll out two-thirds of the chilled pastry on a lightly floured work surface to fit the base and side of the prepared tin. Roll the pastry around the rolling pin, then lift and ease it into the tin, gently pressing to fit the side. Roll out the remaining pastry into a round, large enough to cover the top.

Spoon the filling into the pastry, smoothing over the surface. To make the glaze, mix the egg yolk with 1 tablespoon water and brush it over the pastry edges. Place the pastry lid over the filling, gently pressing to remove any air bubbles, and press the pastry edges together to seal. Cut a slit in the top of the pastry to allow the steam to escape, then brush with the remaining glaze. Mix together the sugar and cinnamon and sprinkle over the pastry.

Bake on the bottom shelf of the oven for 1 hour, or until the pastry is golden. Remove from the oven and allow to cool completely in the tin before serving.

Cocoa and date crostata is best eaten the day it is made.

ROASTED PUMPKIN, GARLIC AND PECORINO PIE
SERVES 6–8

375 g (13 oz/3 cups) plain (all-purpose)
 flour
1 teaspoon sea salt
125 ml (4 fl oz/$\frac{1}{2}$ cup) extra virgin
 olive oil
1 egg
80 ml (2$\frac{1}{2}$ fl oz/$\frac{1}{3}$ cup) iced water

FILLING
1.5 kg (3 lb 5 oz) jap or kent pumpkin,
 peeled, seeds removed, then cut into
 2 cm ($\frac{3}{4}$ inch) chunks
6 whole, unpeeled garlic cloves
60 ml (2 fl oz/$\frac{1}{4}$ cup) extra virgin olive oil
3 eggs, lightly beaten
100 g (3$\frac{1}{2}$ oz/1 cup) grated pecorino
 cheese
2 teaspoons chopped marjoram
$\frac{1}{2}$ teaspoon freshly grated nutmeg

Sift the flour and sea salt into a large bowl and make a well
in the centre. In a small bowl, whisk together the olive oil,
egg and iced water. Pour the mixture into the well in the
flour. Mix using a flat-bladed knife until a rough dough forms,
adding a little more iced water if necessary. Turn out onto
a lightly floured work surface, then knead for 3 minutes, or
until smooth. Gently press together into a flat disc, cover with
plastic wrap and refrigerate for 2 hours.

Meanwhile, preheat the oven to 200°C (400°F/Gas 6).

To make the filling, put the pumpkin and unpeeled garlic
cloves in a large roasting tin, drizzle with the olive oil and toss
to coat. Roast for 30 minutes, or until the pumpkin and garlic
are tender. Remove from the oven and allow to cool slightly.
When cool enough to handle, squeeze the garlic cloves out of
their skins, into a bowl. Add the pumpkin and mash together
using a fork, then stir in the eggs, cheese, marjoram and
nutmeg. Season with sea salt and freshly ground black pepper.

Grease a 16 x 26 cm (6$\frac{1}{4}$ x 10$\frac{1}{2}$ inch) rectangular
shallow baking tin. Roll out two-thirds of the pastry on a
lightly floured work surface to 2 mm ($\frac{1}{16}$ inch) thick, to fit the
base and sides of the prepared tin. Roll the pastry around the
rolling pin, then lift and ease it into the tin, gently pressing
to fit the sides. Trim the edges, cover with plastic wrap and
refrigerate for 30 minutes.

Heat the oven to 190°C (375°F/Gas 5). Spoon the filling
into the chilled pastry case, smoothing over the surface.

Roll out the remaining pastry on a lightly floured surface,
then cut into strips about 2 cm ($\frac{3}{4}$ inch) wide, long enough to
fit diagonally across the pie. Arrange the pastry strips across
the top of the pie, spacing them 1 cm ($\frac{1}{2}$ inch) apart, and
sealing them at each end. Trim the ends to neaten.

Bake for 1 hour, or until the pastry is crisp and golden.
Serve warm or at room temperature.

Roasted pumpkin, garlic and pecorino pie is best eaten
the day it is made.

TOMATO, GOAT'S CHEESE AND CARAMELISED ONION FLAN
SERVES 6

200 g (7 oz/1²/₃ cups) plain (all-purpose) flour
¼ teaspoon salt
120 g (4¼ oz) cold unsalted butter, chopped
60 ml (2 fl oz/¼ cup) iced water

FILLING
2 tablespoons olive oil
3 onions, thinly sliced
60 g (2¼ oz/½ cup) crumbled goat's cheese
3 roma (plum) tomatoes, sliced 5 mm (¼ inch) thick
½ teaspoon rosemary
6 egg yolks
2 eggs
250 ml (9 fl oz/1 cup) pouring (whipping) cream

Sift the flour into a large bowl and add the salt. Using your fingertips, lightly rub in the butter until the mixture resembles coarse breadcrumbs. Make a well in the centre, then add the iced water to the well. Mix using a flat-bladed knife until a rough dough forms. Turn out onto a lightly floured work surface and gently knead until just smooth, then gently press together into a ball. Form into a flat disc, cover with plastic wrap and refrigerate for 30 minutes.

Lightly grease a 25 cm (10 inch) loose-based round tart tin. Roll out the chilled pastry on a lightly floured work surface until 3 mm (¹/₈ inch) thick. Roll the pastry around the rolling pin, then lift and ease it into the tin, gently pressing to fit the side. Trim the edges, cover with plastic wrap and refrigerate for 30 minutes.

Meanwhile, preheat the oven to 200°C (400°F/Gas 6).

To caramelise the onion, heat the olive oil in a large, heavy-based frying pan, add the onion, then cover and cook over low heat, stirring often, for 30 minutes, or until the onion has reduced in volume and is golden.

Prick the base of the chilled pastry case with a fork. Line with baking paper and half-fill with baking beads, rice or dried beans. Bake for 20 minutes, then remove the paper and beads and bake for a further 10 minutes, or until the pastry is golden. Remove from the oven and allow to cool slightly. Meanwhile, reduce the oven temperature to 160°C (315°F/Gas 2–3).

Spread the caramelised onion evenly over the pastry case. Scatter the goat's cheese over, top with the tomato slices and sprinkle with the rosemary. In a bowl, whisk the egg yolks, eggs and cream until smooth and well combined. Season with sea salt and freshly ground black pepper, then carefully pour into the pastry case.

Bake for 30–40 minutes, or until the filling has just set. Remove from the oven and allow to cool slightly in the tin before slicing. Serve warm or at room temperature.

Tomato, goat's cheese and caramelised onion flan is best eaten the day it is made.

PUMPKIN PIE
SERVES 8

150 g (5¹/₂ oz/1¹/₄ cups) plain
 (all-purpose) flour
2 teaspoons caster (superfine) sugar
100 g (3¹/₂ oz) cold unsalted butter,
 chopped
80 ml (2¹/₂ fl oz/¹/₃ cup) iced water
ice cream or whipped cream, to serve
 (optional)

GLAZE
1 egg yolk
1 tablespoon milk

FILLING
2 eggs
140 g (5 oz/³/₄ cup) soft brown sugar
500 g (1 lb 2 oz) pumpkin (winter
 squash), cooked and cooled, then
 mashed
80 ml (2¹/₂ fl oz/¹/₃ cup) pouring
 (whipping) cream
1 tablespoon sweet sherry
1 teaspoon ground cinnamon
¹/₂ teaspoon ground nutmeg
¹/₂ teaspoon ground ginger

Lightly grease a 23 cm (9 inch) round pie dish.

Sift the flour into a large bowl. Stir in the sugar. Using your fingertips, lightly rub in the butter until the mixture resembles breadcrumbs. Make a well in the centre, then add 60 ml (2 fl oz/¹/₄ cup) of the iced water to the well. Mix using a flat-bladed knife until a rough dough forms, adding a little more iced water if necessary.

Gather the dough together and roll out between two sheets of baking paper until large enough to cover the base and side of the pie dish. Roll the pastry around the rolling pin, then lift and ease it into the pie dish, gently pressing to fit the side. Trim away the excess pastry and crimp the edges.

Roll out the pastry trimmings until 2 mm (¹/₈ inch) thick. Using a sharp knife, cut out leaf shapes of different sizes, then score vein markings onto the leaves. Cover the pastry-lined dish and the leaf shapes with plastic wrap and refrigerate for 30 minutes.

Meanwhile, preheat the oven to 180°C (350°F/Gas 4).

Prick the base of the chilled pastry case with a fork. Line with baking paper and half-fill with baking beads, rice or dried beans. Place the pastry leaves on a baking tray lined with baking paper. To make the glaze, mix together the egg yolk and milk and brush over the leaves.

Bake the pastry case for 10 minutes, then remove the paper and baking beads and bake for a further 10 minutes, or until the pastry is lightly golden. Meanwhile, bake the pastry leaves for 10–15 minutes, or until lightly golden. Remove from the oven and set aside to cool slightly.

To make the filling, whisk the eggs and sugar together in a large bowl. Add the remaining ingredients and stir together well. Pour the mixture into the pastry case, smoothing over the surface, then bake for 40 minutes, or until the filling has set. If the pastry edges begin to brown too much during cooking, cover them with foil.

Remove from the oven and leave to cool to room temperature in the dish. Decorate the top of the pie with the pastry leaves. Serve with ice cream or whipped cream, if desired.

Pumpkin pie is best eaten the day it is made.

ITALIAN ALMOND TORTE
SERVES 8

125 g (4¹/₂ oz/1 cup) plain (all-purpose)
  flour
55 g (2 oz/¹/₄ cup) caster (superfine) sugar
60 g (2¹/₄ oz) cold unsalted butter,
  chopped
2 tablespoons iced water

FILLING
50 g (1³/₄ oz/¹/₃ cup) blanched almonds
55 g (2 oz/¹/₄ cup) caster (superfine) sugar
100 g (3¹/₂ oz) marzipan
100 g (3¹/₂ oz) unsalted butter, softened
2 eggs
¹/₄ teaspoon natural almond extract
2 teaspoons orange zest
85 g (3 oz/²/₃ cup) plain (all-purpose)
  flour
¹/₂ teaspoon baking powder
160 g (5¹/₂ oz/¹/₂ cup) apricot jam,
  warmed and sieved

TOPPING
1 egg, lightly beaten
25 g (1 oz/¹/₄ cup) flaked almonds

Grease a 20 cm (8 inch) spring-form tin.

Sift the flour into a large bowl. Stir in the sugar. Using your fingertips, lightly rub in the butter until the mixture resembles breadcrumbs. Make a well in the centre and add almost all the iced water to the well. Mix using a flat-bladed knife until a rough dough forms, adding a little more water if necessary.

Turn onto a lightly floured work surface and lightly knead until smooth. Roll out the pastry to fit the base and side of the prepared tin. Roll the pastry around the rolling pin, then lift and ease it into the tin, gently pressing to fit the side. Trim the edges to 1.5 cm (⁵/₈ inch) from the top of the tin. Cover with plastic wrap and refrigerate for 30 minutes.

Meanwhile, preheat the oven to 180°C (350°F/Gas 4).

Prick the base of the chilled pastry case with a fork. Line with baking paper and half-fill with baking beads, rice or dried beans. Bake for 10 minutes, then remove the paper and baking beads and bake for a further 10 minutes. Remove from the oven and set aside to cool.

To make the filling, put the almonds and sugar in a food processor and process for 20 seconds, or until the nuts are coarsely ground. Tip into a small bowl and add the marzipan and butter. Using electric beaters, beat for 5 minutes, or until very light and creamy. Add the eggs one at a time, beating well after each addition. Add the almond extract and orange zest and beat until combined, then transfer to large bowl. Sift the flour and baking powder into the bowl and fold in using a metal spoon.

Spread the jam over the cooled pastry base. Spoon the filling over the jam, smoothing over the surface. Lightly brush the filling with the beaten egg, then scatter the flaked almonds over the top.

Bake for 30 minutes, or until the filling has set and is golden brown. Remove to a wire rack, release the sides of the tin and leave to cool completely.

Italian almond torte will keep for up to 3 days, stored in a cool place in an airtight container, or can be frozen in an airtight container for up to 4 weeks.

BAKED CUSTARD TARTS WITH RHUBARB

MAKES 8

400 g (14 oz/3¼ cups) plain
  (all-purpose) flour
½ teaspoon salt
165 g (5¾ oz/1⅓ cups) icing
  (confectioners') sugar
200 g (7 oz) cold unsalted butter,
  chopped
2 egg yolks, mixed with 125 ml
  (4 fl oz/½ cup) iced water

FILLING
½ vanilla bean, or ½ teaspoon natural
  vanilla extract
250 ml (9 fl oz/1 cup) milk
250 ml (9 fl oz/1 cup) pouring
  (whipping) cream
4 eggs
145 g (5 oz/⅔ cup) caster (superfine)
  sugar
400 g (14 oz/8 thin stalks) rhubarb,
  trimmed, then cut into 2 cm (¾ inch)
  lengths
95 g (3¼ oz/½ cup) soft brown sugar
½ teaspoon ground cinnamon
1 teaspoon lemon juice

Sift the flour, salt and icing sugar into a large bowl. Using your fingertips, lightly rub in the butter until the mixture resembles coarse breadcrumbs. Make a well in the centre, then add the egg yolks to the well. Mix using a flat-bladed knife until a rough dough forms. Turn out onto a lightly floured work surface, gently knead until smooth, then gently press together into a ball. Form into a flat disc, cover with plastic wrap and refrigerate for 30 minutes.

Lightly grease eight loose-based tartlet tins, measuring 10 cm (4 inches) in diameter and 3 cm (1¼ inches) deep.

Roll out the chilled pastry on a lightly floured work surface until 3 mm (⅛ inch) thick. Cut the pastry into eight rounds large enough to fit the base and side of the tartlet tins. Ease the pastry into the tins, pressing gently around the edges to fit. Trim the edges, then cover with plastic wrap and refrigerate for 30 minutes.

Meanwhile, preheat the oven to 200°C (400°F/Gas 6).

Prick the base of the chilled pastry cases with a fork. Line with baking paper and half-fill with baking beads, rice or dried beans. Bake for 15 minutes, then remove the paper and beads and bake for a further 7–8 minutes, or until the pastry is golden.

Remove the pastry from the oven and leave to cool. Reduce the oven temperature to 160°C (315°F/Gas 2–3).

Meanwhile, make the filling. Split the vanilla bean down the middle and scrape the seeds into a saucepan (or put the vanilla extract in a saucepan). Add the milk and cream, then bring just to the boil. Whisk the eggs and caster sugar in a bowl until thick and pale. Whisk the milk mixture into the egg mixture, allow to cool a little, then strain into a bowl.

Pour the custard into the pastry cases and bake for 25–30 minutes, or until the filling has just set. Remove from the oven and increase the temperature to 180°C (350°F/Gas 4).

Put the rhubarb, sugar, cinnamon, lemon juice and 2 teaspoons water in a small baking dish, toss to combine, then cover with foil and bake for 30 minutes.

Remove the cooled tartlets from the tins and, just before serving, spoon the rhubarb and juices over the top. Serve warm or at room temperature.

Baked custard tarts are best eaten the day they are made.

TREACLE TART
SERVES 6

280 g (10 oz/2¼ cups) plain
   (all-purpose) flour
140 g (5 oz) cold unsalted butter,
   chopped
90 ml (3 fl oz) iced water

FILLING
350 g (12 oz/1 cup) golden syrup,
   treacle or dark corn syrup
25 g (1 oz) unsalted butter
1 teaspoon ground ginger
140 g (5 oz/1¾ cups) fresh white
   breadcrumbs

1 egg, beaten
icing (confectioners') sugar, for dusting
   (optional)

Sift the flour into a large bowl. Using your fingertips, lightly rub in the butter until the mixture resembles fine breadcrumbs. Make a well in the centre, then add the iced water to the well. Mix using a flat-bladed knife until a rough dough forms, adding a little extra water if necessary.

Gently gather the dough together, then roll out into a circle between two sheets of baking paper, to fit the base and side of a 20 cm (8 inch) round, fluted, loose-based tart tin. Line the tin with the pastry and trim the edges, reserving the excess pastry.

Re-roll the pastry scraps on the baking paper into a rectangle measuring about 20 x 10 cm (8 x 4 inches). Using a sharp knife or fluted pastry wheel, cut the pastry into long strips 1 cm (½ inch) wide. Cover with plastic wrap and refrigerate, along with the pastry-lined tin, for 30 minutes.

Meanwhile, preheat the oven to 180°C (350°F/Gas 4).

To make the filling, put the golden syrup, butter and ginger in a small saucepan and stir over low heat until the butter has melted. Stir in the breadcrumbs, then pour the mixture into the pastry case.

Lay half the chilled pastry strips on a sheet of baking paper, leaving a 1 cm (½ inch) gap between each strip. Interweave the remaining strips to form a lattice pattern, then place on top of the pie, using the baking paper to help invert the lattice onto the pie. Brush the lattice with beaten egg.

Bake for 30 minutes, or until the pastry is lightly golden. Remove from the oven and leave to cool in the tin.

Serve warm or at room temperature. Just before serving, lightly dust with icing sugar, if desired.

Treacle tart will keep for 3 days, stored in a cool place in an airtight container.

PECAN PIE WITH BOURBON CREAM

SERVES 6

185 g (6½ oz/1½ cups) plain
(all-purpose) flour
125 g (4½ oz) cold unsalted butter,
chopped
2 tablespoons iced water

FILLING
200 g (7 oz/2 cups) pecans
3 eggs
50 g (1¾ oz) unsalted butter, melted
and cooled
125 g (4½ oz/⅔ cup) soft brown sugar
235 g (8½ oz/⅔ cup) light corn syrup
1 teaspoon natural vanilla extract

BOURBON CREAM
250 ml (9 fl oz/1 cup) pouring (whipping)
cream
1 tablespoon icing (confectioners') sugar
2 teaspoons bourbon

Sift the flour into a large bowl. Using your fingertips, lightly rub in the butter until the mixture resembles breadcrumbs. Make a well in the centre, then add the iced water to the well. Mix using a flat-bladed knife until a rough dough forms, adding a little extra iced water if necessary.

Turn out onto a lightly floured work surface and lightly knead until smooth. Roll the pastry out to a 35 cm (14 inch) round. Roll the pastry around the rolling pin, then lift and ease it into a 23 cm (9 inch) flan (tart) tin, gently pressing to fit the side. Trim the edges.

Roll out the pastry trimmings on a piece of baking paper to a rectangle about 2 mm (¹⁄₁₆ inch) thick, then cover the pastry sheet and pastry case with plastic wrap and refrigerate for 30 minutes.

Meanwhile, preheat the oven to 180°C (350°F/Gas 4).

Prick the base of the chilled pastry case with a fork. Line with baking paper and half-fill with baking beads, rice or dried beans. Bake for 15 minutes, then remove the paper and baking beads. Bake for a further 15 minutes, or until the pastry is lightly golden. Remove from the oven and leave to cool completely in the tin.

Spread the pecans over the cooled pastry base. Put the remaining filling ingredients in a large bowl with a pinch of salt. Whisk together well, then pour over the pecans.

Using a small, sharp knife, cut narrow strips from half the chilled pastry rectangle. From the remaining pastry, cut out small stars using a biscuit (cookie) cutter. Arrange the strips and stars decoratively over the filling.

Bake for 45 minutes, or until the filling is firm. Remove from the oven and leave to cool completely in the tin.

Meanwhile, make the bourbon cream. Using electric beaters, whip the cream and icing sugar in a small bowl until soft peaks form. Using a metal spoon, fold the bourbon through until just combined. Refrigerate until required.

Serve at room temperature with the bourbon cream. Pecan pie is best eaten the day it is made.

STRAWBERRY AND RHUBARB TART

SERVES 6–8

200 g (7 oz/1²/₃ cups) plain (all-purpose)
  flour
55 g (2 oz/¹/₄ cup) caster (superfine) sugar
100 g (3¹/₂ oz) cold unsalted butter,
  chopped
1 egg, mixed with 2 tablespoons
  iced water

FILLING
100 ml (3¹/₂ fl oz) milk
125 ml (4 fl oz/¹/₂ cup) pouring
  (whipping) cream
1 teaspoon natural vanilla extract
a wide strip of lemon peel, white pith
  removed
6 egg yolks
55 g (2 oz/¹/₄ cup) caster (superfine) sugar
2 teaspoons plain (all-purpose) flour
300 g (10¹/₂ oz) rhubarb, trimmed, then
  cut into 2 cm (³/₄ inch) lengths
250 g (9 oz/1²/₃ cups) small strawberries,
  hulled

Sift the flour into a large bowl. Stir in the sugar. Using your fingertips, lightly rub in the butter until the mixture resembles breadcrumbs. Make a well in the centre, then add the egg to the well. Mix using a flat-bladed knife until a rough dough forms, adding a little extra iced water if necessary. Turn out onto a lightly floured surface, then gently press together into a ball. Form into a flat disc, cover with plastic wrap and refrigerate for 30 minutes.

Meanwhile, preheat the oven to 200°C (400°F/Gas 6). Grease a 30 cm (12 inch) loose-based tart tin.

Roll out the chilled pastry between two sheets of baking paper until 4 mm (¹/₈ inch) thick. Roll the pastry around the rolling pin, then lift and ease it into the prepared tin, gently pressing to fit the side. Trim the excess pastry, leaving 5 mm (¹/₄ inch) above the tin. Prick the base with a fork, line with baking paper and half-fill with baking beads, rice or dried beans.

Bake for 15 minutes, then remove the paper and baking beads and bake for a further 8 minutes, or until lightly golden. Remove from the oven and leave to cool in the tin.

Reduce the oven temperature to 180°C (350°F/Gas 4). Place a baking tray on the centre shelf of the oven.

To make the filling, put the milk, cream, vanilla and lemon peel in a heavy-based saucepan and gently heat over low heat for 8 minutes, or until just below boiling point. Remove and set aside to infuse for 10 minutes. Discard the lemon peel.

Put the egg yolks, sugar and flour in a food processor. With the motor running, gradually add the infused milk and blend until the custard is smooth. Pour into the tart case and arrange the rhubarb and strawberries over the top.

Place the tart on the baking tray in the oven and bake for 35–40 minutes, or until the filling has set. Check the tart after 20 minutes — if it is browning too quickly, cover the top with foil. Remove from the oven and leave to cool in the tin.

Serve warm or at room temperature.

Strawberry and rhubarb tart is best eaten the day it is made.

HONEY AND PINE NUT TART

SERVES 6–8

250 g (9 oz/2 cups) plain (all-purpose) flour
1 1/2 tablespoons icing (confectioners') sugar
115 g (4 oz) cold unsalted butter, chopped
1 egg, mixed with 2 tablespoons iced water

FILLING
235 g (8 1/2 oz/1 1/2 cups) pine nuts
175 g (6 oz/1/2 cup) honey
115 g (4 oz) unsalted butter, softened
115 g (4 oz/1/2 cup) caster (superfine) sugar
3 eggs
1/4 teaspoon natural vanilla extract
1 tablespoon almond liqueur
1 teaspoon finely grated lemon zest
1 tablespoon lemon juice

icing (confectioners') sugar, for dusting
crème fraîche or mascarpone cheese, to serve

Lightly grease a fluted, loose-based tart tin measuring 25 cm (10 inches) in diameter and 3.5 cm (1 1/2 inches) deep.

Sift the flour and icing sugar into a large bowl. Using your fingertips, lightly rub in the butter until the mixture resembles fine breadcrumbs. Make a well in the centre, then add the egg to the well. Mix using a flat-bladed knife until a rough dough forms. Turn out onto a lightly floured work surface, then gently press into a ball. Roll out to a circle 3 mm (1/8 inch) thick. Roll the pastry around the rolling pin, then lift and ease it into the prepared tin, gently pressing to fit the side. Trim the edges.

Roll out the pastry scraps and cut out three leaf shapes for decoration. Cover the pastry case and leaves with plastic wrap and refrigerate for 30 minutes.

Meanwhile, preheat the oven to 190°C (375°F/Gas 5) and place a baking tray on the middle shelf.

Prick the base of the chilled pastry case with a fork. Line with baking paper and half-fill with baking beads, rice or dried beans. Bake on the heated tray for 10 minutes, then remove the tart, leaving the tray in the oven. Reduce the oven temperature to 180°C (350°F/Gas 4).

To make the filling, spread the pine nuts on a baking tray and roast in the oven for 3–5 minutes, or until golden. Heat the honey in a small saucepan until liquid, then cool.

Using electric beaters, cream the butter and sugar until light and fluffy. Add the eggs one at a time, beating well after each addition. Stir in the pine nuts, remaining filling ingredients and a pinch of salt. Spoon into the tart case, smooth over the surface and arrange the three pastry leaves in the centre.

Place the tart tin back on the hot baking tray and bake for 20 minutes, or until the filling is golden. Cover the top with foil and bake for a further 20 minutes, or until the filling has set. Remove from the oven and leave to cool in the tin.

Serve warm or at room temperature, dusted with icing sugar and with a dollop of crème fraîche or mascarpone.

Honey and pine nut tart will keep for up to 3 days, stored in a cool place in an airtight container, or can be frozen in an airtight container for up to 4 weeks.

DATE STRUDEL
SERVES 8

185 g (6½ oz/1½ cups) plain (all-purpose) flour
150 g (5½ oz) cold unsalted butter, chopped
60 ml (2 fl oz/¼ cup) iced water
melted butter, for brushing
1 tablespoon icing (confectioners') sugar

FILLING
200 g (7 oz) ricotta cheese
100 g (3½ oz) cream cheese
2 tablespoons ground almonds
2 teaspoons finely grated orange zest
250 g (9 oz) fresh dates, pitted and roughly chopped

Sift the flour into a large bowl. Using your fingertips, lightly rub in the butter until the mixture resembles fine breadcrumbs. Make a well in the centre, then add almost all the iced water to the well. Mix using a flat-bladed knife to a slightly sticky dough, adding a little more water if necessary.

Turn out onto a lightly floured work surface and press together until almost smooth — do not overwork the dough. Roll out on a sheet of lightly floured baking paper to a neat 20 x 40 cm (8 x 16 inch) rectangle, keeping the corners as square as possible. Fold the top third of the pastry down and fold the bottom third of the pastry up over it.

Make a quarter-turn to the right, so that the open edge of the fold is on the right. Re-roll the pastry, dusting lightly with flour if it is sticky, to form a 20 x 40 cm (8 x 16 inch) rectangle, and repeat the folding step as above. Cover with plastic wrap and refrigerate for 30 minutes.

Remove the pastry from the refrigerator and repeat the previous step. Refrigerate for a further 30 minutes.

Repeat the rolling, folding and turning process for a final time, then refrigerate the pastry for another 30 minutes. (The folding and rolling process is essential to give the pastry its flaky character.)

Meanwhile, preheat the oven to 210°C (415°F/Gas 6–7).

Cut the chilled pastry in half. Roll each portion out on a sheet of baking paper, making one 15 x 30 cm (6 x 12 inches) and the other about 17 x 32 cm (6½ x 12½ inches).

To make the filling, put the ricotta, cream cheese, almonds and orange zest in a food processor and blend until smooth. Stir in the dates. Spread the filling in a flat mound on the smaller piece of pastry, leaving a 1 cm (½ inch) border.

Using a small, sharp knife, cut decorative slashes into the larger pastry sheet. Carefully lift it onto the filling, then press the edges to seal. Brush with melted butter and dust with half the icing sugar. Using the baking paper, lift the strudel onto a baking tray and bake for 30 minutes, or until the pastry is crisp and golden.

Remove from the oven and dust with the remaining icing sugar. Serve warm or at room temperature.

Date strudel is best eaten the day it is made.

Sweet ricotta tarts with walnut crust
SERVES 4

WALNUT CRUST

200 g (7 oz/2 cups) walnut halves
or pieces

3 teaspoons plain (all-purpose) flour

2 tablespoons raw or golden caster
(superfine) sugar

40 g (1½ oz) unsalted butter, melted

FILLING

300 g (10½ oz/1¼ cups) ricotta cheese

100 g (3½ oz/½ cup) raw or golden
caster (superfine) sugar

125 g (4½ oz/½ cup) crème fraîche or
sour cream

2 eggs

30 g (1 oz/¼ cup) plain (all-purpose) flour

1 teaspoon natural vanilla extract

2 teaspoons lemon juice

Preheat the oven to 170°C (325°F/Gas 3). Grease four loose-based tart tins measuring 10.5 cm (4 inch) in diameter and 2.5 cm (1 inch) deep. Line the bases with baking paper.

To make the walnut crust, put the walnuts, flour and sugar in a food processor. Using the pulse button, process until the nuts are very finely chopped — take care not to over-process or the nuts will be oily. Remove and reserve 3 tablespoons of the walnut mixture for dusting over the baked tarts. Scatter half the remaining mixture over the base and sides of the prepared tins, pressing the mixture on to thinly coat.

Add the melted butter to the remaining walnut mixture and process for 10 seconds, or until combined. Divide among the tart tins and press firmly over the bases. Set the tins on a baking tray and bake for 10 minutes. Remove from the baking tray and set aside to cool.

Meanwhile, make the filling. Clean out the food processor, add the ricotta and sugar and process for 15 seconds, or until smooth. Add the remaining ingredients and process until just combined. Divide among the tarts, smoothing over the surface. Put the tarts back on the baking tray and bake for 15–18 minutes, or until the filling has set. Remove from the oven and allow to cool in the tins before turning out.

Cover each tart with two strips of paper and, using the reserved walnut mixture, dust two parallel lines over the surface of each. Serve at room temperature.

Sweet ricotta tarts will keep for up to 3 days, stored in an airtight container in the refrigerator.

LITTLE LIME TARTLETS
MAKES ABOUT 24

250 g (9 oz/2 cups) plain (all-purpose)
   flour
2 teaspoons caster (superfine) sugar
1 teaspoon finely grated lime zest
125 g (4^1/$_2$ oz) cold unsalted butter,
   chopped
1 egg yolk, mixed with 2 tablespoons
   iced water

FILLING
125 g (4^1/$_2$ oz/^{1}/$_2$ cup) cream cheese,
   softened
115 g (4 oz/^{1}/$_2$ cup) caster (superfine)
   sugar
2 egg yolks
2 tablespoons lime juice
160 g (5^1/$_2$ oz/^{1}/$_2$ cup) sweetened
   condensed milk

Sift the flour and a pinch of salt into a large bowl, then stir in the sugar and lime zest. Using your fingertips, lightly rub in the butter until the mixture resembles breadcrumbs. Make a well in the centre, then add the egg yolk to the well. Mix using a flat-bladed knife until a rough dough forms, adding a little more iced water if necessary. Turn out onto a lightly floured work surface, then gently press together into a ball. Form into a flat disc, cover with plastic wrap and refrigerate for 30 minutes.

Meanwhile, preheat the oven to 180°C (350°F/Gas 4). Brush two 12-hole patty pans or mini muffin tins with oil.

To make the filling, put the cream cheese, sugar and egg yolks in a bowl and beat using electric beaters until smooth and thickened. Add the lime juice and condensed milk and beat until well combined.

Roll out the chilled pastry between two sheets of baking paper until 3 mm (1/8 inch) thick. Using a 7 cm (2^3/4 inch) fluted, round cutter, cut out rounds from the pastry. Gently press the pastry into the prepared muffin holes. Lightly prick each one three times with a fork and bake for 10 minutes, or until the pastry is just starting to turn golden.

Remove the tins from the oven and spoon 2 teaspoons of the filling into each tartlet case. Bake for a further 5 minutes, or until the filling has set. Remove from the oven and leave to cool slightly before removing from the tins. Allow to cool completely before serving.

Little lime tartlets will keep for up to 3 days, stored in an airtight container in the refrigerator.

MANGO AND PASSIONFRUIT PIES

MAKES 6

400 g (14 oz/3 1/4 cups) plain
 (all-purpose) flour
165 g (5 3/4 oz/1 1/3 cups) icing
 (confectioners') sugar
200 g (7 oz) cold unsalted butter,
 chopped
2 egg yolks, mixed with 2 tablespoons
 iced water
1 egg, lightly beaten
icing (confectioners') sugar, for dusting
whipped cream, to serve

FILLING
60 ml (2 fl oz/1/4 cup) strained passionfruit
 pulp
1 tablespoon custard powder or instant
 vanilla pudding mix
3 ripe mangoes (900 g/2 lb), peeled,
 sliced and chopped
80 g (2 3/4 oz/1/3 cup) caster (superfine)
 sugar

Sift the flour and icing sugar into a large bowl. Using your fingertips, lightly rub in the butter until the mixture resembles coarse breadcrumbs. Make a well in the centre, then add the egg yolks to the well. Mix using a flat-bladed knife until a rough dough forms. Turn out onto a lightly floured work surface, then gently press together into a ball. Form into a flat disc, cover with plastic wrap and refrigerate for 30 minutes.

Grease six 10 x 8 x 3 cm (4 x 3 1/4 x 1 1/4 inch) fluted, loose-based flan (tart) tins or round pie dishes.

Roll out two-thirds of the chilled pastry between two sheets of baking paper until 3 mm (1/8 inch) thick. Cut out six bases to fit the prepared tins. Gently press them into the tins and trim the edges. Refrigerate for 30 minutes.

Meanwhile, preheat the oven to 190°C (375°F/Gas 5).

To make the filling, put the passionfruit pulp and custard powder in a small saucepan and mix together well. Stir over medium heat for 2–3 minutes, or until the mixture has thickened. Remove from the heat, then stir in the mango and sugar.

Roll out the remaining pastry between two sheets of baking paper until 3 mm (1/8 inch) thick. Cut out six pie lids. Re-roll the pastry trimmings and cut into shapes for decoration.

Divide the filling among the pastry cases and brush the edges with beaten egg. Top with the pastry lids and press the edges to seal. Trim the edges and decorate the tops with the pastry shapes. Brush with beaten egg and dust with icing sugar.

Bake for 20–25 minutes, or until the pastry is golden. Remove from the oven and leave to cool in the tins.

Serve warm or at room temperature with whipped cream.

Mango and passionfruit pies are best eaten the day they are made.

Real lemon pie

Serves 8

FILLING
4 thin-skinned lemons
460 g (1 lb/2 cups) caster (superfine) sugar
4 eggs, lightly beaten

310 g (11 oz/2 1/2 cups) plain (all-purpose)
   flour
80 g (2 3/4 oz/1/3 cup) caster (superfine)
   sugar
225 g (8 oz) cold unsalted butter,
   chopped
2–3 tablespoons iced water
milk, for brushing
pouring (whipping) cream, to serve

Start making the filling a day ahead. Wash the lemons well, then dry. Peel two lemons, removing all the white pith with a small, sharp knife, then slice the flesh very thinly, removing any seeds. Leave the other two lemons unpeeled and slice very thinly, removing any seeds. Place in a bowl with the sugar and stir until the lemon slices are coated. Cover and leave to stand overnight.

Sift the flour and a pinch of salt into a large bowl, then stir in the sugar. Using your fingertips, lightly rub in the butter until the mixture resembles breadcrumbs. Make a well in the centre and gradually add most of the iced water to the well, mixing with a flat-bladed knife until a rough dough forms, adding a little extra iced water if necessary.

Turn out onto a lightly floured work surface, then gently gather the dough together. Divide in half and roll each portion into a 30 cm (12 inch) circle. Cover with plastic wrap and refrigerate for 30 minutes.

Meanwhile, preheat the oven to 180°C (350°F/Gas 4). Lightly grease a 23 cm (9 inch) pie dish that is at least 3 cm (1 1/4 inches) deep.

Roll one sheet of pastry around the rolling pin, then lift and ease it into the pie dish, gently pressing to fit the side. Cover all the pastry with plastic wrap and refrigerate for 20 minutes.

Meanwhile, finish preparing the filling. Measure out 750 ml (26 fl oz/3 cups) of the lemon slices and liquid. Place in a bowl with the beaten eggs, stirring to mix well.

Spoon the mixture into the chilled pastry case, then cover with the pastry circle, trimming the pastry and crimping the edges to seal. Re-roll the pastry scraps and cut out decorative shapes. Place on top of the pie and brush with milk.

Bake for 50–55 minutes, or until the pastry is golden brown. Remove from the oven and allow to cool slightly. Serve straight from the dish, with cream for drizzling over.

Real lemon pie is best eaten the day it is made.

VARIATION

For an **apple pie**, toss 5 peeled, cored and thinly sliced apples in 3 tablespoons caster (superfine) sugar with a pinch of cinnamon. Fill the pie, cover with a pastry lid and make some slashes in the top. Dust with caster sugar and bake for 50 minutes.

batters

Before modern, heat-controlled stovetops were invented, many sweet and savoury goods were cooked on a griddle — a thick, flat, cast-iron contraption suspended over a fire — or in a large frying pan held over a low fire. Pikelets, scones, pancakes, crepes and fritters all evolved from these times, and represent but a sprinkling of the world's many flat, griddle-type 'cakes'.

Testament to their sheer deliciousness, such morsels remain popular around the globe today, even though many started life as ascetic foods for Lent. Shrove (or Pancake) Tuesday, for example, is celebrated in Britain just before the 40-day fasting of Lent begins. Pancakes were widely eaten on Pancake Tuesday in an effort to use up supplies of lusciously rich butter, milk and eggs, which were forbidden during Lent.

Russian blini, perfectly delicious little rounds of yeast-risen, buckwheat-flour pancakes, were eaten during the Russian pre-Lent 'butter week' when meat was forbidden, but dairy products and fish (including caviar) could be indulged in at will. Today, the eating of blini is most closely associated with accompaniments such as melted butter, sour cream and caviar.

The birthplace of crepes — those most large, gossamer-thin and delicate of batter goods — was on the streets of Paris, where they were made to order in a big, flat pan, spread with a variety of fillings, then served folded into quarters. These fillings could be as simple as a slick of butter and a sprinkle of sugar, or slices of ham and cheese.

Waffles probably had their origins in medieval 'wafers', which were thin, crisp cakes cooked between heated irons. Sometimes these irons had indentations in them, such as a coat of arms or a honeycomb pattern, which is the surface pattern most often found on modern waffles.

It is believed the Dutch pilgrims brought the idea of waffles (which they called *wafels*) with them to America in 1620. A century and a half later, Thomas Jefferson brought a waffle-iron back with him from France, after which 'waffle parties' became a feature of upper-crust American life.

The modern American-style waffle, based on a wheat-flour batter leavened with bicarbonate of soda (baking soda), has much in common with the famed Brussels waffle, which is made from a batter that is raised with yeast and lightened with whisked egg white. The French have their own waffles (in France they are called *gaufre*), as do the Scandinavians and the modern-day Dutch. There are also many regional waffles throughout Europe and mainly they are eaten as a sweet snack.

In Spain, the batter-based pick-me-up of choice is the churro. Churros are based on a very simple mixture of sugar, flour, eggs and butter, stirred to form a thick batter, which is forced through a piping (icing) bag fitted with a star tube and deep-fried in lengths. Churros can be either straight or curled. It is thought they were 'invented' by nomadic shepherds who had no access to fresh baked goods while tending their sheep in the hills. Churros could be cooked in a pan over an open fire, providing a simple means of enjoying some small, sweet treat on a daily basis. These days, churros are common breakfast fare in Spain, most often served with a cup of thick, bitter-sweet hot chocolate.

Many of these batter-based foods have now come to be associated with weekend breakfasts or brunch.

Notes for brilliant batters

One of the golden rules for making any batter based on wheat flour is not to overmix it once you have added flour to the wet ingredients. Networks of proteins (gluten) quickly build up once you start beating wet flour, and this will make the end result tough.

For this reason, beware of making batter mixtures in a food processor as it is very easy to over-process and toughen the batter using one of these. A wire whisk is a good mixing implement as it will mix quickly and efficiently and also smooth out any lumps in the mixture.

Always cover the mixed batter and let it rest for at least 10 minutes (some recipes stipulate longer), to allow the gluten in the flour to relax. Also, batters thicken on standing as the liquids absorb the flour. If you are able to let your batter stand for at least 45–60 minutes, any small lumps in the mixture will break down. Just remember to give the batter a gentle stir before you cook it as it will separate slightly on standing. If it is a batter that is lightened by the addition of a few stiffly beaten egg whites, fold those in at the last minute, after the resting period.

When cooking pancakes, pikelets (griddle cakes) or any other batter that requires a frying pan, choose one with a heavy base (such as a cast-iron pan) or one that is specially designed for the task, such as a crepe pan. The thick base will disperse heat evenly — and although the pan will heat slowly, it will hold the heat at the required temperature. Don't choose buckled pans or those with thin bases as your batters could either burn easily or not cook through evenly.

Many waffle and pancake recipes use buttermilk as the liquid of choice — and for good reason. When used in conjunction with bicarbonate of soda (baking soda), it neutralises its flavour and helps promote its action. The acids in buttermilk also help tenderise the flour.

Most batter recipes will be simple and involve no special equipment or techniques — particularly if making pancakes, Yorkshire puddings (similar to American popovers) or pikelets. Some batters are a little more demanding to work with, and some do need special equipment (such as waffles, which require a special cooking iron).

Crepes, although not difficult to make, do require a certain knack. The batter is thin and needs to be ladled and quickly swirled into a hot, greased pan in such a way as to thinly coat the pan. It is then briefly cooked, then flipped and cooked on the other side. Often it takes a few first less-than-perfect crepes before you get into the swing of cooking them.

The batter must be the perfect consistency, like very thick pouring (whipping) cream. If too thin, it won't coat the pan properly; too thick and the crepes will be thick and rubbery. You can always thin down a crepe batter that is too thick by stirring in a little extra milk, although it is not recommended to try and thicken one by adding extra flour.

The pan needs to be just lightly greased (butter is the best fat). Too much butter and the mixture will slide off the surface of the pan; too little and the batter will stick. The pan also needs to be just the right temperature — hot enough that the mixture sets almost as soon as it hits the pan, but not so hot that it quickly burns.

While this all makes crepe-making sound tricky, it really isn't. A little practice is all it takes to get the right temperature, batter consistency and amount of butter in the pan. Making crepes is a lot of fun — and leftovers can easily be frozen for another time.

CORN BREAD
SERVES 6

oil, for greasing
125 g (4¹/₂ oz/1 cup) self-raising flour
150 g (5¹/₂ oz/1 cup) fine polenta
1 teaspoon sea salt
1 egg
250 ml (9 fl oz/1 cup) buttermilk
60 ml (2 fl oz/¹/₄ cup) olive oil

Preheat the oven to 220°C (425°F/Gas 7). Generously oil a 20 cm (8 inch) ovenproof cast-iron frying pan and place it in the oven for 10 minutes to heat.

Sift the flour into a large bowl, stir in the polenta and sea salt and make a well in the centre. In a bowl, mix together the egg, buttermilk and olive oil, then add to the well in the dry ingredients and stir until just combined. Do not overmix.

Pour the batter into the hot frying pan and bake for 25 minutes, or until the bread is firm to the touch and golden brown.

Cut into wedges and serve warm or at room temperature.

Corn bread is best served the day it is made, but can be frozen in an airtight container for up to 6 weeks.

MINI LEMON PIKELETS
MAKES ABOUT 25

125 g (4$^{1}/_{2}$ oz/1 cup) self-raising flour
80 g (2$^{3}/_{4}$ oz/$^{1}/_{3}$ cup) caster (superfine)
  sugar
2 teaspoons finely grated lemon zest
1 egg
125 ml (4 fl oz/$^{1}/_{2}$ cup) milk
melted butter, for brushing
90 g (3$^{1}/_{4}$ oz/$^{1}/_{3}$ cup) lemon curd
whipped cream, to serve

Sift the flour into a large bowl, then stir in the sugar and lemon zest. Make a well in the centre.

In a small bowl, mix together the egg and milk, then add to the well in the flour mixture all at once. Using a wooden spoon, stir until a smooth batter forms.

Place a heavy-based frying pan over medium heat and brush with melted butter. Drop heaped teaspoonfuls of the batter into the pan, about 3 cm (1$^{1}/_{4}$ inches) apart. Cook for 2 minutes, or until golden underneath, then turn and cook the other side for 1–2 minutes, or until golden. Remove the pikelets to a plate and repeat with the remaining batter.

Allow the pikelets to cool slightly. Serve topped with lemon curd and whipped cream.

Mini lemon pikelets are best served the day they are made, but can be frozen in an airtight container for up to 6 weeks.

MOCHA WAFFLES WITH ESPRESSO SYRUP
MAKES 8 WAFFLES

ESPRESSO SYRUP
170 g (6 oz/³/₄ cup) caster (superfine)
  sugar
125 ml (4 fl oz/¹/₂ cup) brewed espresso
  coffee
60 ml (2 fl oz/¹/₄ cup) pouring (whipping)
  cream

250 g (9 oz/2 cups) plain (all-purpose)
  flour
2 tablespoons unsweetened cocoa powder
2 teaspoons baking powder
¹/₂ teaspoon salt
310 ml (10³/₄ fl oz/1¹/₄ cups) milk
2¹/₂ teaspoons instant coffee granules,
  dissolved in 1¹/₂ tablespoons water
115 g (4 oz/¹/₂ cup) caster (superfine)
  sugar
3 eggs, separated
60 g (2¹/₄ oz) unsalted butter, melted, plus
  extra, for brushing
ice cream, to serve (optional)

Put all the espresso syrup ingredients in a small saucepan with 3 tablespoons water. Mix well, bring to the boil, then reduce the heat and simmer for 4–5 minutes. Set aside to cool.

Preheat a waffle iron and heat the oven to 120°C (235°F/Gas ¹/₂).

Sift the flour, cocoa, baking powder and salt into a large bowl and make a well in the centre. Add the milk, coffee, sugar, egg yolks and butter to the well and whisk until smooth.

In a clean, dry bowl, beat the egg whites using electric beaters until firm peaks form. Using a large metal spoon, stir a tablespoon of egg white into the batter to loosen it, then gently fold in the remaining egg white.

Brush the waffle iron with melted butter. Pour about 125 ml (4 fl oz/¹/₂ cup) batter (the amount will vary according to your waffle iron) into the centre of the iron and spread almost to the corners of the grid. Cook for 4–5 minutes, or until crisp and golden. Remove and keep warm in the oven while cooking the remaining batter.

Serve the waffles with the espresso syrup spooned over, with a scoop of ice cream if desired.

Mocha waffles are best eaten immediately. Without the syrup they can be frozen in an airtight container for up to 4 weeks.

BUCKWHEAT BLINI WITH SMOKED SALMON
MAKES ABOUT 40

BLINI

2 teaspoons instant dried yeast
a pinch of caster (superfine) sugar
250 ml (9 fl oz/1 cup) milk, warmed
100 g (3½ oz/¾ cup) buckwheat flour
60 g (2¼ oz/½ cup) plain (all-purpose)
 flour
2 eggs, separated
20 g (¾ oz) unsalted butter
80 ml (2½ fl oz/⅓ cup) vegetable oil

150 g (5½ oz/⅔ cup) crème fraîche
 or sour cream
300 g (10½ oz) smoked salmon,
 cut into 2 cm (¾ inch) strips
50 g (1¾ oz) salmon roe
dill sprigs, to garnish

To make the blini, put the yeast and sugar in a small bowl and gradually stir in the warm milk. Sift the flours into a large bowl and make a well in the centre. Add the egg yolks and yeast mixture to the well, then whisk until a smooth batter forms. Cover with plastic wrap and leave in a draught-free place for 45 minutes.

Melt the butter, allow to cool slightly, then stir into the batter. Season to taste with sea salt and freshly ground pepper.

In a clean, dry bowl, beat the egg whites using electric beaters until soft peaks form. Fold one-third of the egg white into the batter, then gently fold in the remaining egg white until just combined.

Heat 1 tablespoon of the oil in a large, heavy-based frying pan over medium heat. Drop half-tablespoonfuls of the batter into the pan, leaving 3 cm (1¼ inches) in between each blini. Cook for 1 minute, or until bubbles form on the surface. Turn and cook for 30 seconds, or until golden. Remove to a plate and repeat with the remaining batter, adding a little more oil to the pan as needed.

Leave the blini to cool completely.

Spread 1 teaspoon of crème fraîche on each blini and arrange a strip of smoked salmon on top. Spoon ¼ teaspoon of salmon roe on top, garnish with a dill sprig and serve.

Blini are best eaten the day they are made. Without the topping they can be frozen in an airtight container for up to 4 weeks.

CREPES
SERVES 4

60 g (2¼ oz/½ cup) plain (all-purpose)
  flour
2 eggs
250 ml (9 fl oz/1 cup) milk
melted butter, for brushing
maple syrup, to serve (optional)
caster (superfine) sugar, for sprinkling
  (optional)
lemon wedges, to serve (optional)

Sift the flour into a bowl and make a well in the centre. In another bowl, mix together the eggs and milk, then add to the well in the flour, whisking constantly to prevent lumps forming. Cover with plastic wrap and leave to stand for 30 minutes.

Meanwhile, preheat the oven to 120°C (235°F/Gas ½).

Place a 20 cm (8 inch) non-stick crepe pan or frying pan over medium heat. Lightly brush with melted butter, then pour 60 ml (2 fl oz/¼ cup) of batter into the pan and swirl to coat the base evenly. Cook for 1 minute, or until golden underneath, then turn and cook the other side for 30 seconds. Remove, cover with foil and keep warm in the oven. Repeat with the remaining batter to make eight crepes.

Fold the crepes into triangles. Serve drizzled with maple syrup if desired, or serve the crepes sprinkled with sugar, with lemon wedges on the side.

Crepes are best eaten the day they are made, but can be frozen in an airtight container for up to 6 weeks, with a layer of baking paper between each. To use frozen crepes, first thaw them, then cover and reheat in a 150°C (300°F/Gas 2) oven for 5–10 minutes.

CHERRY CLAFOUTIS
SERVES 6–8

melted butter, for brushing
500 g (1 lb 2 oz) cherries, pitted
  (see Note)
90 g (3¼ oz/¾ cup) plain (all-purpose)
  flour
2 eggs, lightly beaten
80 g (2¾ oz/⅓ cup) caster (superfine)
  sugar
1 cup (250 ml/9 fl oz) milk
60 ml (2 fl oz/¼ cup) thick (double/
  heavy) cream
60 g (2¼ oz) unsalted butter, melted
icing (confectioners') sugar, for dusting

Preheat the oven to 180°C (350°F/Gas 4). Lightly grease a 1.5 litre (52 fl oz/6 cup) baking dish with melted butter and spread the cherries over the base of dish.

Sift the flour into a large bowl. Add the eggs and whisk until smooth. Add the sugar, milk, cream and butter, whisking until just combined. Do not overbeat.

Pour the batter over the cherries and bake for 30–40 minutes, or until a cake tester inserted into the centre of the clafoutis comes out clean. Allow to cool slightly, dust generously with icing sugar and serve.

Cherry clafoutis is best eaten immediately.

NOTE: You can use a 700 g (1 lb 9 oz) jar of cherries if fresh ones aren't available. Drain them thoroughly before using.

DATE PANCAKES WITH CHOCOLATE FUDGE SAUCE
MAKES 10–12 PANCAKES

185 g (6½ oz/1 cup) pitted dates,
   chopped
1 teaspoon bicarbonate of soda
   (baking soda)
250 g (9 oz/2 cups) self-raising flour
95 g (3¼ oz/½ cup) soft brown sugar
250 g (9 oz/1 cup) sour cream
3 eggs, separated
melted butter, for brushing
ice cream, to serve

CHOCOLATE FUDGE SAUCE
250 g (9 oz/1⅔ cups) chopped
   good-quality dark chocolate
185 ml (6 fl oz/¾ cup) pouring
   (whipping) cream
50 g (1¾ oz) unsalted butter
1 tablespoon golden syrup or corn syrup
2 tablespoons Bailey's Irish Cream,
   Tia Maria or Kahlua

Put the dates in a small saucepan with 250 ml (9 fl oz/1 cup) water. Bring to the boil, remove from the heat, then stir in the bicarbonate of soda. Leave to cool for 5 minutes. Purée the mixture in a food processor until smooth, then set aside to cool.

Sift the flour into a large bowl. Stir in the sugar and the date purée.

In a bowl, whisk together the sour cream and egg yolks, then add to the flour mixture and stir until smooth. Set aside for 15 minutes.

In a clean, dry bowl, beat the egg whites using electric beaters until soft peaks form. Stir a heaped tablespoon of egg white into the batter to loosen, then fold in the remaining egg white until just combined.

Heat a frying pan over medium heat and brush lightly with melted butter. Pour 60 ml (2 fl oz/¼ cup) of batter into the pan. Cook for 2–3 minutes, or until bubbles form on the surface. Turn and cook the other side for 2 minutes, or until the pancakes are golden and cooked through. Transfer to a warmed plate and cover with a tea towel (dish towel) while cooking the remaining batter, stacking the pancakes between sheets of baking paper to prevent them sticking together, and brushing the pan with melted butter as necessary.

To make the chocolate fudge sauce, put the chocolate, cream, butter and golden syrup in a saucepan. Stir over low heat until the chocolate has melted and the mixture is smooth. Stir in the liqueur.

Serve the pancakes with ice cream, drizzled with the sauce.

Date pancakes are best eaten the day they are made.

CHURROS
SERVES 4–6

110 g (3¾ oz/½ cup) sugar
1 teaspoon ground nutmeg
30 g (1 oz) unsalted butter
150 g (5½ oz/1¼ cups) plain
  (all-purpose) flour
½ teaspoon finely grated orange zest
¼ teaspoon caster (superfine) sugar
2 eggs, lightly beaten
1 litre (35 fl oz/4 cups) vegetable oil,
  for deep-frying

Combine the sugar and nutmeg and spread out on a plate.

Put the butter, flour, orange zest, caster sugar, 170 ml (5½ fl oz/⅔ cup) water and a pinch of salt in a heavy-based saucepan. Stir over low heat until the butter softens and a soft dough forms. Cook for 2–3 minutes, stirring constantly, until the dough forms a ball around the spoon and lightly coats the base of the pan.

Transfer the dough to a food processor and, with the motor running, add the eggs. Do not over-process. If the dough is too soft to snip with kitchen scissors, return it to the pan and cook, stirring over low heat, until it becomes firmer.

Spoon the dough into a piping (icing) bag fitted with a 5 mm (¼ inch) star nozzle.

Heat the vegetable oil in a wide, heavy-based saucepan to 180°C (350°F), or until a cube of bread dropped into the oil browns in 15 seconds. Pipe lengths of batter, 6–8 cm (2½–3¼ inches) long, directly into the oil, a few at a time — an easy technique is to pipe with one hand and cut the batter off with a pair kitchen scissors in the other hand.

Cook the churros for 3 minutes, or until puffed and golden, using tongs to turn once or twice during cooking. Transfer each batch to paper towels to drain. While still hot, toss them in the sugar mixture and serve at once.

Churros are best eaten immediately.

BLUEBERRY PANCAKE STACK
SERVES 4

PANCAKES
185 g (6¹/₂ oz/1¹/₂ cups) self-raising flour
1 teaspoon baking powder
2 tablespoons caster (superfine) sugar
2 eggs
250 ml (9 fl oz/1 cup) milk
60 g (2¹/₄ oz) unsalted butter, melted,
   plus extra, for brushing
155 g (5¹/₂ oz/1 cup) fresh blueberries

100 g (3¹/₂ oz) unsalted butter, softened
maple syrup, to serve

To make the pancakes, sift the flour, baking powder, sugar and a pinch of salt into a large bowl and make a well in the centre. Whisk the eggs, milk and melted butter together in a pouring jug, then pour into the well in the flour mixture all at once, whisking to form a smooth batter. Cover with plastic wrap and leave to stand for 20 minutes.

Meanwhile, heat the oven to 120°C (235°F/Gas ¹/₂).

Place a frying pan over low heat and brush lightly with melted butter. Stir the blueberries into the pancake batter. Pour 60 ml (2 fl oz/¹/₄ cup) batter into the pan and swirl gently to make a pancake about 10 cm (4 inches) in diameter. Cook for 1 minute, or until golden underneath. Turn and cook for about 10 seconds, then transfer to the oven to keep warm while cooking the remaining pancakes.

Using a wooden spoon or electric beaters, beat the softened butter until light and fluffy. Stack the pancakes on individual serving plates and serve warm or cold, with the whipped butter and maple syrup.

Blueberry pancakes are best eaten the day they are made.

Doughnut balls with strawberry sauce

Serves 4–6

STRAWBERRY SAUCE
300 g (10½ oz/2 cups) fresh or thawed
  frozen strawberries
160 g (5½ oz/½ cup) strawberry jam

215 g (7½ oz/1¾ cups) self-raising flour
2 eggs
2 tablespoons olive oil
80 g (2¾ oz/⅓ cup) caster (superfine)
  sugar, plus extra, for coating
vegetable oil, for deep-frying
ice cream, to serve (optional)
fresh strawberries, to serve (optional)

To make the strawberry sauce, put the strawberries and jam in a food processor and blend until smooth. Set aside.

Sift the flour into a bowl. In another bowl, whisk together the eggs, olive oil, sugar and 2 tablespoons water until smooth. Stir in the sifted flour and mix to a soft dough. Using floured hands, roll 2 teaspoons of the batter into a ball, then repeat with the remaining batter.

Fill a wide, heavy-based saucepan one-third full of vegetable oil and heat to 180°C (350°F), or until a cube of bread dropped into the oil browns in 15 seconds. Deep-fry the doughnuts in batches for 5–6 minutes each time, or until cooked through and lightly browned, using tongs to turn once or twice during cooking. Transfer each batch to paper towels to drain. While still hot, roll them in the extra sugar to coat.

Serve hot with the strawberry sauce, and with ice cream and fresh strawberries if desired.

Doughnut balls are best eaten immediately.

CHEESE AND SPINACH PANCAKES
SERVES 4

250 g (9 oz/1¼ cups) cooked, drained
  English spinach, chopped
125 g (4½ oz/½ cup) ricotta cheese
30 g (1 oz/¼ cup) grated cheddar cheese
a pinch of freshly grated nutmeg
25 g (1 oz/¼ cup) grated parmesan cheese
½ teaspoon paprika
40 g (1½ oz/½ cup) fresh white
  breadcrumbs

PANCAKES
125 g (4½ oz/1 cup) plain (all-purpose)
  flour
1 egg, lightly beaten
310 ml (10¾ fl oz/1¼ cups) milk
melted butter, for brushing

CHEESE SAUCE
2 tablespoons unsalted butter
30 g (1 oz/¼ cup) plain (all-purpose) flour
435 ml (15¼ fl oz/1¾ cups) milk
125 g (4 oz/1 cup) grated cheddar cheese

Preheat the oven to 180°C (350°F/Gas 4). Put the spinach, ricotta, cheddar cheese and nutmeg in a bowl and add some freshly ground black pepper. Mix well and set aside.

To make the pancakes, sift the flour and a pinch of salt into a large bowl. Add the egg and half the milk and whisk until smooth, then whisk in the remaining milk.

Place a heavy-based frying pan over medium heat and brush with melted butter. Pour in a thin layer of batter to cover the base. Cook for 2 minutes, or until golden underneath, then turn and cook the other side. Remove to a warmed plate and repeat with the remaining batter to make eight pancakes.

To make the cheese sauce, melt the butter in a saucepan over low heat, then add the flour and cook for 1 minute. Remove from the heat and slowly stir in the milk. Bring to the boil, stirring constantly until thickened. Remove from the heat, then stir in the grated cheese. Season with sea salt and freshly ground pepper to taste.

Divide the spinach mixture among the pancakes, roll them up and place in a greased baking dish. Pour the cheese sauce over the top. Mix the parmesan, paprika and breadcrumbs together and sprinkle over the sauce. Bake for 30 minutes, or until the topping is golden brown.

Cheese and spinach pancakes are best eaten immediately. Without the filling and sauce they can be frozen in an airtight container for up to 4 weeks.

desserts

Baked and steamed desserts such as puddings, crumbles, charlottes and cobblers are homey, hearty delights that tend to be associated with the cold winter months when such comforting food is most appreciated. In days gone by they served the purpose of filling hungry tummies; today we simply adore them for their own sake.

Baked desserts draw upon a range of ingredients and cooking styles, and their core techniques have much in common with other baking disciplines — the creaming of butter and sugar, rubbing butter into dry ingredients and folding in whisked egg whites.

The English tradition of dessert-making has given us 'puddings' — not to be confused with what Americans know of as 'pudding', which is a soft, custard-like preparation. British puddings, of which steamed puddings are a most typical example, have evolved over many centuries from the boiled, sausage-like preparations that were made in ancient times.

It is thought the word 'pudding' derives from the French word *boudin*, which means sausage. The original puddings contained meat and were encased (most likely in intestine), then boiled. The classic Scottish haggis is an example of this kind of dish.

By the seventeenth century, sweet versions were being made, and by the late eighteenth century puddings no longer contained meat. By the nineteenth century, they were the sweet, cake-like preparations we know today and were either steamed or baked. Christmas pudding is one of the few steamed puddings that is still widely known and enjoyed.

The British cooking tradition has given us many styles of puddings. Some traditional puddings are elegant affairs, such as queen of puddings (see page 232), with its delicate, custardy, baked base and ethereal meringue topping. Others started life as stomach-filling food for the poor. Sturdier and made from humble ingredients, they were given colourful names like 'spotted dick' and 'roly-poly'.

In times past, most folk could barely afford meat, so puddings had to practically satisfy hunger. Bread was an important staple, and clever ways to use and extend bread — beyond merely serving it in slices — were conjured. One of the most noteworthy examples is bread and butter pudding, which is still a favourite today. Dishes such as baked fruit charlotte also rely heavily on bread.

It is important for the cook to know that modern bread, with its load of 'improvers' and 'enzymes' — and its utter inability to become stale beyond a spongy softness — is useless for such desserts. To achieve the right texture when making these simple dishes, you must find a good loaf that is without adulteration and that will dry out after a day or two.

Dumplings, heavy and filling, were also most likely developed as a way to dampen the appetite for meat — or even to replace meat altogether. Originally dumplings were boiled, but when the use of ovens became more widespread in the nineteenth century, these and many other traditional types of desserts found their way from the stovetop into the oven and evolved into the baked versions we know today.

The evolution continues. In recent times, many traditional desserts have been updated and lightened, and some given clever flavour twists as chefs and cookery writers have experimented with different ingredients, new fruits and previously unimagined combinations. It is also important to remember that sugar was once a costly ingredient and was therefore used sparingly. Sugar-sweetened desserts were a rarity and not the everyday possibility they have become today, bombarded as we are with pre-made versions on supermarket shelves and in freezer cabinets.

Puddings throughout the ages have been made using an inventive range of ingredients — from sago and tapioca through to cake crumbs and rice. These days though, some of the most appreciated baked or steamed desserts are those based upon fresh fruit.

Once again it is the British who have given the world a good number of these — for example pear and apple dumplings, apple charlotte, apricot and other fruit crumbles. The reasons for this, and the general strength of the English dessert repertoire, are varied. Some are to do with the climate and the range of cereal crops (so perfect for milk-based puddings) that were grown, while others relate more to the country's historical trading activities, which brought all manner of food products its way (spices, citrus fruits, dried fruits, sugar cane), with which eager cooks experimented widely.

Today, however, America is probably most closely associated with excellent hot, baked, fruity desserts. The delicious simplicity of some of North America's best-loved baked desserts originated in the utter abundance of fruits available to early settlers. Amelia Simpson's recipe book *American Cookery*, published in 1796 in New York, contains recipes using fruits such as quinces, damsons, apples, cranberries, currants, grapes, gooseberries, stone fruits, pears and many varieties of berries.

One of the most popular uses for these fruits was — and still is — to sweeten them and bake them under some sort of crust. This crust could be made of a biscuit (scone)-style batter, in which case the dessert is called a 'cobbler', although if the same arrangement is cooked on the stovetop (usually in a cast-iron pan) it is called a 'grunt' or a 'slump'.

Crumbles and crisps are other examples and so very easy to make. With their lovely contrast of a soft, yielding fruit layer and crunchy, baked flour-and-butter topping, these are among the most eagerly anticipated of all the hot desserts.

Ironically, just a few centuries ago, not only was a good variety of fruit, either fresh or dried, not widely available to most people, but it was considered, at least in England, as being unhealthy to eat. Superstitions about eating fruit raw led to the common practice of stewing it into submission and using it in hot puddings and desserts.

Now of course we understand the value of eating raw fruits, but appreciate equally their cooked qualities, especially those of apples, pears, berries, cherries, apricots, plums, tamarillos, lemons and quinces, all of which are beautiful in baked desserts.

With the dwindling of the serving class after World War I, puddings fell into sharp decline. Middle-class and wealthy wives had to cook for their own families and wished to streamline meal preparation, so puddings largely fell by the wayside. In more recent decades we have become even more 'time poor'. And with people concerned about their health and staying slim, desserts are often the first casualty of any associated dietary regime.

Still, a home-made dessert is a wonderful thing and tastes so much better than anything you can buy off the supermarket shelf. When eaten as an occasional treat, there is possibly no other course at the dining table that is met with as much enthusiasm — or gratitude — as a home-baked dessert.

QUEEN OF PUDDINGS
SERVES 6–8

500 ml (17 fl oz/2 cups) milk
50 g (1³/4 oz) unsalted butter
140 g (5 oz/1³/4 cups) fresh white
  breadcrumbs
1 tablespoon caster (superfine) sugar
finely grated zest of 1 orange
5 egg yolks
whipped cream, to serve (optional)

TOPPING
210 g (7¹/2 oz/²/3 cup) orange marmalade
5 egg whites
115 g (4 oz/¹/2 cup) caster (superfine)
  sugar

Preheat the oven to 180°C (350°F/Gas 4). Lightly grease a 1.25 litre (44 fl oz/5 cup) square or rectangular baking dish.

Put the milk and butter in a small saucepan and stir over low heat until the butter has melted. In a large bowl, mix together the breadcrumbs, sugar and orange zest. Stir in the milk mixture and leave to stand for 10 minutes.

Lightly whisk the egg yolks, then stir into the breadcrumb mixture. Spoon into the baking dish and bake for 25–30 minutes, or until firm to the touch. Remove from the oven.

To make the topping, put the marmalade in a saucepan and melt over low heat. Spread evenly over the hot pudding.

In a clean, dry bowl, beat the egg whites using electric beaters until stiff peaks form. Gradually add the sugar, whisking until the mixture is stiff and glossy and the sugar has dissolved.

Spoon the meringue evenly over the pudding and bake for a further 12–15 minutes, or until the meringue is golden.

Serve warm or at room temperature, with whipped cream if desired.

Queen of puddings is best eaten the day it is made.

BUTTERSCOTCH SELF-SAUCING PUDDING
SERVES 4

150 g (5½ oz/1¼ cups) self-raising flour
45 g (1½ oz/¼ cup) soft brown sugar
80 g (2¾ oz) unsalted butter, melted
80 ml (2½ fl oz/⅓ cup) milk
1 egg
whipped cream, to serve

BUTTERSCOTCH SAUCE
140 g (5 oz/¾ cup) soft brown sugar
40 g (1½ oz) unsalted butter, chopped

Preheat the oven to 180°C (350°F/Gas 4). Lightly grease a 1.75 litre (60 fl oz/7 cup) soufflé dish or deep baking dish.

Sift the flour into a large bowl. Stir in the sugar and make a well in the centre. In a small bowl, whisk together the melted butter, milk and egg, then add to the well in the flour mixture and stir until just combined. Spoon the mixture evenly into the prepared dish.

To make the butterscotch sauce, first sprinkle the sugar over the pudding mixture. In a pouring jug, whisk together the butter and 375 ml (13 fl oz/1½ cups) boiling water, then pour over the back of a spoon onto the pudding mixture.

Bake for 35 minutes, or until a cake tester inserted into the centre of the pudding comes out clean — do not push the tester all the way to the base of the dish as sauce has formed there and the tester will be sticky.

Remove from the oven and allow to cool slightly. Serve hot, with whipped cream.

Butterscotch pudding is best eaten the day it is made.

CHOCOLATE FUDGE PUDDINGS
SERVES 8

melted butter, for brushing
150 g (5½ oz) unsalted butter
170 g (6 oz/¾ cup) caster (superfine) sugar
100 g (3½ oz/1⅔ cups) chopped
    good-quality dark chocolate, melted
    and cooled
2 eggs
60 g (2¼ oz/½ cup) plain (all-purpose)
    flour
125 g (4½ oz/1 cup) self-raising flour
30 g (1 oz/¼ cup) unsweetened cocoa
    powder
1 teaspoon bicarbonate of soda
    (baking soda)
125 ml (4 fl oz/½ cup) milk
whipped cream, to serve

CHOCOLATE SAUCE
50 g (1¾ oz) unsalted butter, chopped
125 g (4½ oz/1 heaped cup) chopped
    good-quality dark chocolate
125 ml (4 fl oz/½ cup) pouring
    (whipping) cream
1 teaspoon natural vanilla extract

Preheat the oven to 180°C (350°F/Gas 4). Lightly grease eight 250 ml (9 fl oz/1 cup) metal pudding basins (moulds) with melted butter and line the bases with baking paper.

Using electric beaters, cream the butter and sugar until light and fluffy. Pour in the melted chocolate, beating well. Add the eggs one at a time, beating well after each addition.

Sift the flours, cocoa powder and bicarbonate of soda into a bowl, then fold into the chocolate mixture. Add the milk and gently stir to combine.

Half-fill the prepared moulds with the pudding mixture, then cover each one tightly with greased foil and place in a large, deep baking dish. Pour in enough boiling water to come halfway up the side of the moulds. Bake for 35–40 minutes, or until a cake tester inserted into the centre of the puddings comes out clean.

Just before serving, combine all the chocolate sauce ingredients in a saucepan and stir over low heat until the butter and chocolate have melted and the mixture is smooth.

Pour the chocolate sauce over the hot puddings and serve with whipped cream.

Chocolate fudge pudding is best eaten the day it is made.

SPICED APPLE SPONGE
SERVES 4

850 g (1 lb 14 oz) granny smith apples
30 g (1 oz) unsalted butter
40 g (1 1/2 oz/1/3 cup) raisins
2 tablespoons lemon juice
4 cloves
1 cinnamon stick
a pinch of nutmeg
80 g (2 3/4 oz/1/3 cup) caster (superfine)
    sugar
icing (confectioners') sugar, for dusting
vanilla ice cream, custard or cream,
    to serve

SPONGE TOPPING
2 eggs
80 g (2 3/4 oz/1/3 cup) caster (superfine)
    sugar
finely grated zest of 1 lemon
30 g (1 oz/1/4 cup) self-raising flour
30 g (1 oz/1/4 cup) cornflour (cornstarch)

Preheat the oven to 180°C (350°F/Gas 4). Peel and core the apples, then slice each one into eight wedges. Melt the butter in a large frying pan, add the apples and cook over high heat for 7 minutes, or until browned, stirring occasionally.

Add the raisins, lemon juice, cloves, cinnamon, nutmeg, caster sugar and 125 ml (4 fl oz/1/2 cup) water and stir to combine. Bring to the boil, then reduce the heat and simmer for 3 minutes, or until the apples are tender. Remove the cinnamon stick and cloves. Spoon the mixture into a round, deep 2 litre (70 fl oz/8 cup) baking dish.

To make the sponge topping, beat the eggs, sugar and lemon zest in a small bowl using electric beaters for 7–8 minutes, or until light and creamy.

Sift the flour and cornflour into a bowl, then fold into the egg mixture using a large metal spoon.

Spoon the topping over the apples and bake for 30 minutes, or until the sponge is well risen and golden.

Dust with icing sugar and serve hot or warm with ice cream, custard or cream.

Spiced apple sponge is best eaten the day it is made.

PLUM COBBLER
SERVES 6

750 g (1 lb 10 oz) plums
75 g (2¹/₂ oz/¹/₃ cup) sugar
1 teaspoon natural vanilla extract
vanilla ice cream, custard or cream,
   to serve

TOPPING
125 g (4¹/₂ oz/1 cup) self-raising flour
45 g (1¹/₂ oz/¹/₄ cup) soft brown sugar
60 g (2¹/₄ oz) cold unsalted butter,
   chopped
60 ml (2 fl oz/¹/₄ cup) milk
1 tablespoon caster (superfine) sugar

Preheat the oven to 200°C (400°F/Gas 6). Cut the plums into quarters and remove the stones. Put the plums, sugar and 2 tablespoons water in a saucepan and bring to the boil, stirring until the sugar dissolves. Reduce the heat, then cover and simmer for 5 minutes, or until the plums are tender.

Remove the skins from the plums if desired. Stir in the vanilla and spoon the mixture into a 750 ml (26 fl oz/3 cup) baking dish.

To make the topping, sift the flour into a large bowl. Stir in the brown sugar. Using your fingertips, lightly rub in the butter until the mixture resembles fine breadcrumbs. Make a well in the centre, then add 2 tablespoons of the milk to the well. Mix using a flat-bladed knife until a soft dough forms, adding more milk if necessary.

Turn out onto a lightly floured work surface and gently knead until a dough just forms. Roll out the dough until 1 cm (¹/₂ inch) thick, then cut into rounds using a 4 cm (1¹/₂ inch) cutter.

Place the pastry rounds around the edge of the baking dish, overlapping them slightly — not all the plums will be covered. Lightly brush the rounds with the remaining milk and sprinkle with the caster sugar.

Place the dish on a baking tray and bake for 30 minutes, or until the topping is golden and cooked through.

Serve hot or warm, with ice cream, custard or cream.

Plum cobbler is best eaten the day it is made.

PEAR DUMPLINGS
SERVES 6

PASTRY
300 g (10¹/₂ oz/2¹/₃ cups) plain
(all-purpose) flour
125 g (4¹/₂ oz/1 cup) icing (confectioners')
sugar
150 g (5¹/₂ oz) cold unsalted butter,
chopped
2 egg yolks, mixed with 1 tablespoon
iced water

6 firm, ripe pears
100 g (3¹/₂ oz/³/₄ cup) soft goat's cheese,
crumbled
55 g (2 oz/¹/₂ cup) ground almonds
¹/₂ teaspoon ground nutmeg
¹/₂ teaspoon grated lemon zest
55 g (2 oz/¹/₄ cup) caster (superfine) sugar
1 egg, lightly beaten
icing (confectioners') sugar, for dusting
(optional)
custard, to serve

Start by making the pastry. Sift the flour, icing sugar and a pinch of salt into a large bowl. Using your fingertips, lightly rub in the butter until the mixture resembles coarse breadcrumbs. Make a well in the centre, then add the egg yolks to the well. Mix using a flat-bladed knife until a rough dough forms. Turn out onto a lightly floured surface, then gently press together into a ball. Form into a flat disc, cover with plastic wrap and refrigerate for 30 minutes.

Meanwhile, preheat the oven to 180°C (350°F/Gas 4). Grease a large roasting tin.

Leaving the pears whole and unpeeled, core them using an apple corer. Put the goat's cheese, ground almonds, nutmeg, lemon zest and 2 tablespoons of the caster sugar in a bowl. Using a fork, mash to combine well. Fill the pear cavities with the goat's cheese mixture (it's easiest just to use your fingers for this).

Roll out the chilled pastry on a lightly floured work surface until 3 mm (¹/₈ inch) thick, then cut into six 15 cm (6 inch) squares. Lightly brush the squares with beaten egg and sprinkle with the remaining caster sugar.

Drape a pastry square over one of the pears, letting the stalk pierce through it, then fold the pastry down and around the pear to completely enclose it. Press the edges together to seal, trimming where necessary, and reserving the pastry scraps. Repeat with the remaining pastry squares and pears.

Using a small knife, cut 12 leaf shapes from the pastry scraps. Brush the dumplings with the remaining egg and attach two pastry leaves to the top of each, pressing firmly to secure.

Transfer to the roasting tin and bake for 35–40 minutes, or until the pastry is golden and the pears are tender.

Dust with icing sugar if desired and serve hot, with custard.

Pear dumplings are best eaten immediately.

Spiced quince charlottes
Serves 4

450 g (1 lb/2 cups) caster (superfine) sugar
1 vanilla bean
1 cinnamon stick
1 teaspoon ground allspice
1 kg (2 lb 4 oz/4 large) quinces, peeled,
    cut into quarters and cored
500 g (1 lb 2 oz) brioche (see Note)
butter, for spreading
custard, to serve

Preheat the oven to 180°C (350°F/Gas 4).

Put the sugar in a saucepan, add 1 litre (35 fl oz/4 cups) water and stir over medium heat until the sugar has dissolved. Split the vanilla bean down the middle and scrape the seeds into the saucepan. Add the vanilla pod, cinnamon stick and allspice, then remove from the heat.

Place the quince quarters in a large baking dish and pour the syrup over. Cover with foil and bake for 3 hours, or until the quince is very tender and ruby-red. Drain the quince, reserving the poaching syrup.

Thinly slice the brioche and spread each piece with butter. Cut out a circle from eight slices of brioche and use four of them to line the base of four 250 ml (9 fl oz/1 cup) charlotte moulds or ovenproof bowls, placing them buttered side down. Reserve the other brioche slices for the top.

Cut the remaining brioche into 2 cm (³/₄ inch) wide fingers, long enough to fit the height of the moulds. Press the brioche vertically around the sides of the dishes, overlapping slightly.

Divide the quince among the moulds and cover with the four reserved brioche slices. Set the moulds on a baking tray and bake for 20 minutes. Remove from the oven and allow to cool for 10 minutes, then turn the charlottes out onto serving plates.

Serve warm or at room temperature, with custard for drizzling over and with the reserved poaching syrup, if desired.

Quince charlottes are best eaten the day they are made.

NOTE: Brioche is a rich, buttery bread with an almost cake-like texture. It is available from some bakeries. If you prefer, you could instead use a loaf of sliced white bread (remove the crusts first).

APPLE AND RHUBARB CRUMBLE
SERVES 6

4 golden delicious apples
9 rhubarb stalks, trimmed and cut into
    4–5 cm (1¹/₂–2 inch) lengths
grated zest of 1 lemon
80 g (2³/₄ oz/¹/₃ cup) caster (superfine)
    sugar
125 g (4¹/₂ oz) unsalted butter, chopped
125 g (4¹/₂ oz/1 cup) plain (all-purpose)
    flour
1 teaspoon ground cinnamon
thick (double/heavy) cream or custard,
    to serve

Preheat the oven to 180°C (350°F/Gas 4).

Peel and core the apples, then slice thinly. Place in a medium-sized baking dish with the rhubarb. Sprinkle with the lemon zest and 2 tablespoons of the sugar, then dot with 40 g (1¹/₂ oz) of the butter.

Sift the flour into a large bowl. Using your fingertips, lightly rub in the remaining butter until the mixture resembles breadcrumbs. Stir in the remaining sugar and the cinnamon.

Sprinkle the mixture over the apple and rhubarb and bake for 1 hour, or until the topping is browned and the juices are bubbling.

Serve warm or at room temperature, with thick cream or custard.

Apple and rhubarb crumble is best eaten the day it is made.

LEMON DELICIOUS

SERVES 4

melted butter, for brushing
30 g (1 oz) unsalted butter, softened
170 g (6 oz/³/₄ cup) caster (superfine)
   sugar
1 teaspoon grated lemon zest
3 eggs, separated
30 g (1 oz/¹/₄ cup) plain (all-purpose) flour
125 ml (4 fl oz/¹/₂ cup) lemon juice
375 ml (13 fl oz/1¹/₂ cups) milk, warmed
icing (confectioners') sugar, for dusting
vanilla ice cream, to serve

Preheat the oven to 180°C (350°F/Gas 4). Brush a 1.5 litre (52 fl oz/6 cup) baking dish with melted butter.

Put the butter, sugar, lemon zest and egg yolks in a bowl. Using electric beaters, beat until light and creamy. Sift the flour into a bowl. Working in two batches, fold the flour into the egg mixture, alternating with the lemon juice and milk.

In a clean, dry bowl, beat the egg whites using electric beaters until soft peaks form. Pour the pudding batter down the inside of the mixing bowl into the beaten egg white, then gently fold to just combine.

Pour the mixture into the prepared dish and place the dish in a roasting tin. Pour enough warm water into the tin to come halfway up the side of the baking dish. Bake for 40 minutes, or until the pudding is puffed and golden.

Remove from the oven, dust with icing sugar and serve hot or warm, with ice cream.

Lemon delicious is best eaten the day it is made.

VARIATION
To make **lime delicious**, use lime zest and lime juice in the pudding instead of lemon.

CHRISTMAS PUDDING

MAKES 1 LARGE OR 2 SMALL PUDDINGS

500 g (1 lb 2 oz) mixture of raisins,
   currants and sultanas (golden raisins)
300 g (10½ oz/1⅔ cups) other mixed
   dried fruits, chopped
50 g (1¾ oz/⅓ cup) mixed peel
   (mixed candied citrus peel)
125 ml (4 fl oz/½ cup) dark ale
2 tablespoons rum or brandy
grated zest and juice of 1 orange
grated zest and juice of 1 lemon
225 g (8 oz) suet, grated
245 g (9 oz/1⅓ cups) soft brown sugar
3 eggs, lightly beaten
200 g (7 oz/2½ cups) fresh white
   breadcrumbs
90 g (3¼ oz/¾ cup) self-raising flour
1 teaspoon mixed (pumpkin pie) spice
¼ teaspoon freshly grated nutmeg
¼ teaspoon salt
60 g (2¼ oz/heaped ⅓ cup) roughly
   chopped blanched almonds

Prepare the fruit a day ahead. Put all the dried fruit in a large bowl with the mixed peel, ale, rum and all the citrus zest and juice. Mix together, then cover and leave overnight.

The next day, add the remaining ingredients and stir to combine well — the mixture should fall heavily from the spoon. If it is too stiff, add a little more ale.

Grease a 1.25 litre (44 fl oz/5 cup) pudding basin (mould) or two 570 ml (20 fl oz) pudding basins. Line the base with baking paper.

Sit the empty basin in a large saucepan on a trivet or upturned saucer, then pour enough cold water into the saucepan to come halfway up the side of the basin. Remove the basin and bring the water to the boil.

Spoon the fruit mixture into the pudding basin.

Cut a sheet of baking paper and a sheet of foil large enough to fit comfortably over the top and come halfway down the sides of the basin.

Lay the baking paper on top of the foil, to form a double layer. Grease the paper, then fold a pleat in the centre. Invert the double sheet over the pudding, so the greased paper is facing down, then fold it down over the edge of the pudding basin.

Cover with a tight-fitting lid if your basin has one. Tie a double piece of kitchen string securely around the rim of the basin, just under the lip, and run another piece of string across the top to make a handle.

Carefully lower the basin into the boiling water, onto the trivet. Reduce the heat so the water is at a fast simmer. Steam the large pudding for 8 hours, and the smaller puddings for 6 hours, checking the water level regularly, and topping up to the original level with boiling water as needed.

If you are making the pudding ahead of time to reheat later, steam the large pudding for only 6 hours, then steam it for another 2 hours on the day you would like to eat it. Steam the smaller puddings for 5 hours, and for another 1 hour on the day you would like to eat them. You can part-cook the pudding up to 4 weeks ahead.

Christmas pudding will keep for 4 weeks stored in a cool place in an airtight container, or can be frozen in an airtight container for up to 6 months.

Sticky golden sponge pudding
SERVES 6

125 g (4½ oz/1 cup) self-raising flour
120 g (4¼ oz) unsalted butter, softened
115 g (4 oz/½ cup) caster (superfine) sugar
1 teaspoon natural vanilla extract
2 eggs
2 tablespoons milk
175 g (6 oz/½ cup) golden syrup, treacle or dark corn syrup, plus extra, for serving
custard or whipped cream, to serve

Lightly grease a 1 litre (35 fl oz/4 cup) pudding basin (mould). Sit the empty basin in a large saucepan on a trivet or upturned saucer, then pour enough cold water into the saucepan to come halfway up the side of the basin. Remove the basin and bring the water to the boil.

Sift the flour into a bowl. Using electric beaters, cream the butter and sugar until light and fluffy. Stir in the vanilla. Add the eggs one at a time, beating well after each addition, and alternating with a little sifted flour.

Using a large metal spoon, gently fold in the remaining flour, then add the milk and stir to just combine. Pour the golden syrup into the base of the pudding basin and spoon the batter over the top.

Cut a sheet of baking paper and a sheet of foil large enough to fit comfortably over the top and come halfway down the sides of the basin.

Lay the baking paper on top of the foil, to form a double layer. Grease the paper, then fold a pleat in the centre. Invert the double sheet over the pudding, so the greased paper is facing down, then fold it down over the edge of the pudding basin. Tie a double piece of kitchen string securely around the rim of the basin, just under the lip, and run another piece of string across the top to make a handle. Cover with a tight-fitting lid.

Carefully lower the basin into the boiling water, onto the trivet. Reduce the heat so the water is at a fast simmer. Steam for 2 hours, checking the water every 30 minutes, and topping up to the original level with boiling water as needed.

Remove the pudding from the saucepan and test with a cake tester or by pressing the top gently — it should be firm in the centre and well risen. If it is not quite cooked, cover and continue steaming until done.

Turn the pudding out onto a serving dish. Serve warm with custard or whipped cream, with warmed golden syrup passed separately.

Sticky golden sponge pudding is best eaten the day it is made.

STICKY ORANGE AND PASSIONFRUIT PUDDING
SERVES 6

375 g (13 oz/3 cups) plain (all-purpose)
  flour
1$\frac{1}{2}$ teaspoons baking powder
200 g (7 oz) cold unsalted butter,
  chopped
45 g (1$\frac{1}{2}$ oz/$\frac{1}{2}$ cup) desiccated coconut
300 ml (3$\frac{1}{2}$ fl oz) pouring (whipping)
  cream
160 g (5$\frac{1}{2}$ oz/$\frac{1}{2}$ cup) orange marmalade
2 tablespoons passionfruit pulp
cream, ice cream or custard, to serve

PASSIONFRUIT SYRUP
125 ml (4 fl oz/$\frac{1}{2}$ cup) orange juice
170 g (6 oz/$\frac{3}{4}$ cup) caster (superfine)
  sugar
60 ml (2 fl oz/$\frac{1}{4}$ cup) passionfruit pulp

Sift the flour, baking powder and a pinch of salt into a large
bowl. Using your fingertips, lightly rub in the butter until
the mixture resembles fine breadcrumbs. Stir in the coconut.
Using a flat-bladed knife, mix in most of the cream, adding just
enough to form a soft dough.

Turn out onto a lightly floured work surface, then knead
briefly. Roll the dough out between two sheets of baking paper
to make a 25 x 40 cm (10 x 16 inch) rectangle.

Spread the marmalade over the dough and drizzle with
the passionfruit pulp. Roll up lengthways into a log. Cover
with plastic wrap and refrigerate for 20 minutes, or until firm.

Meanwhile, preheat the oven to 180°C (350°F/Gas 4).
Grease an 18 cm (7 inch) round, deep cake tin and line the
base with baking paper.

Cut the chilled dough into 2 cm ($\frac{3}{4}$ inch) rounds and
arrange half of them over the base of the prepared tin. Place
a second layer over the gaps where the bottom slices join.
Put the cake tin on a baking tray.

Put all the passionfruit syrup ingredients in a saucepan
with 60 ml (2 fl oz/$\frac{1}{4}$ cup) water. Stir over low heat, without
boiling, until the sugar has dissolved. Bring to the boil, then
pour the syrup over the pudding.

Bake for 50 minutes, or until a cake tester inserted into
the centre of the pudding comes out clean.

Remove from the oven and leave in the tin for 15 minutes,
before very carefully turning out into a serving dish.

Serve hot, with cream, ice cream or custard.

Sticky orange and passionfruit pudding is best eaten the
day it is made.

index

Published in 2008 by Murdoch Books Pty Limited
www.murdochbooks.com.au

Murdoch Books Australia
Pier 8/9
23 Hickson Road
Millers Point NSW 2000
Phone: +61 (0) 2 8220 2000
Fax: +61 (0) 2 8220 2558

Murdoch Books UK Limited
Erico House, 6th Floor
93–99 Upper Richmond Road
Putney, London SW15 2TG
Phone: +44 (0) 20 8785 5995
Fax: +44 (0) 20 8785 5985

Chief Executive: Juliet Rogers
Publishing Director: Kay Scarlett

Design Manager: Vivien Valk
Project Manager: Janine Flew
Editor: Katri Hilden
Design concept: Sarah Odgers
Design: Alex Frampton
Production: Nikla Martin
Photographer: George Seper
Stylist: Marie-Helénè Clauzon
Food preparation: Joanne Glynn

National Library of Australia Cataloguing-in-Publication Data
Author: Kitchen, Leanne.
Title: The baker / author, Leanne Kitchen.
Publisher: Sydney : Murdoch Books, 2008.
ISBN: 9781741960976 (hbk.)
Series: Kitchen, Leanne. Butcher/Baker series
Notes: Includes index.
Subjects: Baked products.
Dewey Number: 641.815

Printed by 1010 Printing International Limited in 2008. PRINTED IN CHINA.

CONVERSION GUIDE: You may find cooking times vary depending on the oven you
are using. For fan-forced ovens, as a general rule, set the oven temperature to 20°C (35°F)
lower than indicated in the recipe. We have used 20 ml (4 teaspoon) tablespoon measures.
If you are using a 15 ml (3 teaspoon) tablespoon, for most recipes the difference will not
be noticeable. However, for recipes using baking powder, gelatine, bicarbonate of soda
(baking soda), small amounts of flour and cornflour (cornstarch), add an extra teaspoon
for each tablespoon specified.

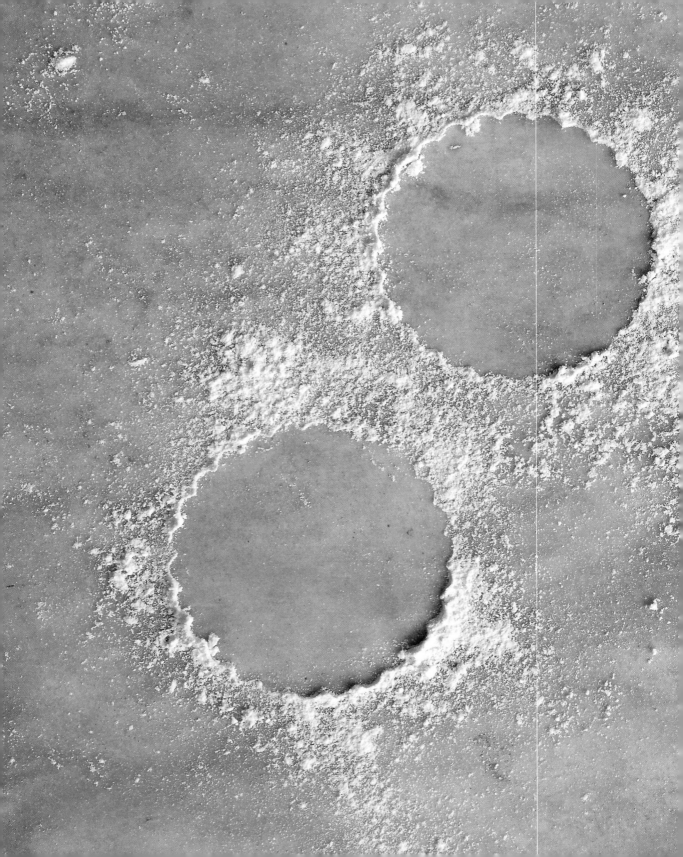